ECONOMIC CRISIS, CIVIL SOCIETY, AND DEMOCRATIZATION:

THE CASE OF ZAMBIA

JULIUS O. IHONVBERE

ECONOMIC CRISIS, CIVIL SOCIETY, AND DEMOCRATIZATION:

THE CASE OF ZAMBIA

JULIUS O. IHONVBERE

Africa World Press, Inc.

P.O. Box 1892      P.O. Box 48

Trenton, NJ 08607   Asmara, ERITREA

Africa World Press, Inc.

P.O. Box 1892
Trenton, NJ 08607

P.O. Box 48
Asmara, ERITREA

Copyright © 1996   Julius O. Ihonvbere

First Printing 1996

Cover & Book design: Jonathan Gullery

Library of Congress Cataloging-in-Publication Data

Ihonvbere, Julius Omozuanvbo.
    Economic crisis, civil society, and democratization: the case of
Zambia / Julius O. Ihonvbere.
        p.   cm.
    Includes bibliographical references and index.
    ISBN 0-86543-500-6 (cloth). -- ISBN 0-86543-501-4 (pbk.)
    1. Zambia--Economic policy. 2. Zambia--Economic conditions--1964-
3. Democracy--Zambia. 4. Privatization--Zambia. 5. Non
-governmental organizations--Zambia. 6. Zambia--Politics and
government--1964- I. Title.
HC915.I37   1996
338.96894--dc20   96-12534
                                                    CIP

CONTENTS

To the memory of my father-in-law,
Chief Bamidele E. Najomo (1933-94)
The Unuevboro of Ogbe in Uvwie Kingdom

ACKNOWLEDGEMENTS

This work is the product of the efforts of several individuals and organizations, in most cases, separated by thousands of miles. I cannot thank everyone who assisted my research, especially the hundreds of respondents I interviewed in Zambia. I can only hope that the way I have used their information and materials meets with their approval. I left Texas to Lusaka a very enthusiastic person. I was thrilled by the prospect of studying the democratization process in Zambia. I was particularly thrilled at the opportunity to study the Movement for Multiparty Democracy (MMD). It was my very first visit to Zambia. I came back somewhat disappointed because the obstacles to democratization in Zambia were so numerous and formidable, that my initial enthusiasm was severely dampened. Being from a comparatively richer and clearly more populous African country which has been terribly governed with a very badly managed economy in the last thirty years, I was shocked at how such a common fate was not unique to my own country, Nigeria. In fact, the poverty I witnessed in Zambia, in the context of declining national resources and pressure from creditors, convinced me that no matter how well-intentioned the MMD was, it had very limited chances for successfully consolidating democracy in Zambia. Yet, there is so much to hope for. As a respondent told me, the people are the ultimate guarantors of the nation's future. Governments come and go, presidents come and go, but the Zambian people will always be around to rebuild.

I wish to thank the organizations which funded this project. First is the National Endowment for the Humanities (NEH); their prompt response to my application convinced me that I was on to an important project in an era when funding for subjects on Africa was becoming really scarce. The American Philosophical Society also provided some financial support. To these organizations, I am very grateful.

In Zambia, I met hundreds of very wonderful people who were quite open with their ideas on the democratization process. Though their initial enthusiasm for the process has been dampened by the economic difficulties, I can only hope that their love for Zambia will see them through these very trying times. Hon. Samuel S. Miyanda, member of parliament for Matero and chairman of the Lusaka Central District of the MMD was an invaluable source of information, contacts and support. It was quite an experience following him on the campaign trail as he campaigned for the MMD Lusaka Central District Chairmanship. Hon. Frederick Hapunda former defence minister under United National Independence Party (UNIP) was extremely helpful to me. As MMD member of parliament for Siavonga and chairman of the party in the Southern Province, he was a very important source of information. He was always willing to be interviewed and to explain some of the intricacies of Zambian politics to me. Derrick Chitala, Loveness Malambo, Dianah Nambula, Philip Chilomo, and Petronella Kapijimpanje were extremely supportive of my project. Mrs. Sikasula, and CJ Sikasula, were like family. The staff of the Mamba Collieries Guest House were as hospitable as ever. I would also like to thank Jotham Moomba of The University of Zambia (UNZA), the staff of the libraries at *Times of Zambia*, and others whom I met but cannot immediately acknowledge.

I also wish to acknowledge the support of Munyonzwe Hamalengwa for his long standing support and for putting me in touch with wonderful patriots in Zambia. Since I got to know Hamalengwa in 1979 he has sustained my interest in Zambia. I am happy that, at long last, I visited his country and I am now able to write about important issues in Zambian politics. Linda Poras of the University of Texas at Austin was invaluable in helping me sort out my accounts following each field trip. I am very grateful to her. Elaine David and Suzanne Colwell of the Government Department, The University of Texas at Austin have always been useful in helping me through the complex world of computer usage. I am grateful to them. I would also like to thank my Research Assistant, Prosper Bani for his invaluable support in countless ways. Ola Rotimi Ajayi of the University of Ilorin who was a Fulbright Fellow at the University of Texas at Austin 1993/94 and Anthony Appiah-Mensah of the University of Ghana both read the original manuscript and made useful suggestions. I thank them very much. As well Sunny Uzuh, Daniel Ihonvbere, Athan and Judith Ogoh, George Najomo, Emeka Okenyi, Francis Egbuson, Richard and Mercy Atata, Doyin and Yinka Odunsi, and Chris Okeagu are owed thanks for their support. My academic family in the United States and in many African countries have always been supportive. I particularly wish to thank Pita Agbese, Femi Vaughn, George Kieh, Michael Hanchard, Femi Taiwo, Esi Dogbe, Pade Badru, Tim Shaw, Terisa Turner, Eme Adibe, Amii-Omara Otunu, SDM, Sheila Walker, Gloria Thomas-Emeagwali, and Kelechi Kalu for supporting my work in various ways. I will like to acknowledge with thanks the journals which published portions of this work before the final manuscript was ready: The *Canadian Journal of African Studies, Asian and African Studies*, and *Afrika Spectrum*. These three journals gave my new focus on Zambia the very first public appearances. Finally, I thank my wife Grace, who acted an as unpaid research assistant and my children Oje, Vera, Ikhide, and especially Efe, whose love for the computer cost me several pages whenever he "intervened" without warning! Of course, I alone take full responsibility for the interpretations and conclusions in this work.

Austin, Texas
May 1995.

ABBREVIATIONS

AMWU	African Mine Workers' Union
ANC	African National Congress
BBC	British Broadcasting Corporation
BSA Co.	British South Africa Company
CCMG	Christian Churches Monitoring Group
CCZ	Christian Council of Zambia
CD	Campaign for Democracy
CFF	Compensatory Finance Facility
CHAKA	Christian Alliance for the Kingdom of Africa
CJA	Commonwealth Journalists Association
CNN	Cable News Network
CNU	Caucus for National Unity
CNU	Congress for National Unity
COZ	Credit Organization of Zambia
CPA	Consumer Protective Association
CPA	Commonwealth Parliamentarians Association
CPU	Commonwealth Press Union
COZ	Credit Organization of Zambia
CSBZ	Cold Storage Board of Zambia
CUP	Committee for Unity and Progress
DNC	Democratic National Congress
DP	Democratic Process
DPBZ	Dairy Produce Board of Zambia
ECA	Economic Commission for Africa
FINDECO	Finance Development Corporation
FODEP	Forum for Democratic Process
FORD	Forum for the Restoration of Democracy
FRCN	Federal Radio Corporation of Nigeria
INDECO	Industrial Development Corporation
INDP	Interim National Development Plan

IOT	International Observer Team
MDP	Movement for Democratic Process
MFJ	Movement for Freedom and Justice
MINDECO	Mining Development Corporation
MMD	Movement for Multi-Party Democracy
MUZ	Mineworkers Union of Zambia
NADA	National Democratic Alliance
NAMBOARD	National Agricultural Marketing Board
NCCM	Nchanga Consolidated Copper Mines
NERP	National Economic Recovery Plan
NGO	Non Governmental Organization
NPD	National Party for Democracy
NUPTW	National Union of Postal and Telecom Workers
OAU	Organization of African Unity
RDC	Rural Development Corporation
RWUZ	Railway Workers Union of Zambia
SAP	Structural Adjustment Program
TAZ	Theology Association of Zambia
TBZ	Tobacco Board of Zambia
TSPP	The Theoretical Spiritual Political Party
TUC	Trade Union Congress
UNIP	United National Independence Party
UNZA	University of Zambia
UNZASU	University of Zambia Students Union
UPP	United Progressive Party
ZANU-PF	Zimbabwe African National Union-Patriotic Front
ZCTU	Zambia Congress of Trade Unions
ZEMCC	Zambia Election Monitoring Coordinating Committee
ZENA	Zambia Enrolled Nurses Association
ZEWU	Zambia Electricity Workers Union
ZFE	Zambia Federation of Employers
ZIMCO	Zambia Industrial and Mining Corporation
ZIMT	Zambia Independence Monitoring Team
ZNBC	Zambia National Broadcasting Corporation
ZNFU	Zambia National Farmers Union
ZNUT	Zambia National Union of Teachers
ZOFRO	Zambia Opposition Front
ZUFIAW	Zambia Union of Financial Institutions and Allied Workers
ZUM	Zimbabwe Unity Movement

CHAPTER ONE

THE DEMOCRATIC UPSURGE IN AFRICA: ANOTHER FALSE START OR A SECOND LIBERATION?

The breathtaking pace of political change in Africa has surpassed any predictions or expectations.... Almost every country has experienced some form of citizens' pressure for broader public participation in political and economic decision-making. Nearly two dozen authoritarian leaders have been overthrown or forced to share power.

Africa is experiencing a revolution as profound as the wave of independence that began to sweep the continent three decades ago.[1]

Whatever democratic advances have been attained in Africa at this stage are still largely structural and/or constitutional; certainly a strong breath of fresh air, but likely to end up in some countries as only cosmetic and/or temporary. The process has a long way to go in much of the continent.[2]

There is no doubting the fact that a wave of democratization is sweeping across the developing world. In the vast majority of nations, new issues, demands, and alignments are emerging on the political terrain. Popular organizations and communities and "members of all classes found themselves sufficiently empowered to undermine authoritarian rulers. The astonishing discovery that mass participation could actually help topple governments hitherto impervious to the demands of their own people has made popular involvement in government the starting point for reconstructing political order...."[3] Largely a response to frustrations with authoritarian rule and the suffocation of civil society, the end of the Cold War and the new disposition towards support for popular movements have invigorated these efforts. Military dictatorships have been forced to accommodate popular interests and to organize open elections. Presidents-for-life have been forced to reexamine their claims to permanent control of political power and to open up political spaces. In many developing social formations, a new political culture is emerging, with popular groups forming new alliances, asking new questions, initiating new programs, and expanding political spaces through demands for social justice, equity, accountability, participation, human rights, and democracy. These demands and the new strategies designed to achieve them—mainly through multiparty political activities—have altered the overall character of the political landscape to a great extent.

The domestic political struggles have been effectively complemented (and in most cases encouraged) by developments in the global system. As indicated earlier, the end of the Cold War significantly reduced the relevance of the tyrants and decadent political rulers of the southern hemisphere. Since alliances with developing nations could no longer be based on Cold War ideologies and interests, democracy has become the basis for forging new relationships in a post-Cold War world. Unfortunately, consistency has not been part of this new relationship. The model of democracy being prescribed—and in most cases, forced on—developing formations has tended to be the *liberal democratic* one which reflects the interests and experiences of the developed social formations. In large measure, this model has overlooked the historical experiences and political balances and interests in underdeveloped formations. As well, the model assumes that existing conditions in developing societies necessarily approximate the conditions in the developed societies in their early periods when the institutions and structures of liberal democracy were initiated and institutionalized. The African experience demonstrates how transplanted institutions and processes of liberal democracy fail to become routinized because of existing structural deformities and contradictions arising from the region's historical experiences and postcolonial alignment and realignment of social forces.

The Western powers that had earlier supported dictators and brutal governments—such as those in Zaire, Equatorial Guinea, Kenya, Nigeria, the Sudan, and Somalia, to use African examples—have begun to make new demands on their former allies. "Good governance" is now demanded as a precondition for further support. Good governance has become part of the package of *political conditionalities* imposed on Third World leaders by Western lenders, donors, and creditors as preconditions for further economic support. In Kenya, it was the only way to get Daniel Arap Moi to reach some accommodation with domestic constituencies and allow popular elections. The election saw the opposition win a hundred seats in parliament. In Malawi, Kamuzu Banda, the country's president-for-life was forced to make concessions to civil society when British aid was slashed in half. Even in Nigeria, limited sanctions from the European Community, Canada, the United States, and the United Kingdom were important in forcing General Ibrahim Babangida to unveil his "hidden agenda" and leave office in disgrace. The reality today in Africa is that things are no longer the same. Throughout the continent, the old order

3

is being challenged, and the present one will not only surely change but might never be reconstituted in the same way, no matter what happens in the next decade and beyond. To be sure, there will be countless failures, compromises, betrayals, and diversions in this new march for empowerment, participation, and democracy. Such setbacks will only tend to strengthen democratic constituencies as opportunists are steadily weeded out of the struggles against the neocolonial African state. In some sense, one might even argue that the current crisis in Africa (see below) is good because it is demystifying the state and its agents and laying bare the political landscape thus making competition against the repressive state possible without external support.

The African Crisis: Perspectives and Interpretations

In its 1989 report on sub-Saharan Africa, the World Bank gave further credence to the growing assumption that African economies were in crisis because of the absence of good governance, decentralization, accountability, and less government intervention in the economy. In his introduction to the report, Barber Conable, the World Bank's president noted that "A root cause of weak economic performance in the past has been the failure of public institutions. Private sector initiative and market mechanisms are important, but they must go hand in hand with *good governance*—a public service that is efficient, a judicial system that is reliable, and an administration that is accountable to its public."[4] As a strategy to promote good governance, Conable suggested the urgent need for a process for "empowering ordinary people, and especially women, to take greater responsibility for improving their lives—measures that foster grassroots organization, that nurture rather than obstruct informal sector enterprises, and that promote nongovernmental and intermediary organizations."[5] Finally, the Bank made the categorical declaration that consolidating the gains of structural adjustment was not enough; that African governments must address "fundamental questions relating to human capacities, institutions, governance..."; that "ordinary people should participate more in designing and implementing development programs"; that the state should "no longer be an entrepreneur, but a promoter of private producers"; and that "Africa needs not just less government but better government—government that concentrates its efforts less on direct interventions and more on enabling others to be productive."[6]

At a general level these are very worthy positions even if they are not new. For over a decade, African and Africanist scholars have drawn attention to the *political* nature and context of the African crisis. It was contended that the economic crisis which was manifested in crippling foreign debts and high debt-servicing obligations, declining foreign aid and investments, rising bankruptcies, unemployment and inflation, institutional decay and infrastructural disintegration, crime, insecurity, and rising malnutrition and social decay, were largely symptoms of serious political deformities, distortions, and disarticulations. The Economic Commission for Africa (ECA) admits that Africa is experiencing a crisis of "unprecedented and unacceptable proportions," and that "the political context of socio-economic development has been characterized, in many instances, by an over-centralization of power and impediments to the effective participation of the overwhelming majority of the people in social, political and economic development."[7] This position, while not denying the severity of the economic crisis, simply emphasizes the need to focus on the political environments of waste, repression, violence, insecurity, and instability that make economic programs impossible to implement no matter how well-intentioned.

When the World Bank and Conable talk about "good governance" and "empowering ordinary people" there is a seeming trivialization of an otherwise serious problem. The issues are conceptualized and addressed outside the historical experience and environment of Africa. There is an assumed harmony among and within social forces and classes. In fact, when "ordinary people" are empowered, what are they expected to do with the power? Are they expected to shake hands with the ruthless exploiters and oppressors of yesterday? Will they ever have the same socioeconomic and political interests as those who had become outrageously wealthy from looting the public purse? Can their "empowered" institutions and communities serve the interests of the dominant elites, including military dictators? Will their interests suddenly become the same as those of foreign capital just because the magic of "good governance" has been invoked?

What the questions above signify is that there are more fundamental issues to be addressed than cataloging the characteristics of "good governance." To be sure, *political conditionality* enables donors, creditors, and lenders to put pressure on recalcitrant, corrupt, and repressive leaders in Africa. We cannot however overlook the fact that these same African leaders were in many instances installed, nurtured, and sustained over the years by the same external interests which have now turned against them. Many African leaders have perfected the art of brutal and inhuman politics, divide-and-rule tactics, and a total commitment to retention of power through the asphyxiation of civil society. As well, political conditionality has made it possible to justify the redirection of aid and investment to other parts of the world. This has contributed to the further marginalization of Africa in the international division of labor, a situation noted by African leaders and nongovernmental organizations in the *African Charter for Popular Participation in Development and Transformation*: "We...observe that given the current world political and economic situation, Africa is becoming further marginalized in world affairs, both geopolitically and economically."[8] More importantly, political conditionality simply complements the *economic conditionality* already imposed on poverty-stricken, debt-ridden, and desperate African states by the World Bank, the International Monetary Fund (IMF), and other creditors.

In the majority of African states, development planning, financial matters, and public policy were already being determined, influenced, or severely constrained by the policies, interests, and power of such creditors. Political conditionality, therefore, would create a platform for using the disbursement of foreign assistance to condition, influence, and determine the context of politics, the political agenda, and the overall ideological content of politics. Once there is complementarily between economic and political conditionalities—and once African leaders, prodemocracy activists, politicians, bureaucrats, intellectuals, researchers, business men and women, as well as grassroots organizations come to imbibe and accept the ideology of international capitalism as the driving force behind their activities—then Africa once again, in spite of the end of the Cold War, will have lost the ability to be original, creative, and independent in fashioning an internally driven agenda for reconstruction, growth, and development.

Richard Sandbrook, in a recent study of the African predicament and the implications of the World Bank's new agenda and emphasis on "good governance," has noted that it is important not to lose sight of the "broader ideological implications" of this strategy. According to Sandbrook, "(s)ince their creation, the IMF and the World Bank have consistently aimed to integrate as many national economies as possible into a multilateral global capitalist economy....Both agencies have encouraged, in countries receiving their loans, monetary, fiscal, and trade policies which *extend the sway of international market forces.*"[9] Since the main concern was with the *process* of governance rather than with the ideological specificity of political change, the

World Bank and Western governments hardly concern themselves with the nature and character of the *state*. Policies of desubsidization, deregulation, commercialization, privatization, devaluation, and so on, prescribed by the World Bank only succeed in breaking down domestic constituencies to make the political landscape more receptive to liberal political prescriptions. While the World Bank never anticipated that its "reform" programs would push the masses to the edge of militant, even violent resistance and struggles for democracy, its policies have also created an atavistic environment and badly damaged the legitimacy of the state and dominant elites. This is the only way we can comprehend the fact that though the unequal distribution of the pains of adjustment promoted largely unanticipated political pressures, the content of these pressures has largely reflected a sort of subservience to Western liberal political models and prescriptions. The impression one gets from public statements from international financial institutions and Western governments is that what African states now need in order to get out of their current state of decay, conflicts, crises, and near disintegration are liberal democratic political models and institutions. But will "good governance" as conceptualized and defined by the donors and lenders change the African State? Make it more efficient and effective? Increase its legitimacy, stability, and hegemony? Or democratize its institutions and processes to make it more accessible to and reflective of the interests of the people? What will happen to the current custodians of state power who have actually precipitated the current crisis in Africa and who continue to benefit from the reproduction of the status quo? Will multiparty elections resolve these contradictions? We do not think so.

The greatest defect of the "good governance" prescription is that it addresses the *symptoms* of the African predicament rather than the structural causes. The timely and interesting piece by Robert D. Kaplan in the *Atlantic*

Monthly addresses the well known stories and predicaments of Africa. While Kaplan does document the African reality, sometimes sensationally and at times in overstretched, anecdotal, and descriptive terms, the largely ahistorical and unanalytical nature of his essay reduces its worth in terms of revealing the structural roots of the crisis of politics, power, and production in Africa. Even the World Bank's *Governance and Development* demonstrates not just a "bureaucratic" approach to the issue of governance, but focuses on institutional matters outside the social context of the very institutions which have been destroyed by bad governance.10 Inefficiency, waste, mismanagement, corruption, hiring of ghost workers, overgenerous allowances to political elites and bureaucrats, and—in the Bank's own words—"the appropriation of the machinery of government by the elite to serve their own interests" are largely manifestations of more structural and historically determined coalitions, contradictions, and crises.[11] These conditions are not necessarily either *natural* or spiritually determined. They are the precipitates of particular forms of social relations, political balances, power relations, alignment and realignment of class forces, and the region's location and role is a highly exploitative and very competitive international division of labor. Without addressing the structural roots of the crisis, the prescription of good governance would simply fail to resolve any of the immediate or longer-term problems of Africa. As well, because the political terrain is so repressive, hostile, uncertain, unstable, and undemocratic; the state, its custodians, and agencies have been unable to contain or mediate the forces of economic, social and political decay and disintegration. Elites loot the treasuries because they can get away with it. The dominant classes privatize the state and its resources because civil society is deformed, weak and highly factionalized. Economic policies fail because they largely reflect the narrow interests of the dominant classes and those of foreign capital. The widespread human rights abuses, mindless corruption, waste, and the subversion of the goals of nationhood which have characterized the majority of African social formations since political independence cannot be divorced from inherited structural contradictions and dislocations.[12] It is doubtful if mere insistence on good governance, even the imposition of political conditionalities will resolve these deep-rooted problems. When foreign aid is denied and countries are isolated until they meet the dictates of the donors and lenders, who actually suffers? To what extent have Western-imposed sanctions affected the Iraqi elite? How much of the sanctions imposed on Libya has affected Ghadaffi and the Libyan bourgeois class? The Haitian elite did not crumble under the yoke of "international" sanctions and a US naval blockade; in fact, the departing military elite managed to win substantial financial gains for itself before retiring into luxurious exile. The truth of the matter is that cutting foreign aid, redirecting investment, and the like do not have much of an impact on the elites. It is the already impoverished masses who suffer the most; and when the elites do yield to such pressures, more often than not they have already designed ways to accommodate and domesticate political prescriptions dictated or imposed by Western powers. Under such conditions, concessions to civil society becomes more of a survival strategy, a sort of tactical political manoeuver. Robert Bates captures very accurately the survival tactics employed so perfectly by Africa's dictators:

> In normal times, the power of government opposition is sufficient to cripple all efforts at political reform. But there is a time when these governments themselves become champions of the rule of law. They do so when they are about to fall. At the time of their political demise, tyrants become converts to civil liberties. On their political deathbeds, they seek an expanded role for due process, restrictions on the

use of the police and the judicial system, an independent judiciary, and the rule of law. When they are about to pass from the political scene, they acquire a vested interest in civil liberties. They want legal and political shelters from the lust for revenge on the part of the citizenry they once repressed.13

Unfortunately for prodemocracy groups which have become so hungry for power, they fall for the bait set by the more experienced dictator and begin to internalize the struggle for power. This was exactly why the Campaign for Democracy in Nigeria failed to prevent the remilitarization of Nigerian politics.[14] This is also why Rawlings and Moi were returned to power in Ghana and Kenya respectively. Because the goals, actors, institutions, methods, and political styles have only been whitewashed and repackaged under a new liberal democratic label, many of the new political movements have become undemocratic, dormant, conservative, visibly opportunistic, and irrelevant to the yearnings of the masses of Africa.

The Contradictions and Limitations of Political Liberalization: Some Theoretical Issues

In spite of the fact that many hitherto "powerful" and almost "invincible" regimes have been forced to accept their own illegitimacy in Africa, recent literature on democratization in the developing world has tended to be rather pessimistic about the prospects for democracy under very difficult conditions.[15] This pessimism arises from the difficulty of matching the so-called preconditions of democracy with the practice of democracy in poverty-stricken, nonindustrialized, debt-ridden, politically unstable, foreign-dominated, and marginal economies in an increasingly complex and competitive global system. Four preconditions are usually identified in the literature as necessary not just for the process of democratization, but also for democratic consolidation.

The first precondition is that some degree of capitalist development is necessary for the survival or consolidation of democracy. In the words of Samuel P. Huntington, "economic development, industrialization, urbanization, the emergence of the bourgeoisie and of a middle class, the development of a working class and its early organization, and the gradual decrease in economic inequality all seem to have played some role in the movements toward democratization in northern European countries...."[16] This was an elaboration of the 1959 postulation of Seymour Lipset that "the more well-to-do a nation, the greater the chances that it will sustain democracy."[17] Such a process of "modernization" and wealth creation was expected to promote higher literacy levels, education, a vibrant mass media, and a middle class with interest in peace, predictable politics, and political security. Can this be the case for Africa? Barrington Moore, Jr. talks of the importance of having an autonomous and productive bourgeoisie as a precondition for democracy. The assumption is that such a bourgeoisie would be interested in predictability, stability, and legality and would thus seek to streamline the content and context of politics largely to promote bourgeois hegemony and private accumulation.[18] Such a bourgeoisie would be interested in a national project and this would necessarily encourage an interest in citizenship, law and order, rights to property, and the routinization of political processes.

This obviously draws heavily on some experiences in Europe. Yet, it holds out little or no promise in Africa, where the state plays the role of the bourgeoisie, in spite of structural adjustment programs. The largely unproductive, factionalized and fractionalized, corrupt, and dependent bourgeois classes in Africa have yet to move into sectors of the economy that will reduce the importance of politics as a mode of accumulation. The state remains the largest investor, employer, importer and exporter, and the struggle within and between social classes (especially the bourgeois classes) is to penetrate and control its institutions and resources in order to facilitate private, clan, and class accumulation to the detriment, usually, of collective or national growth and development. The state is used by the elites for accumulation rather than legitimation purposes. This erodes its tenuous legitimacy and promotes instability and the endless need to rely on the manipulation of primordial loyalties in order to dominate the political landscape.[19] In the struggle to use the state to facilitate private accumulation, all rational and legal norms are thrown to the winds as elites in their factions confront each other in a battle to control the state. Of course, once state power is captured by hook or crook, usually by crook, the process of privatizing and looting it dry begins immediately. The state relies on manipulation and repression, and ends up looking and acting more like an army of occupation than an institution capable of organizing production and exchange and in initiating a viable national project.

On all indicators of development, the vast majority of African states, to take a regional example, are doing so badly that all theories/models of growth and development are being called into question.[20] This would mean that democracy has no future whatsoever in Africa. We might do well therefore to accept Huntington's explanation that while "Economic factors have significant impact on democratization" they are not "determinative. An overall correlation exists between the level of economic development and democracy, yet no level or pattern of economic development is in itself either necessary or sufficient to bring about democratization."[21] In fact, Robert Pinkney has noted that "Countries in Eastern Europe achieved many of the other developments without democracy, while countries such as Botswana and the Gambia (sic. before the 1994 military coup), with few of the developments described, have sustained pluralist systems."[22]

The second precondition for democracy is the existence

of established political culture or traditions. This has been defined by Georg Sorensen as "the system of values and beliefs that defines the context and meaning of political action."[23] African states would do no better on this count. Whatever the legacies of a precolonial and precapitalist communalist culture and tradition might have been, the reality is that possessive individualism, the profit motive, and the atomization of the individual through direct and/or indirect incorporation into the marketplace have steadily eroded the traditional African systems of values. Today, the experience of Africa since the turn of the century has been one of colonial capitalist brutalization, exploitation, and underdevelopment; elite competition and corruption; coups and counter-coups; massive human rights violations; a political tradition of violence, intolerance, and the manipulation of primordial loyalties; religious intolerance and conflicts; and the widening of the gap between the poor and the rich due to misplaced priorities and narrow vision on the part of the dominant classes.[24] These divisions, conflicts, contradictions, and conditions of instability and distrust have directly militated against consensual politics or the generation of a "prodemocratic consensus" capable of promoting democracy.[25]

The third precondition for the survival of democracy relates to what Moore Jr. describes as "a vigorous and independent class of town dwellers" which has been "an indispensable element in the growth of parliamentary democracy. No bourgeois, no democracy."[26] Although it is well known that the bourgeoisie does not always work for democracy, most developing formations have not been favored with the existence of a disciplined, creative, patriotic, productive, and rational dominant class either. In Africa particularly, in spite of some gains and postcolonial realignment of political forces, the bourgeoisie is still largely mired in a sea of conflicts, violence, ethnic-regional-religious contradictions, and problems of leadership and succession. In many social formations, the bourgeoisie has no identity, as it still collectively carries the social and psychological domination of settler and other forms of colonialism. Though located in urban centers, it is still essentially a rural bourgeoisie pretending to be modern, enlightened or sophisticated. The experiences of Liberia, Somalia, Togo, the Sudan, Mozambique, and even Nigeria, attest clearly to the absence of this prerequisite for democracy: the elites do not engage in consensual politics; political competition is normless; and critical issues of the national question continue to mediate bourgeois and state hegemony.

Finally, a fourth set of preconditions for the survival of democracy are the "economic, political, ideological, and other elements that constitute the international context for the processes that take place in single countries."[27] These prerequisite external determinations of the conditions for democratization advanced by Marxists and others who subscribe to forms of dependency theory hold somewhat true. Their contention that the nature and context of international global capitalist domination and exploitation drained resources, encouraged the brain drain, made regimes more desperate, and tied nations to the geostrategic and other needs of the metropole remains very valid in spite of the end of the Cold War. Poverty, debt and debt-servicing, natural disasters, declining investment, closure of credit lines, falling levels of foreign aid, declining commodity prices, rising prices of imports and interest rates, and increasing powerlessness in the international system reduce possibilities for growth, accumulation, savings, and democracy in most developing formations.[28] Of course, the current global balance of power which has the United States as the dominant military power has evinced some demonstration of a relationship between democratization and growing US influence and power. Clearly, U.S. interest in democracy in developing nations is designed to expand markets, and consolidate American global hegemony. This has been visibly articulated in U.S. interest in South Africa and Russia to take two examples where foreign aid and other support represent a sort of investment for the future.

With the end of the Cold War and the apparent triumph of the market as determined by the growing influence and power of the World Bank and the IMF, most developing nations are now engaged in a struggle to toe the lines of US policy and become "democratic" on the US model in order to satisfy the new political conditionalities of Western governments, bankers, donors, and nongovernmental organizations. The "democratic" tag has become a major component of foreign aid and other negotiations between poor nations and lenders as well as donors. In this instance, the democratization agenda lacks the required roots for survival and consolidation. In other instances of imposition of democracy through military threats or force, as we have seen in the case of Haiti, it fails to satisfy the other prerequisites: some appreciable degree of capitalist development; a political culture favorable to democracy; experience with resolving major issues of politics and development in the past; and a fairly strong location and role in the international division of labor. Thus, even in Haiti, based on the preconditions above, and in spite of all the publicity and cost, there is little reason to expect democracy to thrive. The threat or use of sanctions, foreign aid, investment, support for rebel movements, and the granting of special privileges do not in themselves bring about democracy, even if, in some instances, they ease the burden on the state and its custodians and thus encourage them to reach some accommodation with civil society and embark on political reforms (as was the case in Kenya, Malawi, and Ghana). Yet, as Pinkney notes,

> Many of the lessons for the Third World arising out of the literature appear to be negative. Most Third World countries have not enjoyed economic devel-

opment cited by Lipset, or the civil cultural attitudes cited by Almond and Verba. The sequences in development conducive to democracy in the West have not generally occurred in the Third World, and the 'developmental crises' have frequently crowded in on one another over a short period of time. Institutional developments have generally been limited. We have seen that most Latin American states, despite their long period of independence, have built only rudimentary links between government and governed, while the more recently independent states of Africa and Asia have had little time to develop institutions.[29]

Perhaps, there is need to move away from these eurocentric explanations and assumptions about the preconditions for democracy. If we are to adhere to them, there will be no reason to discuss democracy in Africa, as none of the preconditions apply. Yet, the truth is that what the literature outlines as *preconditions* are actually the very reasons or *goals* for which Africans struggle. As Terry Lynn Karl has rightly noted, "what the literature has considered in the past to be the *preconditions* of democracy may be better conceived in the future as the *outcomes* of democracy. Patterns of greater economic growth and more equitable income distribution, higher levels of literacy and education, and increases in social communication and media exposure may be better treated as the products of stable democratic processes rather than prerequisites of its existence (emphases added)."[30] It is precisely this observation that has set the new agenda for a holistic and dialectical study of the specific challenges to democracy and democratization by looking at particular experiences. This has the advantage of avoiding the transposition of experiences, prevents undue generalization across regions and continents, and encourages the need to pay attention to specificities and political dynamics within each social formation or region. We can only better appreciate the sacrifices, strategies, institutions, alignments, and realignments behind these struggles through historical and holistic approaches to particular situations and cases rather than through generalizations.

The Challenges of Democracy/Democratization in Africa

Democracy in Africa shares some basic features with democracy in other parts of the world revolving around issues of personal and collective liberties, basic freedoms, rights, and obligations.[31] These rights and freedoms are often enshrined in constitutions, even under military juntas. However, the extent, expression, and enjoyment of these freedoms and rights are conditioned and determined by issues of power, politics, and production, as well as exchange relations. They are also conditioned by the location and role of particular formations in the global division of labor, the interest of external powers in local political balances and relations, and the nature and direction of struggles in civil society. The rapid alignment and realignment of political forces in civil society, and the preparedness of ruling elites to forge a consensual political terrain to facilitate class or group projects also affect the nature of democracy and the enjoyment of basic rights and liberties. As Salim A. Salim has argued, "democracy is not a 'revelation'. How it is expressed, how it is given concrete form, of necessity, varies from society to society. Consequently, one should avoid the temptation of decreeing a so-called 'perfect' model of democracy and of exporting it wholesale or imposing it on another society."[32] It is quite true, as Martin Klein has noted, that "Democracy is not an abstract ideal. People do not choose democracy because they read about it. Democracy has invariably risen out of a struggle against autocracy."[33]

Today, from the World Bank and the International Monetary Fund, to Western governments and credit clubs, the "demand for democracy" has become a critical aspect of their relations with the very countries they have traditionally dominated and exploited. Any serious effort at understanding the challenge or dilemmas of democracy in Africa must, therefore, pay due attention to the region's historical experiences, the implications of that experience, and the contemporary interplay of social and political forces. Without dwelling too much on this, the record of postcolonial African elites and the postcolonial state throughout the 1960s and 1970s was one of consolidating and legitimizing neocolonial and unequal relations, reproducing underdevelopment, and backwardness. Since the 1960s, Africa has simply moved from one crisis to the other. Politics became warfare. Conditions of instability, corruption, waste, poverty, uncertainty, disillusionment, and violence encouraged military adventurists to hijack popular struggles in the majority of African states. Democracy was thrown out of the political terrain in virtually all African states. In those countries like Senegal, Kenya, and Zambia where the military had not terminated the democratic processes, individuals, their protegees or a clique of elites simply privatized the state in the "interest of the nation," relying on bogus "ideologies" like Humanism, Nyayoism, Authenticity, Uhuru, and the like. There was hardly a difference between Nigeria and Kenya though the latter had a parliament and the former was under military rule: regimes were corrupt and intolerant, the press was not free, academics and social critics were persecuted, civil society was suffocated, opposition was banned, and both nations were subservient to foreign capital. The general condition of political cynicism, economic vulnerability and decay, social dislocation, and peripheralization in the global capitalist system, deepened the African crisis and made it vulnerable to dictates from the outside on political and economic matters. More importantly, the rapid economic deterioration made the elites more desperate and unwilling to tolerate opposition. This led to coups and countercoups, civil strife, wars, and the wanton abuse of human rights. The last issue ever considered by such repressive regimes (often supported by *both* super powers in the name of a so-called Cold War) was democracy.

Of course, the difficult conditions arising from economic and social dislocation and decay compounded the challenges to democracy. This was the more so in the context of deep primordial cleavages and general failure of the state to provide for the underprivileged. It was quite easy therefore for voluntary associations, religious bodies, ethnic associations, and individuals with dubious sources of wealth to take over the functions of the highly weakened state. This way, it was easy for counter-bases of power and authority to emerge beyond the state demanding the loyalty of the people. Where the state had failed to act as a state, the people turned to primordial associations and crass individualism. The people generally regarded the state not just as enemy but as a force to be challenged, cheated, and demystified. There is no way in which such a state could ever promote a democratic agenda or inspire people to higher levels of political consciousness and patriotism. Let us consider other challenges to democracy.

Economic Liberalization and Democratization in Africa

The issues touched on above are neglected in more popular explanations of the problems of liberal democracy in Africa, especially the role played by the West in nurturing, sustaining, and reproducing despotic regimes in Africa. Explanations have tended to focus on the more superficial aspects of political change in the region. It is precisely this sort of focus that has convinced donors, lenders, and Western governments that the agenda for Africa's democratic enterprise can be set from the outside. As well, it is assumed that a combination of economic and political restructuring programs, under the supervision of IMF and

World Bank officials with emphasis on the implementation of orthodox monetarist programs, will promote an "enabling environment" which in turn will promote democracy, stability, growth, accountability, and development.

Of course, African leaders, afraid of the "pressures from below" and recognizing that the alignment and realignment of political forces would deprive them of the lucrative and comfortable but exploitative locations in their respective political economies, have been quick to accept political prescriptions from the West. In most cases, they have had no choice. Having bankrupted their respective countries, and manipulated primordial loyalties to the maximum as part of their divide-and-rule politics, the forging of an alliance with more powerful external forces has been the only option left for most of them. Pressures from debt, debt-servicing, unemployment, ethnic and religious upheavals, closure of credit lines, increasing bankruptcies, rising militancy among nonbourgeois constituencies, and restlessness within the military and security networks for a variety of reasons, have exposed the tenuous hold on power and exposed the leaders to direct challenges by the people.[34]

Ironically, the structural adjustment program has helped significantly in promoting the democratization agenda in two unintended ways: first, it took away from the state and its custodians the resources, autonomy, and capacity to repress, bribe, intimidate, and manipulate nonbourgeois forces. With no money, with worthless currencies that have been badly devalued, with the closure of credit lines, and with investors moving to Eastern Europe and relocating capital while holding back on new investments, African leaders found themselves to be almost irrelevant in the geostrategic and economic calculations of the former Cold War masters.[35] They now had to face the wrath of the people. Secondly, the proletarianization of the middle classes brought an army of bureaucrats, intellectuals, and professionals into the ranks of workers, peasants, and the unemployed. Policies of retrenchment; desubsidization; introduction of new levies, taxes, and fees; as well as the repressive environment required to force orthodox adjustment on the populace—all these factors increased the militancy of nonbourgeois forces even as they demystified the state, its institutions, and its custodians. This encouraged popular groups to form new organizations, revive dormant ones, ask new questions, and make new demands on the state for accountability, participation, social justice, and the meeting of basic human needs. Though unintended, the impoverishment, repression, marginalization, brutalization, exploitation, and humiliation which nonbourgeois forces and vulnerable groups suffered from the orthodox structural adjustment programs and from the elites in Africa contributed significantly to the renewed interests in democracy, democratization, empowerment, and the need to mount a fundamental challenge to the dictators on the African political landscape.

To be sure, elections have taken place all over the continent, even in South Africa. Military governments have been forced to make concessions to civil society and reach accommodation with or give way to popular groups (Mali and Benin); some have been forced to civilianize themselves in order to remain politically relevant (Ghana); one-party states have been transformed in less than a year into multiparty states (Zambia); presidents-for-life have been compelled to restructure their political positions and perspectives on politics and power (Malawi); dictators who were darlings of the West have been pressured into holding multiparty elections through the withholding of foreign aid disbursement (Kenya and Malawi); and in Nigeria, popular groups succeeded in driving the discredited dictator from power and the remilitarization of the political landscape in November 1993 took very serious cognizance of the new power, influence, and capabilities of the prodemocracy constituencies. Yet, these changes, important as they are, have not altered the purpose of politics, the nature of politics, the character of the elites, the nature of the repressive state, the character of society, the conditions of dependent accumulation and foreign domination, and the peripheral location and role of African formations in the international division of labor.

Unfortunately for Africa, the current tendency to equate elections with democracy and give the impression that the mere existence of several political parties means that democracy exists has reduced the focus on prodemocracy and civil liberties constituencies at the grassroots. As the African situation has clearly demonstrated, elections may take place, a multiplicity of parties may dominate the political terrain, but the elitist, exploitative, violent, manipulative, and in many instances pedestrian and predatory character of politics remains intact. If one reads Chinua Achebe's *A Man of the People*, published in 1966, one will be struck with how so little has changed in the nature of the actors, the role of money in politics, the place of religion, region, and ethnicity, the diversionary politics of the elites, political opportunism and defensive radicalism, as well as the unrepentant abuse of power.[36] This unchanging vortex of politics, dominated by an old guard and (more recently) by their younger protegees (the so called "new breed" politicians) has made it impossible for the people to empower themselves and their communities in order to determine and dictate the content and context of national politics. These—even more than the crisis of dependence, vulnerability, foreign domination, and underdevelopment—are the real challenges to democratization in Africa.

Evaluating the Democratization Process

It has become necessary, therefore, to take a step back from the current euphoria surrounding the democratization process in Africa. This is necessary to avoid another "false start" in the political process which might culminate in the abortion or subversion of Africa's so-called "second revolution."[37] Already we are witnessing traces of defensive radicalism; ideological and political opportunism and posturing; a concentration on aping Western models, institutions, and traditions; and the politics of manipulation, violence, and diversion. Michael Bratton and Nicolas van de Walle contend that the "dynamic process of protest and reform is nascent in Africa, and the future course of regime transitions is highly uncertain."[38] They warn that "the partial liberalization of authoritarian regimes does not amount to a transition to democracy" and that the results of elections to date do not "provide any guarantee that competitive politics will be institutionalized."[39] Samuel Decalo is even more pessimistic about the future of liberal democracy in Africa. As he noted in the second opening quote, the on-going democratic changes are superficial and are incapable of articulating an alternative political program for a fundamental transformation of African politics.[40] The insecurity and instability of the new democracies, the ability of the "old buzzards" to outfox the prodemocracy movements, the opportunism and divisions within the ranks of the opposition, and the remilitarization of politics in locations such as Niger, Nigeria, and The Gambia, clearly provide reasons for pessimism. Why are scholars so pessimistic about the democratic enterprise in Africa?

It is very clear that the prerequisites discussed earlier do not exist in Africa. Yet, any focus on those prerequisites is like condemning Africa to eternal political bondage under dictatorships which have practically ruined the continent.[41] Because a distinction is not often drawn between democracy and *democratization*, it has become rather easy for African leaders to accommodate the *features* and institutions of liberal democracy while suffocating and dividing civil society at the grassroots. As well, because the current agenda for democracy in Africa as sponsored and pursued by the neocolonial state has been set by Western donors and

Western governments, African leaders have tried as much as possible to stick to the foreign-generated agenda so as to ensure that the lines for foreign aid and credit are kept open. The leaders have used democracy to give some form of legitimacy to regimes with longstanding reputations for brutality, corruption, and gross inefficiency. For instance, Rawlings in Ghana and Moi in Kenya used *elections* to relegitimize their exploitative and repressive regimes in a continent and global order which seems to be rejecting despotism. While the demands of donors and lenders for political pluralism were satisfied, this did not create much room for democratic deepening or economic autonomy of such governments.[42]

In the context of ongoing recomposition of political, strategic, and economic relations in the emerging global order, Africa has boundless opportunities to restructure political and economic spaces with an agenda which acknowledges its historical experiences, specificities, balance of forces, and location and role in the international division of labor. Such an agenda will require leaders to reach out to their respective peoples, discard traditional patterns, structures, and institutions of politics, and reach accommodation with constituencies hitherto marginalized and repressed, such as women, minorities, and ethnic and religious interests. Unfortunately, even with the best of intentions, Africa's deepening economic crisis and desperate social conditions make the processes of democratization, and democratic consolidation very challenging.

The African condition today is, to say the least, very pathetic. As Lance Morrow put it recently, Africa is in a "scramble for existence."[43] It is quite obvious that conditions of deepening civil crisis, increasing marginalization in the global system, and increasing vulnerability to external penetration, domination, manipulation, and exploitation, have had three main consequences: First, it has exploded the invincibility of the state and opened it up to challenges

25

from disadvantaged constituencies; second, it has made the state, its agents, and its agencies more desperate and repressive in some instances, and willing to make concessions to civil society in others; and third, it has made Africa more of a pawn in the hands of international finance institutions like the IMF and the World Bank and thus created a major opening for the political and ideological manipulation of the continent. This has encouraged the imposition of models of democracy which are, more often than not, out of tune with African realities and aspirations. This excessive influence of foreign institutions has created a huge "credibility deficit" among African governments thus further eroding the ability of the state to organize a genuine transition to democracy.

In the midst of the confusion, instability, conflicts, and contradictions generated and/or accentuated by the policies of the IMF and the World Bank, attention has shifted away from the struggles of the people at the grassroots level; from the limitations of the so called prodemocracy movements; from the required preconditions for the survival of democracy; and from the urgent need for a strengthened civil society. Rather, Western governments, donors, and creditors have drawn a direct linkage between democracy and development; sung the praises of the market; imposed political conditionalities on African states; and assumed that regimes which had spent decades suffocating civil society and oppressing their peoples during the implementation of structural adjustment can be expected to open up civil society, respect human rights, and cultivate democratic traditions. In fact, there is not one single example in Africa were orthodox structural adjustment has led to more democracy, increased political stability, national unity, the provision of basic needs for the masses, growth, and development. In spite of vitriolic propaganda, and the determination to showcase Ghana as a successful experiment through the massive infusion of loans and other financial support, adjustment has deepened class antagonisms and conflicts, delegitimized the state, marginalized the masses from the elites, and created conditions for the strengthening of neocolonial relations and further marginalization in the global capitalist system. Adjustment in Ghana has more than quadrupled the country's foreign debt, eroded its national autonomy, and rendered the Cedi almost worthless.[44] As Georg Sorensen has observed:

> Nowhere does the consolidation of democracy face larger obstacles than in sub-Saharan Africa, where the foundation on which democracy must be built, is very weak. The African state has failed both economically and politically. In general, Africans are as poor today as they were thirty years ago. At the same time, the large majority of African states have so far failed to institutionalize any form of effective rule, be it authoritarianism or democracy....[45]

One can now effectively make the argument that since the ongoing efforts at democracy are still conducted within the parameters of the dictates, ideals, perceptions, and needs of lenders and donors, they would be cosmetic, tenuous, and superficial even if they cost huge amounts of money. In spite of the widespread enthusiasm for democratization in Africa, the current processes are informed and driven more by elite interests and struggles to survive the pressures both from below and from the outside. Sorensen has argued that such Western-instigated drives for democracy would be "counterproductive" because:

> The Western countries themselves are examples of the fact that democracy cannot be installed overnight; it is a long-term process of gradual change. When quick fixes of imposing multiparty systems, for example, are substituted for the long haul of patiently paving the way for a democratic polity, the result may be that a thin layer of democratic coating is superimposed upon a system of personal rule without changes in the basic features of the old structure.[46]

The Neocolonial State and Democratization

It is incredible that the entire world seems to be taken in by the so-called democratization processes in Africa when the brutal, unstable, non-hegemonic, and grossly inefficient neocolonial state has remained intact. The state, under the control of very conservative and corrupt political forces, has survived the "changes" in every country that has conducted so-called multiparty elections. The very survival of this state which has historically failed to meet the basic needs of the majority or guarantee basic freedoms, provides a clear pointer to the fact that "there is not much hope that the recent democratic openings will progress into consolidated democracies."[47] Given that the current "transitions" in Africa are dominated, influenced, conditioned, and operated largely by the very same elites who subverted the early democratic experiments, collaborated with military juntas, and ruined African economies, there is every reason to see their new conversion to democracy as a temporary retreat strategy to remain politically relevant and to strengthen their hold on the state which is in reality a means to rapid primitive accumulation.[48] In case after case, "incumbent leaders have preempted the new winds of democracy and have succeeded in staying in power by engineering transitions from above."[49] Where they have been defeated, they have, as in Zambia with Kenneth Kaunda, continued to loom large in the political sphere; and in other instances, they have succeeded in being part of the process of (s)electing their successors. In this way, the old political traditions, alliances, and institutions have remained intact, even if in temporary abeyance to allow "things to cool down."

One can indeed argue that since the vast majority of the democratization agendas do not include programs aimed at dismantling and reconstructing the oppressive neocolonial state and its institutions that have been at the heart of Africa's predicaments since the colonial days, there is no way the tenuous victories will not be easily confused, incorporated, and domesticated by contradictions and coalitions arising from the distorted economic sector and negative political, even cultural attitudes largely aided by ethnic, regional, personal, and religious interests. The Zambian example, where the Movement for Multiparty Democracy (MMD) struggled to come to power—only to be more faithful to the World Bank and donors and virtually retain all of Kenneth Kaunda's ministers and institutions—is a typical case in point. Frederick Chiluba has not succeeded in *changing* anything in Zambia and this has made Kenneth Kaunda's popularity increase in what Huntington has referred to as "authoritarian nostalgia."[50] In fact, Kaunda is already contemplating a return to power in an attempt to cash in on the crisis of democratic consolidation which has plagued the MMD government since its spectacular victory in 1991.

Finally, to the extent that Africa is unimportant in the geostrategic and political calculations of the West, especially the United States—a position informed by a combination of ignorance, discrimination, fear, insecurity, and racism—democratizing nations are unlikely to receive the sort of support which Russia, for example, is receiving from the United States and other Western powers and institutions.[51] As well, the absence of a strong constituency for Africa in the United States (or anywhere outside Africa for that matter) means that no democratization effort will receive support like Haiti did even where clear movements towards liberal democracy are terminated, as has been the case in Nigeria. Sorensen points out that "no additional aid seems to be forthcoming as a result of the democratic openings. Current public opinion in the North seems to be that starvation and death are more acceptable in Africa than elsewhere or are unavoidable there. In other words, the conditions that are being imposed concerning democratization do not promise more aid if they are met; they promise less aid if they are not met."[52] This complicates the predicament of the beleaguered African state which is already under extreme pressure. This has the possibility of forcing the desperate state to return to repression, political posturing, propaganda, and the manipulation of primordial loyalties in order to retain control of the political landscape.

The reality of Africa, in spite of vitriolic propaganda from African dictators, opportunistic politicians, and so called prodemocracy leaders is that, as long as the current custodians of the state remain in power, democracy in Africa will remain a mirage—in as much as the institutions, structures, and social relations with which the elites dominated and repressed society remain unchanged; in as much as the masses of the people are not empowered and society is not opened up for mass political action; and in as much as the economic dislocation and crisis inherited at political independence in the 1960s continue. It is impossible to carry out a viable and credible political restructuring and transformation in a political economy dominated and controlled by the very class forces and interests which ran down the various economies, accumulated huge and unprecedented foreign debts, repressed and tried to eliminate all popular organizations, mortgaged their respective economies to foreign interests, and showed little or no concern for the terrible living conditions of the masses of the people. How can leaders like Arap Moi in Kenya, Eyadema in Togo, Abacha in Nigeria, and Mobutu in Zaire, to name a few, preside over the process of democratization except at levels unlikely to challenge the enshrined traditions of corruption, repression, waste, and mismanagement?

One of the major reasons why antidemocratic forces held sway for so long in Africa is the very nature and role of the neocolonial state. Largely a continuation of the colonial state; lacking hegemony, credibility, stability, and legitimacy; and presided over by a largely unproductive and weak elite, the state became a direct instrument of oppression and exploitation. Since it easily played the role of capitalist because of the weaknesses of local dominant classes, the struggle to control it was normless, often requiring the use of violence and the manipulation of primordial loyalties by elites who lacked credible bases of support in civil society. Human rights abuses, wanton massacre of nonbourgeois forces, misplaced priorities, inefficiency, subservience to foreign capital and imperialism, and the general exploitation and oppression of the people became the main features and functions of the state in Africa.

It is amazing that there is really not one prodemocracy movement that has the total dismantling—or at least reconstruction—of the state as a primary goal. Rather, what we see are struggles to *replace* the government, to *participate* in government, and to actually continue with the policies and politics of the repressive state. To be sure, some of the more established prodemocracy movements have developed some cosmetic programs for *reforming* rather than *transforming and recomposing* the state. It is even more worrisome to note the sort of persons leading many of the prodemocracy movements: political opportunists, disgraced politicians, old and tired politicians of the first decade of independence, retired military officers, persons who have been marginalized from existing exploitative power structures, and professional politicians and petty-bourgeois lawyers. The political interests and consciousness of these persons have seriously conditioned the nature and operations of prodemocracy movements in the region. The hunger for naked power and the urge to become the state has factionalized and seriously weakened the prodemocracy movements in Africa. Little wonder that in Zaire, Zambia, Ghana, Kenya, Togo, and Nigeria, their ranks are splintered, their voices so many and so conflicting that it is often difficult to discern a specific agenda beyond the clamor for a nebulous democratic agenda. Since every leader of a small prodemocracy group wants to be a presidential candidate, they refuse to reach accommodation with each other and fail to present a united front to challenge the incumbent government. In Ghana the boycott of the parliamentary elections did not prevent the National Democratic Congress (NDC-the PNDC without the "P"!) led by Rawlings from securing the support of some fringe parties and giving some legitimacy to the elections. In Zambia today, there are over 34 opposition parties, all with their eyes on the presidency even when they lack an understanding, much less a program for reform and recovery in the country. The majority of the so called opposition parties have been formed by dismissed and disgraced politicians and ministers who are simply interested in occupying the state house: all other things will follow! In Nigeria, in spite of the unprecedented victory of the Campaign for Democracy (CD) over the Ibrahim Babangida junta and the ongoing struggles against General Abacha's dictatorship, new prodemocracy movements like the National Conscience (NC) and the Democratic Alternative (DEAL) are being formed by the "new" democrats everyday. This simply divides the opposition, creates diversions, and weakens the ability to present a holistic agenda for political renewal to the people. It is thus easy to agree with Claude Ake's position that "the self-appointed agents of democratization in Africa are implausible. They are not so much supporting democracy as using it...the African elite support democracy only as a means to power, the international development agencies support it as an asset to structural adjustment and Western governments support it ambiguously torn between their growing indifference to Africa and their desire to promote their own way of life."[53] Specifically, on the hollowness of the new democratic agenda as it relates to the character of the neocolonial state, Ake is very instructive:

> One of the most remarkable features of democratization in Africa is that it is totally indifferent to the character of the state. Democratic elections are being held to determine who will exercise the powers

of the state with no questions asked about the character of the state as if it has no implications for democracy. But its implications are so serious that elections in Africa give the voter only a choice between oppressors. This is hardly surprising since Africa largely retains the colonial state structure which is inherently anti-democratic, being the repressive apparatus of an occupying power. Uncanningly, this structure has survived, reproduced and rejuvenated by the legacy of military and single-party rule. So what is happening now by way of democratization is that self-appointed military or civilian leaders are being replaced by *elected dictators* [emphasis added].[54]

It is no wonder therefore, that in less than five years of struggle, many of the prodemocracy movements have become exhausted and are in disarray. The hopes for a "quick kill" and capture of power now unrealizable, many are forging alliances with incumbent regimes, joining military *juntas*, or converting themselves into Non-Governmental Organizations (NGOs)!

The Limits of Elections as Democracy

This is where the current wave of elections which are ushering in liberal democratic forms of governance in various shades are most defective. Of course, it is "utopian to expect democratic norms to be an immediate success." It is true that "Many of Africa's new leaders will fail. Some will revert to autocratic methods. Some will prove as corrupt as their predecessors. Some will prove incompetent. Some will founder on the shoals of ethnic conflict. The struggle is, alas, one that must be fought over and over again...."[55] Yet, as Catherine Newbury has rightly noted, "liberal democracy (is) an important first step, providing possibilities for political organization that have been stifled under authoritarian regimes."[56] However, where the ongoing democratic processes seem to be focusing "mainly on political procedures and practice (liberal democracy), while excluding peasants and workers,"[57] while actually trying to stifle prodemocracy constituencies, there is a need to examine them critically and rise beyond euphoria and the superficial, attractive as these may appear.

Of course, it is important to raise the issue of democratization under difficult conditions. The social and economic crisis makes it difficult for the people to tolerate the slow process of reform and recovery, and to be patient with some of the new leaders like Chiluba in Zambia. The people have suffered for so long and have been exploited by local and international forces for too long. Unfortunately, the prodemocracy groups and new political parties all campaigned promising change, better government, human rights, and the provision of basic needs. On coming to power, they confronted empty treasuries, huge internal and foreign debts, pressures/demands from bankers and other lenders, and "political conditionalities" imposed by donors. They also had to deal with a global system in which Africa was largely unimportant to global geostrategic and economic calculations, and where foreign interests and aid were shifting to other regions of the world. It is therefore pertinent to ask: Can Africa really *democratize* when it remains the most poverty-stricken, least industrialized, most marginal, most debt-distressed, most vulnerable, most foreign-dominated, and most crisis-ridden region in the world? Are there any indications that the global economy will become more favorable to African participation?[58] Will terms of trade improve so as to enable African economies to generate more foreign exchange? Will debt relief become a serious part of global debt negotiations? Will Africa's current, almost irrelevant, but certainly marginal place in the economic and geostrategic calculations of the developed countries (especially the United States) improve because so-called multiparty elections have been held? Will more investors and donors return to Africa? Will the international arms dealers from the East and West change their manipulative and exploitative trade relations with Africa to promote less emphasis on wars, security, and the expansion of the military? Will current patterns of resource extraction and transfer abroad be restructured to favor Africa? Finally, will African elites accept the need for a drastic restructuring of the political landscape in such a manner as to render them relatively powerless and virtually accountable to the popular will?

It has been argued by several Africans and Africanists that the democratic struggles in Africa are hampered by "the implementation of structural adjustment programmes, violent ethnic upheavals, the difficulty with which new hegemonic coalitions are being forged and the resistance of the military to returning to their barracks."[59] It is clear, therefore, that more than any other region in the world and more than at any point in history, the task of successful transition to democracy—and the more challenging task of effectively sustaining and reproducing democracy—in Africa could easily be subverted on its own terms.

In view of the points above, it is clear that democracy must go beyond mere elections, important as these are. Only a structural transformation of the social formation, a dismantling and reconstruction of institutions, and the full inclusion of the people in the initiation and implementation of socioeconomic and political programs can give elections the relevance they deserve in the political culture and process. The current Western (especially American) emphasis on multiparty elections is escapist, diversionary, and of limited leverage in the context of the very deep roots and wide implications of the African predicament. As we have seen in The Gambia, in Niger, and in Nigeria, elections, even where they are monitored by scores of foreign observer groups, hardly prevent the return of the military—clearly one of the most serious challenges to democracy and peace in the continent.

The Military and the Democratization Process

The military remains one of the major obstacles to democratization in Africa. In spite of the controversial roles of Thomas Sankara in Burkina Faso, Jerry Rawlings in Ghana, and Mummar Ghadaffi in Libya, the record of the African military has been one of disaster. The situation in Zaire under Mobutu Sese Seko, Togo under Gnassingbe Eyadema, Ethiopia under Mengistu Haile Mariam, Benin under Matthew Kerekou, Somalia under Said Bare, and the Sudan under Jaffer Nimeiri attest to this fact. The Nigerian case amply demonstrates that the military, as an undemocratic commandist organization, is incapable of initiating, nurturing, and consolidating democracy in Africa. It has relied on brutish force, intimidation, and wanton human rights abuses to stifle civil society and assert its own control over society.[60] The promulgation of decrees and edicts which nullify the jurisdiction of the law courts, the proscription of trade unions and student unions, the subversion of the course of justice, intolerance of opposition, and general inability to appreciate or understand the meaning of accountability to civil order have made it impossible for the African military to promote the process of democratization. As every instance of military dictatorship in Africa has demonstrated, the military is as corrupt, factionalized, and fractionalized as the political class. Discipline and professionalism have been so badly eroded that the army is at best a badly structured and badly run organization which sits on the people, suffocates civil society, destroys creativity and originality, and squanders scarce resources on the defense of the looters of the national treasury.

The truth is that the military has no business being in power irrespective of the circumstances. The excuse of political conflicts and the loss of direction by corrupt politicians does not justify the intervention of the military, which, in any case, has hardly done any better. The intervention of the military has been encouraged by the fragmentation and weaknesses of civil society. The damage which the Babangida and Abacha *juntas* have caused in Nigeria clearly attests to the dangers of military misrule in Africa. The singular act of terminating the march to a Third Republic cost the debt-ridden nation over N50 billion. The military has arrogated to itself the right to determine for the people which government is good or bad. It acts as if there are two parties in Africa: the military and the people. Since it controls or monopolizes the legal control of the means of coercion, it sees itself as the senior or stronger party. It has refused to let the political process mature, get routinized and institutionalized, and has refused to allow politicians to learn from their mistakes, align and realign their loyalties and interests, and forge the required linkages with their respective constituencies to sustain democracy. The African military refuses to believe that democracy relies upon the fact that differences and contradictions exist and that the solution is to negotiate and reconcile these differences to the highest degree possible. The African military does not believe that democracy makes room for politicians and political actors to "agree to disagree", and that social pluralism is the very strength of democracy. As a largely parasitic organization, it has continued to drain scarce resources, thus making it difficult if not impossible for new democratic governments to survive.[61]

To be sure, the military has been able to intervene at will and get willing supporters in its determination to stamp out democracy from Africa because the political elite has been very opportunistic and weak when it comes to challenging military dictatorships. The political elite in Africa has not accepted democracy, much less democratization, as a viable agenda for checking the intervention of the military in politics on a permanent basis. Their political parties have been divided along ethnic, regional, even religious lines; they have relied on propaganda, lies, and divisions in their political contestations; and like previous governments, they have looted the treasury without restraint. In fact, the political elite, traditional and religious leaders, intellectuals of all ideological persuasions, and business persons rush and fall over each other to welcome the military, seek political appointments and contracts, bad-mouth the previous government, and congratulate the military for chasing away "irresponsible" politicians. Historically, this has been the experience of Nigeria, where several leaders of the human rights and prodemocracy community melted into the Abacha junta following the November 1993 coup—without apologies—including Alhaji Baba Gana Kingibe, the elected running mate of Chief M.K.O. Abiola. Such acts erode the credibility of the political elite in the eyes of both the military and the people. And one of the reasons why the military has hated the university system, and intellectuals in particular, is the opportunistic, subservient, and sycophantic postures of many African academics.[62] Ordinary people easily become discouraged and apathetic when they see the radicals, activists, "fire eaters," Marxists, and democrats of yesterday—who organized "National Conferences," protest marches, even acts of sabotage, against the neocolonial state—now hobnobbing, wining and dining military officers legendary for their shallow thinking, corruption, repression, and other atavistic modes of behavior. As well, since the elites who are supposed to be lords in their ethnic enclaves have so openly welcomed the military, who is to stop the officers from arrogating to themselves the right to determine, condition, and structure the context and content of national politics?

The new democratic agenda in Africa must design clear and popular programs to contain the military and subject it to civil society. This can be done through constitutional and political means. The overall goal is to thoroughly educate the people and the military about the primacy of the popular will and to get communities, organizations, and all institutions to design ways to resist the military through acts of civil disobedience that will render nations ungovernable to military adventurists. This will be difficult and will take some time, but the process must be initiated by the more serious prodemocracy movements.

In a global system where there is so much discrimination, inequality, poverty, exploitation, and racism, the challenges and predicaments catalogued above should alert us all to the difficulty of building viable democratic systems based on liberal Western notions of democracy in developing formations. This is the more so when such notions are tied to foreign aid or trade: the baggage of political conditionalities imposed from the West on poverty-stricken and often desperate nations. Today, many leaders are forced to accept Western-dictated political reforms because multiparty elections and the tag of "democracy" bring international recognition, and are now being used by investors as major criteria for doing business with African states irrespective of the depth and sustainability of such exercises. As well, religious fundamentalism, opportunistic nationalism, ethnic conflicts, and the contradictions arising from unresolved issues in the national question pose very serious challenges to the democratic agenda in Africa. Without doubt, in Liberia, Nigeria, the Sudan, Somalia, Rwanda, Burundi, and Togo (to mention only the hot spots of crisis in Africa), the democratic agenda has taken a back seat to efforts to resolve the national question, reconstitute the state, and mediate contradictions and conflicts within and between political constituencies. For the weak and vulnerable, the uncertainty they face on a daily basis on the frontline of struggle or in their respective refugee camps is how to survive the hell right here on earth, a hell created by African elites and their foreign masters and allies.

The problems, constraints, and contradictions outlined above would give the general impression that the current processes of political liberalization in Africa are at best another false start. This is because the process is not creating a fundamental change or break with the past. It is still dominated by the elites who had suffocated civil society and banished democracy from the political landscape for decades. It is taking place in an increasingly difficult world system which is hardly favorable to Africa. Yet, the changes do have some meaning and possibilities. These can only be exploited, however, if domestic communities and constituencies seize the initiative to deepen the political processes, reconstruct the political agenda, get directly involved in politics, and forge new sociopolitical relations to strengthen civil society. The Zambian experience since 1991 demonstrates this paradox of change without change and the difficulty of consolidating procedural liberal democracy in a crisis-ridden political economy.

This can be done by rejecting politicians who lack presence and a record in the community; by opposing and rejecting politicians who have been disgraced in their previous positions; by democratizing their community-based organizations; by networking with other democratic organizations; by sponsoring leaders from their respective organizations to participate in politics; and by generating resources through collective work to reduce reliance on the state and corrupt politicians. In addition, as the politicians expose their opportunism through the collaboration with the military and elite-dominated political parties, the people and their organizations must hold them permanently responsible for the devastation of their communities. The people must be prepared, through their organizations, to oppose the military through acts of civil disobedience or simultaneous withdrawal of services whenever such adventurists terminate democratic experiments. The people and their communities must insist, as a precondition for participation in the political process, the inclusion of their needs and ideas in the planning and implementation of public policies. Finally, the people and their communities must insist on constitutionalism, respect for democratic institutions and traditions, the supremacy of the popular will, and their involvement in the construction of a new political and economic agenda for renewal and recovery by forming their own political parties or forging an alliance with parties that are clearly sympathetic to the people, self-reliance, and development.

Notes

1. "News Analysis: People Power—'Unstoppable,'" *Africa News* (December 23, 1991—January 6, 1992).
2. Samuel Decalo, "The Process, Prospects and Constraints of Democratization in Africa," *African Affairs* 91(1992):8.
3. Nelson Kasfir, "Popular Sovereignty and Popular Participation: Mixed Constitutional Democracy in the Third World," *Third World Quarterly* 13, 4 (1992):587.
4. World Bank, *Sub-Saharan Africa: From Crisis to Sustainable Growth-A Long-Term Perspective Study*, (Washington, D.C.: World Bank, 1989), p. ix (emphasis added).
5. Ibid., p. ixi.
6. Ibid., pp. 2-5.
7. Economic Commission for Africa, *African Charter for Popular Participation in Development and Transformation*, (Addis Ababa: ECA (E/ECA/CM.16/11), 1990), p. 17.
8. Ibid., p. 18.
9. Richard Sandbrook, *The Politics of Africa's Economic Recovery*, (Cambridge: Cambridge University Press, 1993), p. 4 (emphasis added).
10. World Bank, *Governance and Development*, (Washington, D. C.: World Bank, 1992).
11. World Bank, *Sub-Saharan Africa*, p. 192. On Robert Kaplan see his article "The Coming Anarchy," *Atlantic Monthly* (February 1994). For a critique see Carol Lancaster, ""The Coming Anarchy,"" *CSIS Africa Notes* 163(August 1994).
12. Julius O. Ihonvbere, "The 'Irrelevant' State, Ethnicity and the Quest for Nationhood in Africa," *Ethnic and Racial Studies* 17, 1 (January 1994).
13. Robert Bates, "Socio-Economic Bases of Democratization in Africa: Some Reflections," in *African Governance in*

the 1990s (Atlanta: The Carter Center of Emory University, March 1990), p.32.

14. See Julius O. Ihonvbere, "Dead End to Nigerian Democracy?: Explaining The 1993 Abacha Coup in Nigeria," Proceedings of the 1994 Meeting of the Association of Third World Studies, April 1995, and Ajayi Ola-Rotimi and Julius O. Ihonvbere, "Democratic Impasse: Remilitarization in Nigeria," *Third World Quarterly* 15, 4 (1994).

15. See Claude Ake, "Is Africa Democratizing?" *The Guardian* (Lagos) (December 12, 1993); Mohammed B. Alam, "Democracy in the Third World: Some Problems and Dilemmas," *Indian Journal of Politics* XX, 1-2 (January-June, 1986); Michael Bratton and Nicolas van de Walle, "Popular Protest and Political Reform in Africa," *Comparative Politics* 243, 4 (July 1992); and Samuel P. Huntington, *The Third Wave: Democratization in the Late Twentieth Century*, (Norman: University of Oklahoma Press, 1991).

16. Huntington, *The Third Wave*, p. 39.

17. S. M. Lipset, "Some Social Requisites for Democracy: Economic Development and Political Legitimacy," *American Political Science Review* 53, 1 (1959):79.

18. See Barrington Moore, Jr., *The Social Origins of Dictatorship and Democracy*, (London: Allen Lane, 1967).

19. See Claude Ake, "Is Africa Democratizing?" (op. cit.); and Peter Anyang'Nyongo, "Democratization Processes in Africa," *CODESRIA Bulletin* 2 (1991).

20. See the lamentations of African leaders in speeches delivered at the opening session of the Kampala Forum, Kampala, Uganda, May 19, 1991 reproduced in Olusegun Obasanjo and Felix G. N. Mosha, (eds.), *Africa: Rise to Challenge-Towards a Conference on Security, Stability, Development and Cooperation in Africa*, (New York: Africa Leadership Forum, 1991).

21. Huntington, *The Third Wave*, op. cit., p. 59.

22. Robert Pinkney, *Democracy in the Third World*, (Boulder: Lynne Rienner, 1994), p. 19.

23. Georg Sorensen, *Democracy and Democratization*, (Boulder: Westview, 1994), p. 26.

24. See George Ayittey, *Africa Betrayed*, (New York: St.

Martin's Press, 1992).

25. For a discussion of similar conditions in Latin America see Terry Lynn Karl, "Dilemmas of Democratization in Latin America," *Comparative Politics* (October 1990).

26. Moore, Jr, *The Social Origins of Dictatorship* (op.cit.), p.418.

27. Sorensen, *Democracy and Democratization* (op.cit.), p.27.

28. See Samuel P. Huntington "Will More Countries Become Democratic?" *Political Science Quarterly* 99, 2 (1984); and Catherine Newbury, "Introduction: Paradoxes of Democratization in Africa," *African Studies Review* 37, 1 (April 1994).

29. Pinkney,*Democratization in the Third World* (op.cit.), p.34.

30. Karl, "Dilemmas of Democratization" (op.cit.), p.5.

31. See Larry Diamond, Juan J. Linz, and Seymour Martin Lipset (eds.), *Democracy in Developing Countries: Africa*, (Boulder: Lynne Rienner, 1988); Dov Ronen, (ed.), *Democracy and Pluralism in Africa*, (Boulder: Lynne Rienner, 1986); and Robert Fatton, "Liberal Democracy in Africa," *Political Science Quarterly* 105 (Fall 1990).

32. Adotey Bing, "Salim A. Salim on the OAU and the African Agenda," *Review of African Political Economy* 50(March 1991):29.

33. Martin Klein, "Back to Democracy," Presidential Address to the 1991 Annual Meeting of the African Studies Association.

34. See Julius O. Ihonvbere and Terisa Turner, "Africa in the Post-Containment Era: Constraints, Pressures and Prospects for the 21st Century," *The Round Table* 328 (October 1993); and Ayesha Imam, "Democratization Processes in Africa: Problems and Prospects," *CODESRIA Bulletin* 2(1991).

35. See Fantu Cheru, *The Silent Revolution in Africa: Debt. Development and Democracy*, (London and Harare: Zed and Anvil, 1989); Michael Chege, "Remembering Africa," *Foreign Affairs* 71, 1 (1991-92); and Michael Clough, "The United States and Africa: A Policy of Cynical Disengagement," *Current History* 91 (May 1992).

36. Chinua Achebe, *A Man of the People* (London: Heinemann, 1966).

37. See Julius O. Ihonvbere and Terisa Turner, "Africa's Second Revolution," *Security Dialogue* 24, 3 (September 1993); and Julius O. Ihonvbere, "Africa's Second Independence: A Political and Economic Overview," *California Newsreel- Library of African Cinema* (1993-1994).

38. Bratton and van de Walle, "Popular Protest and Political Reform" (op. cit.):419.

39. Ibid.:438.

40. Decalo, "The Process, Prospects and Constraints" (op.cit.):8.

41. See Robert Kaplan, "The Coming Anarchy," *Atlantic Monthly* (February 1994).

42. Sorensen, *Democracy and Democratization* (op.cit.), p.30.

43. Lance Morrow, "Africa: The Scramble for Existence," *TIME* (September 7, 1992).

44. See Baffour Ankomah, "Ghana's Reform Programme: How Long Will it be Before the Patient is Cured?" *African Business* (March 1990); and Ross Hammond and Lisa McGowan, "Ghana: The World Bank's Sham Showcase," in Kevin Danaher, (ed.), *50 Years is Enough: The Case Against the World Bank and the International Monetary Fund*, (Boston: South End Press, 1994).

45. Sorensen, *Democracy and Democratization* (op. cit.), pp.50-51.

46. Ibid, p.53.

47. Ibid.

48. See "Whose Democracy," *Africa World Review* (May-October 1992); "Democracy in Africa: Lighter Continent," *The Economist* (February 22, 1992); Julius O. Ihonvbere, "Is Democracy Possible in Africa?: The Elites, The People and Civil Society," *QUEST: Philosophical Discussions* VI, 2 (December 1992); and Julius E. Nyang'Oro, "Reform Politics and the Democratization Process in Africa," *African Studies Review* 37, 1 (April 1994).

49. Sorensen, *Democracy and Democratization* (op.cit.), p.52.

50. Huntington, *The Third Wave* (op.cit.), p.262.

51. "Commentary," *Africa Demos* 1,2(January 1991); and "Commentary: Threats to Africa's Democracies-I," *Africa Demos* I, 1 (November 1991).

52. Sorensen, *Democracy and Democratization* (op.cit.), p.54.
53. Ake, "Is Africa Democratizing?" (op. cit.).
54. Ibid.
55. Klein, "Back to Democracy" (op. cit.).
56. Newbury, "Introduction: Paradoxes of Democratization" (op. cit.):2-3.
57. Ibid., p. 3.
58. See: North South Roundtable, *The Challenge of Africa in the 1990s*, (New York: North South Roundtable, 1991); and Richard Sandbrook and Mohammed Halfani, (eds.), *Empowering People: Building Community, Civil Associations, and Legality in Africa*, (Toronto: Centre for Urban and Community Studies, 1993).
59. *CODESRIA BULLETIN* (1991) cited in Klein, "Back to Democracy" (op. cit.).
60. See Julius O. Ihonvbere, *Nigeria: The Politics of Adjustment and Democracy* (New Brunswick, NJ: Transaction Publishers, 1994).
61. For details on military misrule and brutality in Africa, see: George Ayittey, *Africa Betrayed* (op. cit).
62. See Julius O. Ihonvbere, "The State and Academic Freedom in Africa: How African Academics Subvert Academic Freedom," *Journal of Third World Studies* X, 2 (Fall 1993).

CHAPTER TWO

INDEPENDENCE,
ECONOMIC CRISIS, AND
AUTHORITARIANISM IN ZAMBIA

Zambia, formerly Northern Rhodesia, is a landlocked country with a population of about eight million. With a total
land area of 750,000 square kilometers, it has three main
geographical areas: a high plateau, a range of mountains,
and the southern tip of Lake Tanganyika and part of the
Mwenu Wantipa and Bangweulu Lakes. The country is
bounded in the north by Tanzania and Zaire, in the east by
Malawi and Mozambique, in the south by Zimbabwe,
Botswana, and Namibia, and in the West by Angola. The territory had been colonized in 1889 by the British South
Africa Company (BSA Co.) under charter from the English
crown. Two British protectorates were merged in 1911 to
form Northern Rhodesia. In 1924 the United Kingdom took
over the administration of the territory from the BSA Co.
This takeover was not unrelated to the discovery of vast
amounts of copper deposits in the territory in the 1920s.
The combination of domination by the BSA Co. and the UK
government initiated an unprecedented era of exploitation
in the territory. This discovery of copper culminated in the
emergence of the copperbelt region as the economic nerve

center of British domination of the territory.

In 1953, the Federation of Rhodesia and Nyasaland was created from the union of Northern Rhodesia (Zambia), Southern Rhodesia (Zimbabwe), and Nyasaland (Malawi). The Federation was dissolved after a decade in 1963 due to opposition from the majority African population in Northern Rhodesia, and Nyasaland due to domination by Southern Rhodesia, which was under white rule. This dissolution was made easier by the results of the 1962 elections, which culminated in an African majority in the Legislative Council. The BSA Company under the leadership of Cecil Rhodes, and the later British colonial rule, both had only one major goal in what is today known as Zambia: the ruthless exploitation of the people and resources of the territory for the benefit of investors in the BSA Co. and the British government. As Tony Hodges has noted, "Zambia's plight, put in historical perspective, is stark. From British colonial times, its economy was geared to copper production for export to the industrialized countries of the north...."[1] In fact, the colonial state "accorded little importance to agriculture," thus laying the foundation for crisis in that sector in the post-colonial period.[2] This exploitation laid the foundation for the underdevelopment of the country and for its marginalization in the international division of labor. As Fantu Cheru has rightly noted, "Zambia's current economic crisis cannot be understood in isolation from the pattern of economic development which it inherited from the colonial period. As one of the British colonies in southern Africa, Zambia (then Northern Rhodesia) was developed according to British interests, specializing in the production of copper while its agriculture and indigenous industrial base were allowed to disintegrate."[3] Thus, the struggle for political independence, the character of state, its institutions, and social relations of production, the content and context of politics, and the relations with foreign capital were influenced and determined by the structures laid and nurtured for decades by

British colonialism and other imperialist designs in the territory.

The struggle for political independence had been led by petty-bourgeois elements that succeeded in mobilizing workers and peasants to join in the struggle against colonialism. This "nationalist petty bourgeoisie," according to Munyonzwe Hamalengwa, inherited state power and constituted itself into a bureaucratic bourgeoisie. Through nationalistic economic policies and by using state power, it sought to redress its weaknesses *vis-à-vis* foreign capital in the control of the economic fortunes of the nation."[4] The first crop of leaders had some privileges either through education or family backgrounds which propelled them to political prominence. But, as in other African situations, political opportunism, political posturing, and struggles for limited objectives characterized their relations with foreign capital, the colonial state, and the masses they had mobilized in the struggle for freedom. Since the independence struggle was waged "along populist rather than class lines" and the contradiction was presented as existing between imperialism and the African people, 1964 did not witness a revolutionary or fundamental transformation of the relations of power, production, and exchange in Zambia.

Zambia, like other African colonies, had suffered terribly from the contact with the forces of imperialism, and the industry of mineral extraction, mainly copper, had created rapid urbanization and an urban-based working class. Though the migrant labor system tended to discourage the development of a strong working class, especially as colonial capital preferred to treat workers as "tribesmen," the early history of working-class politics in the country contributed substantially to restless anticolonial politics, the development of working-class consciousness and methods of struggle against capital. Thus working-class involvement in the politics of the country before, during, and after the struggle for political independence is rather well established.

The United National Independence Party (UNIP), which was the dominant nationalist movement in Northern Rhodesia, having broken away from the African National Congress (ANC) in 1958, did receive the support of several important trade unions in the struggle for independence. Its slogan in the struggle for independence was "One Zambia—One Nation," reflecting the strong desire for national unity in the face of strong ethnic loyalties and divisions. On October 24, 1964, Zambia became an independent republic, with Kenneth Kaunda as president.[5]

The Postcolonial State and the Consolidation of the Bureaucratic Bourgeoisie

The UNIP, right at the beginning, showed some tendencies towards authoritarianism. Ironically, it was authoritarianism not by a class but largely by Kaunda, who actually saw himself as the personification of the nation. Aside from a programmed effort to obliterate any other form of opposition and to present himself as the "father" of the nation and the main (if not the only) hero of the struggle, the independence constitution actually named Kaunda as the first president of the republic! The constitution made provisions for a strong chief executive, a unitary state, and a cabinet which was to be selected from the national assembly but would be responsible to the president. With the attainment of political independence, the weak Zambian bourgeoisie immediately decided to use the state to expand its role in the economy and to penetrate sectors hitherto dominated by foreign capital. The state went into joint ventures, partnerships, and other forms of cooperative ventures with foreign business interests. It also created very large and powerful parastatals such as the Zambia Industrial and Mining Corporation (ZIMCO), which in turn controlled the Industrial Development Corporation (INDECO). Other major parastatals included the Mining Development Corporation (MINDECO) and the Finance Development

Corporation (FINDECO). With these corporations the political elite was able to extract surpluses and accumulate capital to support its political programs, while the bureaucratic fraction of the bourgeoisie expanded its ranks and tried to use the bureaucracy for massive primitive accumulation. According to Hamalengwa, this process of expanding state control put vast public resources and privileges at the disposal of the Zambian elite, "from high salaries, free housing, free cars, easy access to loans; from corruption and robbery etc. The high military, security and police officers also shared in this embourgeoisment by being appointed to head government institutions and sharing in the privileges."[6]

As demonstration of its economic nationalism and determination to wrest control of the economy from foreigners, the state under UNIP carried out extensive nationalizations and economic reforms in 1968 and 1969. Kenneth Kaunda used every opportunity from party conventions to press conferences and public statements to criticize foreign-controlled companies, especially in the mining sector, for relying too much on local resource generation rather than bringing in foreign exchange. He was also very critical of the foreign corporations, for their massive repatriation of capital and for not investing sufficiently in the local economy, and for generally contributing minimally to the development of Zambia (which was one of the largest copper producers in the world).[7] The point however, is that extensive state intervention in the economy and the reliance on state corporations for accumulation laid the foundation for the continuing weakness of the elite, and for unbridled corruption, waste, and mismanagement. In any case, the parastatal system was the foundation for the patron-client politics of Kaunda and the UNIP as appointments to lucrative administrative positions as well as access to the services and resources of the parastatals was used to incorporate and domesticate the Zambian elite. Yet, rather than strengthen this elite, excessive state intervention and a robust patronage system simply reproduced its weakness and generally unproductive disposition. The bourgeoisie just could not compete outside the structures of state support and subsidy, and never gave itself the opportunity to be creative and productive. The general enthusiasm which accompanied the attainment of political independence was not carried over to the processes of strengthening the state, building the market, and consolidating the power and productive capabilities of the local bourgeoisie outside the structures of the state.

At the ideological level, the local bourgeoisie devised philosophical rationalizations and justifications for its massive reliance on the state to accumulate and reproduce itself. It did this by critically inserting itself into the fabric of the state, thus legitimizing its monopoly over state resources and the instruments of coercion. In spite of increasing class formation and class crystallization, Kaunda, who dominated the political landscape of the country and imposed his ideas on the nation, denied the existence of classes in the country and came up with the ideology of *humanism*. "Humanism" was to be the national philosophy and socialism the "instrument for building a Humanist society."[8] Its main objectives, as spelled out by Kaunda himself, included, the socialization of the Zambian economy by "the instrument of state control in order to bring this important sector of our life closer to the people who now own it"; greater social security to Zambians; abolition of exploitation and victimization; the establishment of a fair principle of taxation and distribution of wealth; social justice; increased Zambian participation "in and control of their economy thereby putting the destiny of the nation in the hands of its citizens"; free education, to enable every Zambian to receive education "to the best of his or her ability right up to university level"; free medical service; transformation of the armed forces "into an instrument for the service of their fellow men in accordance with Humanism," away from the "heartless instruments of intimidation and terror that they used to be before independence"; construction of infrastructure; rural development and increased agricultural production; the use of the office of investigator general "to deal with abuse of power, corruption, victimization and other forms of injustice"; and the guarantee of a peaceful and just future for all Zambians under the leadership of the party.[9]

In 1976, Kenneth Kaunda moved a step further in trying to concretize his ideological control of Zambia: he declared the ideology of "*Communocracy*." At a meeting of party leaders at the historic Mulungushi Rock in Kabwe, Kaunda defined Communocracy to mean "the control of the economy and social services by the whole community; a step to a government of all the people, by all the people and for all the people."[10] Communocracy was to serve as the ideological weapon for abolishing exploitation and class distinction in Zambia.[11] To date, however, no one really understands what this ideology stood for in the politics of UNIP, the politics of Kaunda, the relations of production and exchange in the country, and Zambia's place in the global order. The greatest indictment of Kaunda and his political ideologies is in the terrible conditions of living, the vulnerability of the economy, and the general state of decay and instability of the nation twenty-seven years after he took office as president of the country. Virtually everyone I interviewed at several locations in the country, but especially in Lusaka, the nation's capital, laughed and asked me to forget "humanism," which was simply an effort on Kaunda's part to leave something to be remembered by and to create the impression that something original was going on in the country!

For Kaunda and his party, the ideology of Humanism was very important. It was the only "viable" instrument with which to build an extensive network of patron-client relations, domesticate political opposition, depoliticize the people away from the deep political consciousness of the anticolonial struggle, and if possible build a personality cult by imposing himself on the nation as leader, teacher, and father. Zambia according to Kaunda faced "the danger of creating two nations within one"—not along the lines of capitalism which creates a bourgeoisie and proletariat, but "between the rural and urban areas."[12] Yet, year after year, the distortions and differentiation along gender, class, regional, and power lines continued to deepen in the country. Neither humanism nor communocracy could halt the slide into economic crisis, redress gross inequalities, or prevent the abuse of power, corruption and human rights abuses. In fact, neither "ideological" positions could prevent the majority of Zambians from becoming poorer in spite of the abundant resources of the country.

Through a variety of mechanisms, the state also tried to control and domesticate the working class in Zambia after political independence. As part of the grand strategy of incorporation, ideological containment, and domestication, the state in 1965 legislated the creation of a central trade union federation—The Zambia Congress of Trade Unions (ZCTU) through the Trade Unions and Trade Disputes (Amendment) Act of 1965. The strategy was to strive to domesticate and incorporate the leadership of the Congress and thus control the politics of the working-class movement.[13] The ruthless exploitation of the working class and the neglect of the basic needs of the vast majority continued after independence, discriminatory wages were paid to African and expatriate workers, and the rights of labor were severely constrained through the retention of colonial legislation against workers' rights. It took several commissions like the Hadow Commission, and numerous strikes against the postcolonial government for some of these constraints to be reversed. What is important here is to note that relations between the state and the working class—which had been mutually distrustful during the struggle for independence—did not improve with independence, largely because the state and the UNIP leadership distrusted labor and sought to domesticate it without resolving the problems and constraints against the working classes.

One major effort at incorporation was the absorption of ZIMCO, the largest corporation in Zambia, which is "an umbrella holding company,...the largest entity within the parastatal sector...the biggest employer of mining, commercial and manufacturing sector," as an "arm, albeit a very important arm of the Party through its government."[14] This way, all workers were to subscribe to and to accept the philosophy of Humanism and to be subservient to the policies of the party. The domestication and incorporation of the working class was a very important aspect of the bureaucratization project and was necessary to consolidate patron-client relations on a national scale. It was also a prelude to declaring the one-party state which Kaunda saw as the final step to his total control of the nation.

In spite of its professed commitments to freedom, the UNIP government retained and continued several mechanisms of repression which the colonial state had employed against the Zambian people. This was in part a measure of its insecurity and failure to impose its hegemony on the social formation. Through the Emergency Powers Act of 1964, the Zambian state simply continued to maintain the emergency powers the colonial state had used to repress nonbourgeois forces, especially the anticolonial forces. In this way, the neocolonial Zambian state showed that it was only marginally different from the colonial state. In 1969, the Emergency Powers Act was amended to continue maintaining the state of emergency indefinitely and this enabled the UNIP government to frequently detain opposition elements, especially journalists, students, union leaders, and workers. Throughout the 1970s, the state descended heavily on the trade unions and did not hesitate to detain labor leaders, even if they were legally on strike. It sponsored pro-government candidates for union positions during elections and relied on frequent wage increases to placate restless mine workers on whose work the economy was heavily dependent.

The concentration of revenue generation on copper exports led to the neglect of agriculture. Although about seventy percent of the population relied on subsistence agriculture, the sector remained under the control of large commercial farms which continued to dominate the production of cash crops, determine prices and the quantity of exports. Policies on rural development and the promotion of agriculture relied more on propaganda and long presidential speeches than on concrete policies capable of mobilizing rural producers, preventing the rural-urban drift, and improving the contribution of agriculture to the nation's gross domestic product. In fact, UNIP saw rural development as a way to control rural producers and rural production. As Michael Bratton has rightly noted, the UNIP "patronage machine did not completely overlook the rural areas. During the 1960s, copper earnings fueled a handout of public resources. Through a program to promote agricultural cooperatives, UNIP distributed jobs, loans, and trading licenses with the aim of building local support for the ruling party and undermining opposition parties. To guarantee a national supply of staple grains, the government provided fertilizer subsidies and panterritorial prices for controlled products."[15] The government, in pursuing this grand strategy, established rural reconstruction centers, intensive development zones, multipurpose cooperatives, the Lima Program and settlement schemes, and other such "innovative" agricultural schemes which failed to improve the rural areas, improve rural income or increase agricultural output. It also set up the huge National Agricultural Marketing Board (NAMBOARD), which enjoyed a monopoly in purchasing all grains from peasant producers. As the International Labour Office (ILO) rightly noted in 1975, "One is struck by a neglect of agriculture, by the low priority given to rural activities in the allocation of economic resources and skilled manpower, and, overall, by the absence of clear and coherent framework for rural development, within which decisions are taken."[16]

The Zambian state confused the proliferation of so called agricultural parastatals (all with a retinue of bureaucrats often paid high salaries and allowances) with the fundamental task of improving the rural areas and empowering rural producers. The creation of the Credit Organization of Zambia (COZ), Dairy Produce Board of Zambia (DPBZ), Cold Storage Board of Zambia (CSBZ), Rural Development Corporation (RDC), National Agricultural Marketing Board (NAMBOARD), Tobacco Board of Zambia (TBZ), and Agricultural Finance Company (AFC) failed to change the situation of agricultural and rural neglect. In spite of this proliferation of agricultural institutions, agricultural output did not increase. Its share of the budget declined from a seven-percent high in 1970 to less than three-percent in 1980, and "the terms of trade for rural dwellers deteriorated more than 5 percent per year," between 1965 and 1980.[17] Although part of a strategy for encapsulating rural producers into the sphere of state control, these parastatals constituted a major drain on state resources due to their corruption, inefficiency, and ineffectiveness. However, the fairly high prices of copper, the country's main export, covered up these failings and inefficiencies until the mid-1970s, when severe imbalances began to erode growth rates and bring about severe deficits.

In sum, the new Zambian state had launched a three-pronged strategy for building hegemony and implementing a national project—ideological manipulation and control; the domestication of nonbourgeois forces, especially the working classes; and state control of the economy through parastatals in order to promote rapid accumulation by the Zambian bourgeoisie. None of these strategies was designed to challenge inherited contradictions and conflicts; to reassure distressed and alienated communities and ethnic groups; to restructure the colonially determined structures and patterns of production and exchange; or to dismantle and restructure inherited repressive and exploitative institutions and social relations in order to mobilize the people and bring them into the main stream of politics and power.

The State and Economic Decay in Zambia

The Zambian economy at independence had been one of the most buoyant in Africa. In the first decade of *political* independence, the economy was relatively stable. Between 1964 and 1969, the price of copper and other exports continued to rise and this enabled the state to execute several projects designed mainly to meet the demands and tastes of the urban-based elite. A decade after political independence, the country enjoyed "a balanced external trading account based on the export of copper. Providing 90 percent of foreign exchange earnings and 53 percent of the government budget, copper revenues enabled major public investments in health, education, and transportation."[18] By the mid-1970s, the Zambian economy was in crisis. From the mid-'70s through the '80s, "growth became erratic...as copper prices dropped sharply in the world market."[19] Mismanagement, corruption, the suffocation of popular groups and opposition elements, excessive dependence on copper exports for foreign exchange earnings, and the proliferation of inefficient and wasteful corporations simply reproduced Zambia's neocolonial inheritances and underdevelopment.

The precipitous decline in copper prices and steep rises in import volumes had far-reaching effects on the ability to pay wages, meet basic needs, keep development projects afloat, and import essential goods including spare parts and inputs for the country's import-dependent industries. As Cheru has noted, "After twenty-five years of independence, Zambia's economic fortunes are still tied to copper, which accounts for 90% of foreign exchange earnings. This dependence on copper has been the main cause of Zambia's vulnerable position in the world economy. A prolonged depression in the world copper industry has affected the performance of the Zambian economy since the mid-1960s."[20] Cheru also notes that the "rapidly dwindling" output of copper from a peak of 710,000 tonnes in 1974 to 463,000 tonnes in 1986, and the failure of government to "diversify the economy and mobilize the population for long-term development" have contributed to the deteriorating economic fortunes of the Zambian economy.[21] For an economy that was so dependent on foreign exchange earnings from a sector which was in itself under the control of powerful profit- and hegemony-seeking transnational corporations, a decline in output and prices (and therefore in foreign-exchange earnings) spelled immediate imbalances and crisis. Thus when copper prices fell precipitously by the mid-1970s, "Capacity utilization in manufacturing declined drastically. Lack of foreign exchange severely limited the capacity of Zambia to import spare parts, fuel and machinery whose value [had] increased dramatically relative to Zambia's traditional exports."[22] Higher oil prices in the early 1970s only made matters worse for Zambia, which is an oil-dependent economy. This occurred at a time of global economic recession, which severely affected aid flows to the country. Given the inability to import needed inputs and spare parts, capacity utilization in all major industries declined:

> In 1982, 21 of the 46 manufacturing companies under the Industrial Development Corporation (INDECO) parastatal were operating with capacity utilization of less than 50%. Industries that are heavily dependent on imported inputs [were] the hardest hit. Some, like Consolidated Tyres, Livingstone Motor Assembly and Mansa Batteries were working at 15-20% capacity in 1983. Some firms had to be

closed completely. Capacity utilization has dropped even further since 1986.

What is not revealed in the above figures is the human dimension of the crisis. As one industry after another closed its doors because of lack of spare parts and basic inputs, thousands of workers were made redundant. In the construction industry, for example, employment dropped to 30,000 as compared to 80,000 ten years earlier.[23]

As the deepening economic crisis led to further retrenchment of able-bodied workers, the working classes responded with strikes. In a society without safety nets and without a strong credit system, opposition to mass lay-offs and deepening economic crisis was inevitable. The government's desperation was evidenced in the decision of the Zambia Consolidated Copper Mines [ZCCM] to end a pension scheme for its workers. When the workers protested against the move, the company sacked 4,364 workers.[24] In early 1986 the government, as part of its cost cutting strategy, shut its embassies in Lisbon and Jeddah and recalled some 32 diplomats.[25] The situation was not helped one bit by the imposition of IMF and World Bank monetarist stabilization and adjustment prescriptions (see below) which led to a further depreciation of the Kwacha. The inflation which accompanied the devaluation of the Kwacha by 20 percent in 1976 and by another 10 percent in 1978, and the unequal distribution of the pains and costs of these developments, led to the strikes of 1978. As usual, the state responded to the strikes by increasing the wages of workers, which only fueled the level of inflation, thus eroding the real value of the wages.

The UNIP-led government had proclaimed Zambia a one-party state in December 1972 and in October 1978, after eliminating all possible opposition, Kenneth Kaunda stood for the country's presidential election as the sole candidate.

This ritual was to be repeated until he was defeated in multiparty elections in 1991. Prior to the 1978 elections, the political elite felt that there was a need to placate the electorate but ignored the need for a comprehensive response to the crisis generated by export concentration. The state also ignored the need to discipline the elite, conserve foreign exchange, and redirect the patterns of accumulation away from import-export activities and distribution to production:

> To make matters worse, despite the economic crisis Zambia was experiencing, the state bourgeoisie were living conspicuously rich and extravagant life-styles. While the workers were being told daily in the *Zambia Daily Mail* and *Times of Zambia* to tighten their belts, the bourgeoisie were "loosening" theirs. The workers were justified in refusing to tighten their belts further.[26]

By the end of 1980, it was clear that the Zambian economy had been hopelessly mismanaged and derailed, and possibilities for recovery in the context of an increasingly difficult international economy were dim. Salaries could not be paid, the country's foreign debt was piling up, imports of essential goods became scanty, foreign investors held back on new investments or repatriated capital as the Kwacha declined in value daily, a thriving parallel market emerged, land speculation became a very lucrative business, and workers and rural people and students became increasingly restless. Inevitably, the political ramifications of the deepening economic and social crisis began to appear. The working class, which was the hardest hit by the deepening crisis, began to shed its populist—even conservative— postures and to adopt more radical and militant political postures. Students and rural people also began to openly criticize and challenge the state. Scholars and human rights activists began to blame Kaunda and the ruling party openly for the numerous problems of the country. Ironically, sections of the bourgeoisie also became more critical of the state of affairs, and this in turn was to prompt a severe crisis within the ruling party, culminating in the expulsion of some members (see below).

Early Calls For Multiparty Democracy

Though the economic crisis was deepening and Kaunda as an individual and as president of the republic was busy looking for scapegoats to blame for his misfortunes, many Zambians were beginning to attribute the problem to the outdated and tired ideas of Kenneth Kaunda, the lack of creativity and vision within the ruling party, the domination of national politics and decisionmaking structures by the old vanguard of the nationalist movement, the generally repressive political atmosphere, and the limitations of the one-party state which Kaunda had forced on the nation. The "frequent packaging and repackaging of the bogus and useless philosophy of humanism now meant little to all Zambians. We were getting bored of all the talk and no action. We felt betrayed by the opulence of the elite and the poverty of the majority. Kaunda was too busy trying to enshrine his name on every institution and piece of stone in Zambia to notice the decay and frustrations below."[27]

The deepening economic crisis and popular pressures and responses forced the increasingly desperate state to become more intolerant. It readily invoked its draconian labor laws, emergency powers, and other manipulative methods to contain popular protests and opposition. These strategies were particularly directed at the ZCTU, which was increasingly becoming the "conscience of the nation" and the bastion of opposition to one party rule and political repression. Kaunda took the ZCTU very seriously because its over 380,000 members had a capacity to overwhelm the ruling party's machine if it decided to directly confront the state on political issues. There were also expressions of opposition from the rural areas through the activities of the Commercial

Farmers' Bureau (CFB), which remained firmly opposed to the involvement of the Zambian state in agriculture.

Demands for democratization, accountability, and change in the governing echelons of the country became evident from the beginning of the 1980s. Elias Chipimo, former Zambian high commissioner to Britain and chairman of the Standard Bank of Zambia, argued in early 1980 that the "multiparty system was the surest way of avoiding coups and eliminating the disgraceful tendency of presidents ending up with bullets in their heads."[28] Rather than appreciate this call for the opening up of the political system and for accountability and political responsibility, Kaunda took it personally and accused former cabinet members and some prominent Zambians of trying to assassinate him and overthrow his government. He issued a 24-hour ultimatum to the Bank to denounce its chairman and distance itself from his views. In a statement released by Sir George Taylor, senior deputy chairman of Standard Bank of London, Chipimo's views, obviously seen as an embarrassment to the bank, were declared "personal." The bank "dissociated itself from political views and comments expressed by its chairman."[29] It had taken a lot of courage for such a highly placed political figure to take such a public stand under Kaunda. But Chipimo "was only expressing the feelings of many Zambians. It was already becoming clear that the UNIP and Kaunda had become arrogant and complacent only because there was no opposition or serious mechanisms for checking their excesses."[30] When the government announced on October 16, 1980, that it had nipped a coup attempt in the bud, the incident provided a good excuse to round up the advocates for multiparty democracy—Elias Chipimo, Patrick Chisanga, Edward Shamwana, Valentine Musakanya, and three senior army officers were detained. Charged in 1982, six of them were found guilty and were sentenced to death in 1983. The sentence was never carried out and they were eventually released, one after the other. But the innocence of a political landscape under the domination and manipulation of Kenneth Kaunda and the UNIP had been broken, the myth of "KK" was exploded, and Zambia was never going to be the same again.

Kaunda and the UNIP Central Committee also went on the offensive, describing the advocates of multiparty politics as "communists" and "devils." They were branded as ambitious politicians whose only interest was in Kaunda's job as president of Zambia. Kaunda had always displayed a rather arrogant position on the emergence of an opposition. There are of course many Zambians who believed that this "arrogance" was a cover for deep fears harbored by Kaunda: he was not so naive as to believe that his repressive and corrupt administration would last for ever, especially in the face of monumental changes within and beyond Africa. In his October 1971 address to the UNIP National Council at Mulungushi Hall, Kaunda described the advocates of multiparty politics as "old leaves on a plant which have outlived their usefulness." He contended that these advocates "gave the Party a poor and undignified image. They created greater problems than they solved. There is no reason for concern. There is, therefore, no need for us to spend too much time discussing opposition elements."[31] Shadreck Soko, a member of the Central Committee, declared that "people harboring ambitions for the presidency while KK is still in power are devils.... It is strange that some of us want to become presidents when Dr. Kaunda is still alive."[32]

By 1988, Kaunda was beginning to "smell" multiparty politics and prodemocracy advocates in every nook and cranny of the country. The truth was that he was becoming more insecure by the day as prominent members of the party and leading scholars and activists were beginning to openly challenge his domination of Zambian politics and his ability to continue in power. In September 1988, he accused traders of teaming up to form a new political party in Zambia.[33] The security forces were specially instructed to "fish out and detain" any person or persons found to be in sympathy with the idea of multiparty politics. Such efforts to suffocate the demands for opening up the political space and respecting the basic rights of Zambians did not deter the advocates for multipartyism. Many of the prominent UNIP members who had been dismissed, demoted, disgraced, or discriminated against began to get together to discuss how to alter the country's political balances. Finding themselves to be without influence, power, and resources outside the party's powerful and pervasive patronage machine, people like Vernon Mwaanga engaged in extensive business activities to strengthen their financial bases. Of course, in doing these they became intricately linked with all sorts of scandals and underhanded business dealings. But this involvement in business was to give them the financial power to fund an opposition movement that was later to see Kaunda and the UNIP out of power.

At a meeting at Garden Motel on the outskirts of Lusaka in July 1990, the prodemocracy advocates issued a statement calling for the immediate registration of voters; for lifting of the state of emergency; for international observers to monitor elections; and for multiparty politics. This meeting was attended by prominent businessmen, intellectuals, former ministers, and politicians—including UNIP sympathizers Vernon Mwaanga, Andrew Kashita, Elias Chipimo, Frederick Chiluba, Mundia Sikatana, Akashambatwa Mbikusita-Lewanika, and Remmy Mushota. By the end of September 1990, the Movement for Multiparty Democracy (MMD) had constituted a formal National Interim Committee. Lusaka businessman Arthur Wina was elected Chairman; former assistant commissioner of police Kelly Walubita was in charge of the security subcommittee; ZCTU chairman general Frederick Chiluba was vice-chairman of the movement and also in charge of Organization and Operations; businessman and former minister for foreign affairs Vernon Mwaanga, also a vice-chairman, was responsible for publicity and public relations; Akashambatwa Mbikusita-Lewanika was secretary and Levy Mwanawasa was chairman of the legal subcommittee.[34] Ephraim Chibwe was in charge of fundraising, while Andrew Kashita was responsible for transportation. Wings for women and youths were created and a full-time secretariat was established. At the same time, the president of the African Bar Association and chairman of the Commonwealth Lawyers Association, Roger Chongwe, came out to declare that the one-party system violates the rights of Zambians to free and fair choice.[35] As Chongwe put it,

> A one party political system allowed the party structure to operate like a parasite on the tax payers money, neglecting the dispensation of basic needs to the people while forcing them into the culture of silence under the guise of peace and stability.[36]

He called on trade union leaders in Zambia to fulfill "the historical mission of trade unions," which is "the pursuit of the establishment of a humane political system which respects the rule of law."[37]

With the open activities of the MMD—which constituted a direct challenge to the one-party state, the state of emergency, UNIP, and Kaunda personally—donations from ordinary Zambians poured into the coffers of the movement. The ability to raise funds through voluntary contributions shocked Kaunda, to say the least, and sounded a very serious note of warning. It was clear than Zambians had been waiting for an opportunity to identify with a new organization, new ideas, new leaders, and of course, new hopes and promises. The police, under orders from Kaunda and his aides, immediately set out to contain the effectiveness and spreading popularity of the movement. Rankin Sikasula, Copperbelt member of the UNIP Central Committee, accused the MMD "of trying to woo support by telling lies, bribing and corrupting the minds of the weak in Zambia."[38]

Premier-general Malimba Masheke also described the MMD as "a band of dishonest people who may plunder the wealth of Zambia if voted into power."[39] Henry Kalenga, secretary general of the outlawed Peoples Redemption Organization (PRO), equally described the MMD as "opportunists who had amassed wealth under UNIP and were now masquerading as liberators of the people of Zambia." Because virtually all the leaders of the MMD had been powerful UNIP members and many had held ministerial appointments in the past, Kalenga cautioned that "when a crab moves from the Kafue river into the Zambezi, it remains the same, it has merely changed the name of the river."[40] When the MMD tried to hold the first organizational meeting of its National Interim Committee at the Luanshya Adult Education Center in Lusaka, the police declared the meeting "unlawful"[41] despite the fact that Miyamba Kazembe of the MMD had a police permit—on the grounds that Kazembe's permit was for an "indoor" meeting while some of the overflow crowd of 400 had to stand outside!

When this trend of harassing the MMD and of impeding to its ability to organize and get its message out to the populace continued, the movement sued the UNIP government. In his ruling, Mr. Justice Bobby Bwalya stated that "the state violated public order Act Articles 22 and 23 of the Constitution which gave any person a right to assemble, associate and demonstrate freely provided one's action did not threaten public peace." It was his learned opinion that the state "acted illegally when it denied the MMD permits to hold public meetings and therefore must pay damages."[42] The MMD also sued the Zambia National Broadcasting Corporation (ZNBC), the *Times of Zambia*, and the *Zambia Daily Mail* for denying them coverage. In December 1990, the MMD was officially launched as a political party and it filed its application for registration. It received its certificate of registration in January 1991. Frederick Chiluba claimed support of the trade unions for the MMD and

Jonathan Simakuni, national chairman of the Mineworkers Union of Zambia (MUZ) reaffirmed the total support of mine workers and the trade union movement for the new political party.[43]

The movement purchased vehicles for its operatives and several bicycles for distribution to villages. It set up district bodies. In Livingstone, for instance, veteran politicians, trade unionists, and businessmen flocked to the MMD. The chair of MMD Livingstone district was a former District Governor for Kalomo, Hamwene Kayunma; former Pemba member of parliament Peter Muunga was in charge of publicity and public relations; and ZCTU district chairman David Maluza was secretary. The movement put out a paid advertisement in the newspapers entitled "National Interim Committee for Movement for Multiparty Democracy— Resolutions and Framework of Action" in August 1990. This was like a public invitation and hundreds of people flocked to the MMD secretariat to purchase membership cards and express solidarity.

This mass movement to join the MMD scared the Kaunda government. It decided to intimidate, as much as possible, those who had joined the movement, or had expressed support for its activities as a way of either coercing them away from continued participation, or discouraging others from following in their footsteps. For instance, Azwell Banda, District Field Officer of the Poultry Producers Association of Zambia (PPAZ) was fired for "unsatisfactory performance" as soon as he was elected Chairman of the MMD in the Eastern Province.[44] Students from the University of Zambia (UNZA) also flocked to the MMD because they believed that the "one-party system of government suppressed political dissension as evident in UNZA where several student publications had been banned for expressing views contrary to those of UNIP."[45] The students also felt that "over the years Kaunda paid just lip service to improving education, liberating Zambia from imperialism, and actually allowing popular groups to participate in politics. The man actually thought that the country belonged to him, his children and a handful of tired politicians."[46]

The registration of the MMD as a political party completely disorganized and restructured the nature of political alliances and allegiances in Zambia. Within weeks, there was a drastic alignment and realignment of political forces. Persons who had been considered to be very loyal to Kaunda and UNIP openly abandoned the ruling party and declared for the opposition. Contrary to Kaunda's October 1971 boast that there was "no cause for alarm" because Zambians were calling for multiparty democracy, "it was clear that UNIP was in trouble. Many of us could not believe it. People just abandoned the old man and the party. He did not leave the stage when the ovation was loud and clear and people simply wanted change and new blood in charge of the country."[47] To be sure, many did so out of frustration within UNIP; out of the desire to identify with the new movement even if they did not believe in it; out of the bandwagon effect; and out of genuine commitment to people's power and democracy.

In December, UNIP was shocked when Humphrey Mulemba, a founding member of UNIP, former party secretary general and member of parliament for Slowezi East, declared for the MMD. In his statement, Mulemba stated that "UNIP hindered the freedom of expression. UNIP had failed to democratize itself over the years and was oppressive in nature."[48] On the first day of January 1991, three Councilors from Choma District, Philip Maambo from Kalindwa Ward; Enoch Kasonkomona from Mabula Ward, and George Nyanga from Mbubala Ward lost their positions as Ward Chairmen as they declared for the MMD. Robinson Nabulyato, former speaker of the National Assembly, also joined the MMD in January. Lusaka businessman Winson Gunboh donated K20,000 to help the movement with registration. Bennie Mwinga, member of parliament for Mazabuka, resigned from UNIP and opted for the MMD; and almost the entire ward executive and the Youth and Women's League as well as 225 other voters of Livingstone's Maramba ward except for vice-chairman Wesley Mwila resigned from UNIP and joined the MMD. In February 1991, the ward chairman for Kalingalinga Simon Chitebula Chiyobeka and two others resigned from UNIP to join the MMD. Other prominent politicians who quit UNIP to join the MMD included Mike Mbewe, secretary Mosi-Oa-Tunya (The Smoke that Thunders) Ward; Stephen Katogi Mulenga, secretary Ndeke Branch of UNIP; vice-chairman of UNIP for Livingstone's Maraba Ward, Wesley Mwila eventually quit; Michael Sata, Kabwata member of parliament; two army officers who discontinued their training abroad to join the MMD; Christian Temp, who was involved in the 1988 abortive coup; former premier Daniel Lisolo; and Daniel K. Kapapa, member of parliament for Kasama. Over 2000 UNIP party cards were handed over to the MMD in Slowezi; eighty-one persons and two officials defected at Ndola to the MMD and 300 in Ndola surrendered their UNIP cards.[49] While quitting UNIP, Stephen Mulenga stated that "it is only a stupid fly which follows a dead body to the grave."[50] This signified a realization that MMD was the winning party—the Bandwagon effect! Michael Sata, a very bright, foxy, and rather traditional but effective politician presented 5,727 voters cards from "workers in parastatals, the civil service and ordinary Kabwata residents who have decided to go with me" to the MMD and, quoting the Book of Proverbs (Chapter 15, Verse 14), and presenting his UNIP Card No. 119602 to the MMD, stated that "intelligent people want to learn but stupid people are stupefied by ignorance."[51] The situation was akin to people rejoicing and identifying with an army of liberation. In fact, "at that time, it was a sign of prestige and enlightenment to identify with the MMD and a sign of conservatism and ignorance to be identified with UNIP."[52] With its membership swollen beyond its expectations, the MMD was set to confront Kenneth Kaunda and UNIP in the October elections.

Intensifying the Struggle for Democracy: The Working Class Takes on the State

Though the leadership of the ZCTU constantly stated that it was not an alternative to the government and had no intention of replacing it, it declared in September 1980, through chairman Frederick Chiluba, that it was warming up for a fight against a government which it perceived as having consistently failed to respond to its demands and improve the living conditions of the workers. Chiluba promised that workers would embark on a national strike before the end of 1980 to press home their demands for better conditions.[53] The ZCTU was clear on the fact that it perceived the government and its poor handling of the economy as the main cause of Zambia's predicaments. The platform for a political showdown between the state and working class was gradually being erected.

The government, as usual, sought to divert attention by initiating a Local Government Administration Bill in parliament aimed at "democratizing" and "decentralizing" the administrative system. It was thought that this would reduce pressure on the central government and localize struggles in the local government, even divide the working classes. Ironically, for a government that was already facing serious challenges, and for an economy that was in deep trouble, the new administrative system was to replace elected mayors with appointed mayors and was to cost a lot of money as 20 additional councilors were to receive salaries totalling over K500,000 per month. The ZCTU opposed this bill and accused the government of financial recklessness. The UNIP government got the Bill through parliament in December 1980 and it went into effect on January 1, 1981 as the Local Administration Act (1980). Workers felt vindicated when neither the government nor the local governments could financially support the new system and in less than five years it had become discredited. The Mineworkers Union of Zambia (MUZ) had ordered its members to boycott elections to the new councils and had threatened to expel members who defied the order. The ZCTU had supported the MUZ's position and the government was convinced that both bodies had ganged up to bring it down.

In January 1981, several union leaders, particularly those of the ZCTU and MUZ leaders were arrested and detained—Frederick Chiluba of the ZCTU; Newsted Zimba, ZCTU secretary general and member of parliament, and his deputy, David Mwila, chairman of the MUZ, and thirteen others. They were also expelled from the country's sole party, UNIP. Since the government was deliberately vague in its pronouncement, it was not certain to the workers if the expulsion from the party also meant expulsion from their respective union positions since the ZCTU had been absorbed into the country's sole political party. This generated more strike actions from the Nchanga Consolidated Copper Mines and several other mines across the country. Bank and Insurance Workers soon joined and the country was grinding to a halt. The government called the strikes "illegal" and described them as the equivalent of a coup, but the workers persisted, as teachers, postal workers, electricity workers, and other public servants called sympathy strikes. It was the announcement of the Minister for Labour that the expulsion did not affect their union positions that put a stop to the strikes and in April 1981, the expelled labor leaders were reinstated in the party. The government's response had been proved to be misguided, it cost the country over K20 million in foreign exchange earnings and over 123,256 man-days.[54] Once again, the working class had challenged the state on political grounds and won. The delegitimization of the Zambian state was moving in a rather fast pace and the increasing power, legitimacy, and influence of the ZCTU and its affiliates was moving in the opposite direction.

The 1980s were devastating for the Zambian economy. There seems to have been a direct correlation between deepening economic and social crisis on the one hand, and the mobilization, militancy, and politicization of the labor movement on the other. The reinstatement of the expelled union leaders into UNIP did not stop further strike actions. Actually, most of the unions had "used the expulsion merely as an excuse to challenge the Kaunda government and put new issues on the political agenda."[55] In July 1981, railway workers went on strike without following state-established procedures for calling strikes. They were opposed to the changes made by government in the management of the railways corporation. A strike by rail workers is as important as a strike by mine workers; both are directly related and the railways are the most important mode of transport in the country. The impact was immediate and devastating. The strike was joined by mineworkers who were opposed to the termination of emergency food allocation. The government had resorted to this form of subsidy in view of the deepening crisis and the scarcity of essential commodities. In the same month, mine workers in Lushanya and Kabwe went on strike in support of university graduate workers who were demanding an end to discriminatory pay structures between Zambians and expatriates. By the end of July, Zambia had experienced over 84 strikes which had not followed established procedures. The state saw these developments as direct evidence of the increasing politicization of labor issues, especially as "sympathy" strikes were becoming commonplace.

The unsteady and insecure Zambian state and UNIP government simply responded by rearresting the labor leaders it had detained a few months earlier. The charge was one of instigating illegal strikes, creating disaffection, and trying to topple the country's government. The detention was challenged at the High Court of Zambia, which ruled that the state had no case against the union leaders, as the causes of the strike action were very glaring and were direct responses to government policies. The labor leaders were released in November 1981. Once again, the union leaders had confronted the state and defeated it in its own courts. As well, the courts had given tacit approval to "illegal strikes" by contending that the conditions of economic disaffection and poverty were sufficient grounds for workers to embark on strike actions for which their leaders could not be held responsible. The popularity of the unions and their leaders soared while the credibility of the government and the party took a downward turn. The increasing number of strikes with political implications began to influence political debates, political consciousness, and the character of working-class alliances:

> ...1981 was the most explosive year as far as class struggles between the state and the labour movement was concerned. There were in all 156 strikes involving 76,776 workers resulting in a loss of 556,408 man-days. These figures indicate an increase compared to strikes which took place in 1980 which were recorded at 121 involving 28,434 workers causing a loss of 79,896 man-days...the workers' struggles were not limited to wage demands only. The overwhelming number of strikes were concerned with other issues i.e. political questions or conditions of employment etc. (66.7%) while 23.7% were concerned with wage demands and 9.6% with collective agreements.[56]

Though 1982 was comparatively peaceful, recording only 39 strikes, the economic crisis continued to deepen. It was becoming clear that if there was an organization or movement placed to unseat the Kaunda government, it was the labor movement. The ZCTU had, through its politics, pronouncements, and relations with the government, "emerged as a viable *de facto* opposition party" in one-party-ruled Zambia.[57] This shift in power relations alarmed the state, which in its panic moved from one error to another. It employed an old trick often resorted to by African leaders:

deny the union of compulsory check-off and starve it of funds; then the union will be unable to operate and it will become dormant. With the compulsory check-off system, the employers deducted all dues from the salaries and wages of workers and passed these on to the unions. The new system would force a huge bureaucracy on the unions, and the collection of dues, being voluntary, would become very difficult. At least, that was the assumption. In 1985, the UNIP government came up with the *Statutory Instrument Number 6 of 1985 (the Trade Unions [Deduction of Subscription] Regulation 1985)*. Issued on January 19, 1985, it revoked previous orders empowering employers to deduct union dues from wages if they went on an illegal strike. Previously, even if workers went on strike, employers still deducted their union dues and continued to pay their wages. Since the government felt that the vast majority—in fact, all—of the strikes in 1981 and 1982 were "illegal," such a move would scare workers from going on strike and industrial peace would be assured. By mid-1985, as demonstration of its resolve to cut short the growing influence and power of the unions and their leaders, the state employed the regulation against the Zambia National Union of Teachers (ZNUT), Zambia Union of Financial Institutions and Allied Workers (ZUFIAW), Zambia Electricity Workers Union (ZEWU), National Union of Postal and Telecommunications Workers (NUPTW), and the Mineworkers Union of Zambia (MUZ). Legal challenges to the new regulation at the Kitwe high court failed. Within the working class movement, the new law was a "clear sign of fear in the government. They were scared of our growing power and unity. We felt that a government that will deprive workers of pay was a bad government."[58]

The state followed up this effort at domesticating the labor movement with a bill introduced in Parliament by the Minister for Labour and Social Services aimed at converting trade unions into so-called "mass organizations" along the lines of the womens' and youth wings of the country's sole ruling party. The main objective here was to politically domesticate or contain the labor movement, bureaucratize its structures, and make it subject to the whims and dictates of Kenneth Kaunda, whose personality dominated the ruling party. The trade unions opposed this move and saw it as a sign of weakness on the part of the government, as well as an effort to stifle all dissenting voices. To Frederick Chiluba, the Chairman of the ZCTU, this was no doubt a steady but unacceptable march towards "political absolutism":

> A trade union movement is a specialist workers' organization which only caters for people in formal employment with distinguishable employers working under prescribed laws.... A trade union cannot be a mass organization because its membership is not open to everyone in the country...like a political party.... True to absolutism the party wants to control absolutely the news media, the church, the trade unions and industry and even football and net ball so that every citizen will exist because of the party, instead of the party existing because of its members who are drawn from the country's citizens.... The one-party system of politics in Zambia requires an independent, free, strong trade union movement to provide positive pressure to check on government excesses so as to ensure accountability of political leadership.[59]

Clearly, the ZCTU was arrogating to itself the power or right to check the excesses of the government and ruling party. This meant that, in one-party Zambia, and with the domineering figure of Kaunda to contend with, the path to conflict between the state and labor was wide open. A measure of the increasing influence of the labor movement was the election of six labor leaders to parliament by the end of the 1980s. Workers were beginning to support, in a political sense, people drawn from their own constituency. The elected members also saw themselves as directly representing—and accountable in the first instance to—the workers. Unfortunately for Kaunda and the Zambian state, deepening socioeconomic crisis, indebtedness, inflation, and the evaporation of foreign aid were to further erode state legitimacy and provide sufficient grounds for the opposition to mobilize, politicize, and move the masses to action.

Economic Deterioration and the Further Delegitimization of the State

In spite of very loud propaganda and several "innovative" programs, the Zambian economy continued to deteriorate. The Third National Development Plan, 1980 to 1984, had hoped to achieve a 4.8-percent per-annum real GDP growth rate, a 1.5-percent per-annum growth in per-capita income; a savings and investment ratio of GDP of 29 percent per-annum; an increase in the share of private consumption in GDP from 43 percent to 51 percent; and diversification of the economy away from a chronic dependence on copper exports. Such projections had been made under the overtly optimistic assumption that the price of copper would remain constant at K1,200 per ton; the terms of trade would remain constant; and the exchange rate would remain constant even after the 1978 devaluation. Of course, "(n)one of the above assumptions materialized during the Plan period." It was "affected by financial crisis as it coincided with the second oil shock of 1979/80 which resulted in reduced demand for most primary commodities including copper.... By 1981..., copper export earnings slumped by 14.6 per cent. The economy's inability to increase other exports resulted in a 20-percent decline in total export earnings and a current account deficit of 22 percent of GDP. The value of the Kwacha depreciated during the Plan period while the terms of trade continued to deteriorate."[60]

By 1983, Zambia had accumulated a $3.5 billion debt and

it was already having serious problems with debt-servicing obligations. According to Tony Hodges, the debt crisis of Zambia must be placed in historical context of colonial underdevelopment, export concentration, and the volatility of copper prices in a global market beyond Zambia's control:

> ...copper still accounts for roughly 90 percent of exports, leaving Zambia overwhelmingly dependent on a single, volatile and, in recent years, generally depressed commodity market. Unable to adapt easily to the deterioration in its terms of trade, Zambia resorted to heavy borrowing, becoming one of the most heavily indebted countries in all of Africa. It is now caught in a debt trap, on top of its chronic dependence on copper. Worse still, Zambia's commercially exploitable copper deposits are expected to run out in 15 to 20 years' time.[61]

Given the severe economic crisis, the government had no other option than to approach the International Monetary Fund and the World Bank for a stabilization and structural adjustment package to "resuscitate and restructure the economy."[62] It needs to be noted, however, that Zambia began to rely on IMF funds and support with the oil price increases of the early 1970s. With these oil prices, "Zambia increasingly became dependent on IMF resources. It made use of resources from the Fund's Oil Facility and was granted several standby agreements. It also began to draw funds from the Extended Facility Fund (EFF) after 1981. Between 1973 and 1978, Zambia was granted three standby arrangements. Whereas the 1973 standby agreement was granted with no conditionality, the other two involved conditionalities requiring the government to put ceilings on the money supply, government credit and devaluation of the Kwacha."[63] These standby agreements did virtually nothing to help the Zambian economy. This was because they addressed the *symptoms* rather than the structural and political *causes* of the Zambian predicament: the character of power, politics, production and exchange relations as well as the role of foreign capital in the underdeveloped and dependent economy of Zambia.

In 1981, the IMF made available to the Zambian government SDR 800, the second largest credit to an African country. The agreement was predicated on improved copper prices and the assumption that the government had the capability to carry out far-reaching reforms to put the economy on track, especially through the diversification of exports away from concentration on copper. The government and the IMF had seriously miscalculated, and the "economic reform programme failed when copper prices continued the downhill slide, worsening the domestic and external financial imbalance."[64] A three-year (1983-85) adjustment package was agreed to with the Fund and Bank and a one year standby agreement was also reached in 1983 to "restore financial stability." A standby agreement was reached for the period 21 October 1985 through April 1987 to implement the devaluation of the Kwacha, price decontrol, interest rate liberalization, import liberalization, reduction of the role of development planning in favor of budgeting, drastic cuts in public expenditures, removal of subsidies on an array of social programs, reduction in government deficit; introduction of credit ceilings on government and private sector borrowing; and the privatization of government-owned enterprises.[65] As is typical in the majority of African states, this new alliance with the Fund/Bank failed to resuscitate the deteriorating Zambian economy.

The reasons for the failure of structural adjustment in Zambia are legion. Export earnings declined to their lowest level in 1982 in spite of IMF intervention. Increased government borrowing and the accumulation of payment arrears on foreign debt eroded the country's creditworthiness and increased its deficit. Copper prices continued to decline and the currency was again devalued by 20 percent in 1983. The cut in food and farm subsidies fueled inflation and generated severe political opposition and unrest. The 1981 standby agreement had collapsed in July 1982, the 1983 standby agreement had been suspended in June 1984, and Zambia had failed to pay its overdue debt to the Fund or meet other declared budgetary goals.

The "home grown" alternative, *Restructuring in the Midst of Crisis* adopted in May 1984, was aimed at addressing foreign exchange scarcity, improving capacity utilization, increasing labor utilization in the production process in order to generate employment, and diversifying the economy away from copper exports. This so-called home-grown alternative failed to produce any results like previous plans.[66] This "new" policy, with emphasis on trimming the size of the state and tight fiscal measures, impressed the IMF and in June 1984 the government reached a twenty-month standby agreement with the Fund for SDR 225 million. Of course, like other previous agreements, it was suspended in February 1985 as the government could not service its $800 million arrears, trim the deficit, diversify the economy, or increase productivity in agriculture and manufacturing. To make matters worse, a government that was on the brink of bankruptcy—which could not supply drugs to hospitals, pay salaries to teachers and civil servants, keep its foreign embassies functioning, or repair damaged roads and other infrastructure—spent an unbelievable $18 million on its twentieth independence anniversary celebrations. As Fantu Cheru has noted:

> At the beginning of 1985, Zambia was on the brink of economic and political disaster. Its foreign debt had grown to $4 billion by June 1984. It owed $725 million to the IMF and $350 million to the World Bank. In 1986, arrears to the IMF alone were around $100 million and this blocked the way to a new Standby agreement. Almost all economic indicators registered a decline. Drastic curtailment in import levels had negative consequences on output,

employment and government revenue. In a desperate bid to stop the disintegration of the state, the Zambian government had to resort to a massive retrenchment programme and unblock the way to new negotiations with the IMF.[67]

These new moves did not do much good for the government or the economy. In fact, "Zambia became steadily poorer, regressing in World Bank nomenclature from a "lower middle income" country to a "low income" status. Per-capita GDP fell in real terms by an annual average of 2.7 percent during the 1970s and by over 3 percent a year in the 1980s. Between 1977 and 1987, real per-capita income fell by a full 26 percent. Meanwhile, the rate of fixed investment fell from 18.2 percent in 1980 to 10.7 percent in 1987.[68] The on-and-off relationship with the Fund reflected the crisis of legitimacy of both the state and the IMF as both bodies preferred to concentrate on superficial issues and on the symptoms rather than the structural causes of the Zambian predicament. The reform policy was implemented half-heartedly by a government that had lost all credibility and lost control of the dynamics of society. Mismanagement and corruption remained commonplace, the rural areas remained neglected, governmental accountability remained very low, and there were no serious structural transformations in the patterns of production and exchange. More importantly, the costs and pains as well as few gains of adjustment were not evenly distributed, the poor bore the brunt of the policies while the rich continued to live a life of opulence. Since there were no programs in place to mitigate the harsh effects of adjustment, the monetarist policies simply deepened alienation from the state, opposition to the policies, political unrest and instability, and an increased commitment of the people to change. Thus, unintendedly, the structural adjustment program contributed significantly to the delegitimization of the state, its institutions and custodians, and to the intensification of the struggle for opening up the political system. Of course the government found it easy to mount a campaign against the Bank and Fund, arguing among other things that "IMF stabilization programmes and conditionality clauses attached to it ignored the structural problems of developing countries like Zambia and the need to focus on pressing social issues."[69] In the UNIP Resolutions of the Ninth General Conference held at the Mulungushi Rock of Authority, Kabwe, in August 1983, the party noted that it was "Gravely concerned by the deteriorating economic situation in the country caused by the world economic recession" and went on to blame its internal failures on the "stiff opposition from vested interests in the country."[70] To make matters worse for Zambia, most of its debts had been contracted on "relatively hard terms and much of it is not reschedulable because it is owed to the multilateral institutions which enjoy 'privileged creditor' status in the international financial system."[71]

In the *Fourth Plan*, the government admitted that it practically achieved nothing under its structural adjustment program:

> The performance of the economy during the Third National Development Plan period was not satisfactory. This performance is reflected in all macro-economic indicators: such as Gross Domestic Product (GDP); Government budget; balance of payments; general price levels, and employment levels. Real GDP grew by 1 per cent throughout the Plan period or an average of 0.2 per cent per annum. The only positive growth rate occurred during 1981 when an impressive 6.2 per cent was achieved. However, this was followed by a negative decline of 2.8, 2.0 and 0.4 per cent in 1982, 1983 and 1984 respectively. Based on the projected growth in real GDP of 4.8 per cent per annum per capita incomes were estimated to grow by 1.5 per cent over the Plan period. The failure of the economy to expand at the envisaged rate, in the face of a higher rate of population growth, led

to a 20 per cent fall in per capita income. The Plan period 1980 to 1984, alone witnessed a 12.1 per cent decline in per capita income or an average of 3.0 per cent per annum.[72]

In fact, for the years 1985-1987, GDP per-capita income declined by 0.1, 0.6, and 3.7 percent, respectively. The country's current account balance in 1985 deteriorated sharply in spite of trade liberalization due to "large outflows of invisibles relative to inflows" and this further weakened the "overall balance-of-payments position." Meanwhile the depreciation of the Kwacha due to devaluation and inflation saw a rapid increase in the value of imports by 124.5 percent to K4,028.6 million as against a 62-percent increase which had occurred between 1984 and 1985. The economy consequently recorded a huge deficit of K2,345.7 million in the invisible account.

Debt-service ratios continued to increase, from 43 percent of export earnings in 1984 to 74 percent in 1985 and 1986; capital inflows actually declined precipitously in 1986; unemployment grew especially as the industrial sector was stagnating; and expatriates fled the mining sector, creating a serious management crisis. By the end of 1986, the over-all balance deficit was K2.1 billion. The standby agreement reached in March 1986—once again, with the IMF, and for SDR 230 million—was to be repaid in two years as well as an additional SDR 69 million from the Compensatory Finance Facility (CFF) had given the economy some breathing space as creditors rescheduled their debts and Sweden actually wrote off $7.7 million owed it by Zambia. But Zambia, as usual, was in no position to meet up with its credit arrears and the facility was suspended in May 1987. Zambia was effectively on the path to total economic crisis. Because the government blamed the IMF and its stabilization-and-adjustment package for the deteriorating conditions of the economy, it imposed a 'ceiling' on debt-service repayments, broke negotiations with the Fund, and terminated the structural adjustment program in May 1987. Needless to say, the IMF lenders and donors were unimpressed by this move as Zambia was fully at the mercy of the outside world. This was because the Zambian elite had done virtually nothing to mobilize the people for the sacrifices required to put the economy back on track or to promote some appreciable level of growth and development. The elites shielded themselves from the deepening crisis and spiralling inflation as much as possible, usually through corruption, the privatization of public resources, and through party patronage. With no domestic constituency to support its defensive radicalism towards the IMF, Zambia was in no position to take drastic steps to extricate itself from the influence and control of the Fund and Bank.

Palliatives and Propaganda: Kaunda and the New Economic Recovery Programme

On May 1, 1987 the Government launched the country's New Economic Recovery Programme (NERP) with the theme "Growth from Own Resources." According to President Kenneth Kaunda, the NERP was made necessary because of

> worsening economic crisis. Between 1980 and 1986 the Zambian economy sunk into deeper crisis caused mainly by continued high prices of oil. This crisis was characterized by a worsening in the country's terms of trade. While export prices rose by 151 percent between 1980 and 1985 this increase was more than offset by a simultaneous increase in import prices which saw the import price index rising to 990.57 as against the 1979 base of 100. This represented a rise in import prices of more than 800 per cent.[73]

President Kaunda noted that "domestic inflation was higher than recorded in previous years reaching a peak of 67 per cent in April 1987"; that there was a drastic decline in capacity utilization "which cut across all sectors of the economy"; and that the country's "heavy external debt burden...turned Zambia into a net exporter of financial resources at a time when the country was in dire need of resources to keep the economy afloat." Kaunda blamed the adoption of an IMF- and World Bank-sponsored Structural Adjustment Program (SAP) for the deepening crisis of the nation and argued that between 1983 and 1985 Zambia "witnessed a faster decline in the country's economic performance." Furthermore, the President lamented the horrendous conditions of the economy by noting that:

> ...by April, 1987 the rate of domestic inflation had reached record levels while capacity utilization in the economy declined with some key industries registering levels as low as 12 per cent. During this period higher interest rates on the world money market resulted in the country's external indebtedness rising from US$3.2 billion in 1980 to US$5.6 billion at the beginning of 1987.[74]

According to the government, the only way out of the problem was to terminate relations with the IMF and to introduce a new domestic economic agenda—the NERP.

The key objectives of the NERP were: to reactivate the economy by maximizing the utilization of domestic resources; to change the structure and pattern of consumption from import dependence to reliance on domestically produced goods and services; and to rationalize the use of foreign exchange as a strategic resource. Thus an Interim National Development Plan (INDP) covering an eighteen month period commencing in July 1987 was drawn up to:

(a) release resources for development by compressing nonessential and luxury imports and limiting debt service payments;

(b) reactivate the economy by increasing capacity utilization in enterprises producing essential or basic goods for export;

(c) stabilize the economy by controlling inflation;

(d) promote a self sustaining economy through increased profitability and reinvestment of profits in enterprises utilizing local raw materials;

(e) diversify exports by promoting nontraditional exports and exports of manufactured goods;

(f) restructure production and consumption patterns so as to use foreign exchange as a strategic resource;

(g) increase employment opportunities through the establishment of village and small-scale industries based on local raw materials;

(h) increase the government capacity to manage the economy; and

(i) reduce subsidies gradually and target them to the needy.[75]

This was actually Kenneth Kaunda's last gamble. The government was aware that its policies had to make a substantial difference from the abandoned structural adjustment program. The people had to see evidence of governmental commitment and an improvement in their living conditions. For the INDP to achieve these goals, its strategies included: severe restriction of imports to mainly essential goods and services; restriction of debt-service payments to 10 percent of net export earnings after deduction of payments in respect of ZCCM, ZIMOIL, Zambia Airways (IATA), and fertilizer imports; controlling inflation through the stabilization of the exchange rate of the Kwacha at K8 to US$1; keeping interest rates fixed at between 15 and 20 percent; establishing a minimum wage, and restricting wage increases to collective bargaining channels; channelling resources and profits from INDP only to enterprises producing essential goods or basic goods for export; diversifying the economy to reduce overdependence on copper; restructuring consumption patterns to conserve foreign exchange and redirecting tastes and values to local products through massive public campaigns; increasing taxes on the importation of luxury items; discouraging capital-intensive and import-oriented industries in favor of labor-intensive industries reliant on local resources; promoting the exportation of manufactured goods; exploiting the nation's regional markets through industrial decentralization; and strengthening the government's management capacity to reorder national priorities and to promote "participatory democracy." To put it mildly, the IMF was not amused or impressed by this so called "indigenous" or "home grown" alternative to its omnipotent prescriptions. It found it irritating that a small and debt-ridden country like Zambia could break relations with it, suspend its debt payment, and impose a limit on debt-servicing obligations. In response, it decided to punish Zambia (see below). Zambia was isolated and left high and dry in its difficulties.

Perhaps, if the government were able to implement these and other policies, particularly its promised commitment to "participatory democracy," there might have been a chance for *some* recovery. Unfortunately, this was not to be. First, the INDP assumed a new commitment from the Zambian bourgeoisie, which actually remained as unproductive, subservient, and decadent as ever, finding it impossible to restructure its largely unproductive, corrupt, wasteful and dependent patterns of accumulation. The bureaucratic faction resisted any effort to reduce its privileges. The parastatals continued to run inefficiently and they found several ingenuous ways around public policies. The ruling party itself remained corrupt and completely incapable of charting or following a new path of socioeconomic and political restructuring. Secondly, with the termination of the structural adjustment program and negotiations with the IMF in 1987, all Fund loans to Zambia were terminated and financial support from the international donor community dried up immediately. Creditors imposed new conditionalities and applied pressures on Zambia while suppliers simply declared Zambia a non-creditworthy state. Finally, and thirdly, the political crisis continued to deepen. Most of the policies introduced were unpopular and easily precipitated unrest across the country.

The removal of subsidies on refined maize meal, the country's staple food, led to a 120-percent increase in the price of "mealie meal." It led to very violent riots in Kitwe and Ndola, major towns in the Copperbelt. Several people died, and over 400 people were arrested by the police. The government was forced to reintroduce the subsidy. In April 1987, in spite of commitment to keep wages down, there were strikes for wage increases, while strikes against a proposed 70-percent increase in fuel prices (especially in Lusaka) again forced the government to rescind the policy. It was becoming increasingly clear to the government that implementing its tough policies in an economy already run down and so badly mismanaged was going to be even tougher. It is important to note at this point that the Zambian bourgeoisie did not behave as if the country were in crisis. It continued to rely on corruption as a major means of accumulation and remained incapable of addressing the country's deepening crisis from a holistic and structural perspective. As Fantu Cheru has noted, "For Zambian elites who make their living off the modern sector, there was no urgency to change the status quo despite some alarming trends in the economy. The nature and severity of the foreign exchange crisis was gravely underestimated. Economic policy continued along the same path based on the belief that the shortfall in copper earnings was a temporary phenomenon."[76]

The government, of course, sought some diversions. In April 1987, it accused South Africa of colluding with some wealthy Zambians and military officers to overthrow it. Some cabinet changes were carried out to give the impression that serious political restructurings were occurring and a new Minister for Finance was appointed. In August 1988,

the government introduced some amendments to the constitution to allow for the expansion of the Central
Committee of UNIP. This meant increasing the membership
from 25 to 68. The purpose was to incorporate more people
who were seen as representing important segments or interests in the country—industrialists, and labor leaders like
the secretary general of the powerful MUZ. At a time when
the party and government were supposed to be downsizing,
it was actually increasing its ranks and creating more
bureaucrats.

In October 1988, six military officers and three others
were accused of trying to overthrow the government. They
were accused of treason and convicted in August 1989.[77]
These developments exposed the increasing fragility and
insecurity of the government. It showed that the government was increasingly vulnerable and was seeking enemies
and scapegoats as well as diversions from its failed economic
and social programs. By 1989, though Kaunda had pur-
portedly won the 1988 election with a 95.5-percent endorsement from the electorate (he was the only candidate, and
voter turnout was only 54 percent), there were several riots
and strikes all over the country, especially in the Copperbelt
and Lusaka. Increases in the prices of essential goods were
resisted again by workers. The government was forced to
resume negotiations with the IMF and in September 1989
it implemented the IMF package by devaluing the Kwacha
and removing several subsidies and price controls and
embarked on a program of mass retrenchment of workers
from the parastatals and bureaucracy. This effectively nul-
lified the INDP and showed that the Kaunda government
had lost control of the Zambian economy and was completely incapable of putting the nation on a viable path to
recovery.

1990 did not witness any improved conditions in Zambia.
The working-class and rural people grew more restless and
militant. Demands for the UNIP government of Kaunda to

quit the political scene began to be heard more frequently. The country reached a new agreement with the IMF again and dispensed with all rhetoric about social concerns for the underprivileged. This was the only way to get international donors to resume aid to Zambia and in July 1990 creditors agreed to a rescheduling arrangement for Zambia's foreign debt. By this time, "basic social services had crumbled, schools lacked books, and hospitals were spurned by all but the indigent. Food riots erupted in the capital, Lusaka in June 1990 after a government effort to decontrol the price of maize meal, the country's staple food, brought large price increases."[78] During the riots "angry protesters in Lusaka sent pointed political messages to Kaunda not only by setting ablaze a national monument commemorating his leadership role in the nationalist struggle, but also by singling out state-owned retail stores as the main target of looting. Citizens now explicitly blamed the single-party system for their economic plight."[79]

Striving for Some Lost Ground: Political Reorganizations and Concessions to the Opposition

The deepening economic crisis put severe pressure on the Kaunda government. Paradoxically, 1990 was also to witness some of the most fundamental and dramatic changes in Zambia's political history. In May, Kaunda announced that a popular referendum on multiparty politics, which was becoming the main political issue and was at the center of national political discourses would take place in October 1990. He made it clear in his announcement that though he and UNIP were not afraid of multiparty politics, he was completely opposed to the idea. As usual, Kaunda invoked the old and already discredited arguments in support of one-party rule. He conceded that those who advocated for multiparty politics would be granted permission to openly campaign for support. This signal from Kaunda generated heated debates and massive and unprecedented alignment and realignment of forces. Ironically, virtually all those who had been victims of Kaunda's repression, who had been dismissed from UNIP or the government, and who had dealings with the labor movement began to regroup. It was as if Kaunda had provided a platform for his opponents to come together under the banner of demand for democracy. At this point it was not really clear if the new groupings were encouraged or motivated by their beliefs in democracy, empowerment of the people, accountability and social justice, or, if they were simply opportunist liberal movements brought together by a common dislike for Kaunda.

In June, Kenneth Kaunda removed Frederick Hapunda as Minister for Defence largely because he was suspected of supporting the mounting movement for multiparty politics. The Minister for Mines, Bernard Fumbel was also removed from office. At the end of June, Mwamba Luchembe, a lieutenant in the Zambian army, announced on state radio that the Kaunda government had been overthrown in a coup d'etat. The coup, though suppressed in that same day, received widespread support all over the country. The coup alarmed Kaunda, who now saw how vulnerable he was to a better-organized coup. The coup also validated Elias Chipimo's earlier statement about sit-tight leaders who are forced to leave office only with a bullet in the head! In July he quickly appointed Lt. General Hannaniah Lungu as Minister for Defence in place of the dismissed Hapunda. July also witnessed the formation of the Movement for Multiparty Democracy (MMD) as an alliance of opponents of the Kaunda government. Led by former Minister of Finance Arthur Wina and by Frederick Chiluba, Chairman of the ZCTU, the MMD gained widespread support in every corner of the country (see above).

The economic difficulties imposed on the people, especially the urban working classes, by the adjustment program, continuing corruption in government, the arrogance of power displayed by the Kaunda government elite, and the general inability to meet the basic needs of the people increased support for the MMD. The increasing support which the MMD was receiving and the rate at which people were decamping from UNIP to join the MMD as well as the open participation of popular former ministers in the MMD forced Kaunda to announce a postponement, to August 1991, of the referendum he had promised to hold in October 1990. The explanation was that there was need for sufficient time to enable people to register to vote in the referendum. The MMD opposed the postponement and argued for a December 1990 date. The referendum was to be done away with completely later. However, another novel development occurred when in August 1990 the National Assembly, dominated by UNIP members, proposed the introduction of a multiparty political system in the country. Kaunda immediately announced his opposition to this call. As the debate intensified, it became obvious that Kaunda would be unable to stand in the way of multiparty politics. Eventually, in September 1990, in an address to the National Council of his party, he supported the call for multiparty politics.

While the credit for this development obviously should go in the first instance to the MMD and other popular groups in the country, it is also important to note that creditors, donors and international finance institutions had come up with political conditionalities for continuing aid to African nations, including Zambia. In any case, the MMD had become such a mass popular movement that Kaunda realized that the very emergence and growing influence of the movement was not only a judgement on his own credibility and popularity, but also that it was pointless to try and wish the MMD away or to think of stamping it out through some political means. Following his acceptance of multiparty politics in September, he proposed an October 1991 date for multiparty elections in Zambia. He also jettisoned the idea of a referendum and called instead for a commission to review the constitution so as to bring it in line with the new multiparty system. These proposals were endorsed by the National Council on September 27, 1990, and in October legislation permitting the formation of other political parties in the country was passed. The country had come full circle and Kaunda had once again been contained and forced to change his political position by a combined force of popular organizations led by the MMD. Between November and December, Kaunda carried out a great deal of administrative and political reorganization within the party and government. He announced his plans to run as presidential candidate for UNIP and managed to contain opposition to this idea within the party among those who felt that Kaunda had become a liability.

The process leading to the 1991 general elections was rough and full of conflicting and complex developments, accusations and counter-accusations, efforts to manipulate the state and its resources, appeals to the masses for support, and violence. By mid 1991, according to Richard Joseph,

> The country was now in receivership to a host of international and bilateral lending agencies. Successive International Monetary Fund stabilization plans had been agreed to but not implemented. Zambia was in arrears on its repayment schedules and spending millions of dollars monthly to subsidize maize sales while failing to pay agricultural producers an attractive price. It was an extreme case of an economy in need of adjustment. The government's ability to resist the growing political opposition was sapped by the increasing reluctance of foreign creditors to keep bailing it out.[80]

Conclusion

The Zambian case demonstrates the classic situation in Africa. Independence is won by an alliance of urban and rural people led by an urban-based petty-bourgeoisie. The new elite appropriates the state and its resources, surrounds

93

itself with political opportunists and sycophants, neglects the basic needs of the people and the rural areas, becomes corrupt, wastes money on prestige-seeking foreign affairs and pet projects, and imposes a one-party state on society. It tries, through legal and extra-legal means, to domesticate and incorporate all opposition elements and relies heavily on defensive radicalism, bogus ideologies, political containment, manipulation of primordial loyalties, lies, propaganda, and diversions. These postures and actions lead to inefficiency, a hyper-bloated bureaucracy, economic decay, and general deterioration. Foreign debts pile up. Terms of trade deteriorate, inflation and unemployment increase to unprecedented proportions, as do crime, prostitution, drunkenness, violence, intolerance, and rural-to-urban migration. Each act of repression, detention, and human rights abuse weakens the state, delegitimizes the leadership, and makes the "one party" vulnerable to coups, political challenges, and other forms of opposition. In the Zambian case, as the UNIP lost control of the economy due to internal mismanagement and irresponsible economic policies as well as a deteriorating price of copper, on which the economy was dependent, it alienated the populace and provoked challenges to its rule.

Without doubt, developments in the global economy and negative repercussions of orthodox stabilization and adjustment policies prescribed by the Fund and the World Bank complicated possibilities for recovery. Fantu Cheru, for instance, gives a lot of attention to the role the IMF and World Bank played in the "bantustanization" of Zambia. He argued that the IMF was very wrong when it advised the Zambian government to devalue its currency and to auction its foreign exchange in the hope that "the auction system would discourage imports and force both producers and consumers to use local materials and consumer goods...that import dependent and capital intensive firms would be forced to curtail imports and instead utilize local labour, thus generating more employment."[81] These developments never occurred in Zambia. The first auction, on 11 October 1985, saw an immediate 53-percent drop in the value of the Kwacha from K2.23 to K5.01. to US$1. Prices increased, hoarding began to characterize the retail sector, unemployment increased, the cost of borrowing and doing business increased tremendously, and small scale industries were threatened. As Cheru has argued:

> Devaluation of the Kwacha failed to stem the tide of imports. Contrary to what the IMF was preaching, there were no restrictions on the kinds of goods which could be imported with the foreign exchange allocated to an importer. Despite the increase in the value of imports as a result of the devaluation, the flood of imports swallowed the country because of an IMF-mandated trade liberalization policy. Local producers shifted their attention from production to retailing of imported goods since they found the latter more profitable than the former. Devaluation had made the cost of production expensive as the price of basic inputs rose sharply.
>
> As the Kwacha depreciated sharply, the cost of many consumer goods increased simultaneously. Essential inputs disappeared while basic consumer goods became too expensive for ordinary citizens to afford.[82]

For Cheru, therefore, the IMF, the World Bank, and other Western bilateral aid institutions are to be held directly responsible for the Zambian condition and the rapid slide towards disaster. This is because, "these institutions and their governments have long supported misguided development projects which, in the final analysis, benefited local elites, Western contractors, consulting firms, and research universities more than the upgrading of Zambia's capacity to plan and implement alternative policies based on local knowledge and resources."[83] Specifically, Cheru notes that these institutions and their governments in the West have employed foreign aid and other assistance to gain "political leverage" in Zambia; bilateral donors have supported IMF initiatives and, while "publicly pledging to help Zambia in its darkest hour, they chose to hold up disbursements of funds until the government reached agreement with the IMF."[84]

There is certainly a lot to be said for this position adopted by Cheru. Without doubt Zambia had, since political independence, been a pawn in the hands of international finance institutions, donors, creditors, and other forces of imperialism, particularly transnational corporations in the extractive industry. They loved Zambia only for its copper. When prices fell, they turned their backs on Zambia and looked for other locations to reap profits. When Zambia reacted to popular pressure and broke relations with the Fund, donors, lenders, and creditors joined the Fund in isolating the country and further complicating possibilities for recovery. But this is exactly where the challenge lies, and why African governments and their political elites must now take most of the blame for their predicaments. They are all aware that the relationship between Zambia and the West has historically been exploitative and unequal. Yet, we have not seen any serious commitment to change, to restructure, to empower the people and their communities, and to stamp out waste, irresponsibility, mismanagement, and corruption. In the midst of the crisis, as Cheru himself noted, the Zambian elite behaved as if nothing were really amiss. The state became more repressive. We did not witness any increased commitment to a structural transformation of the economy, and only lip service was paid to economic diversification, industrialization, agricultural productivity, and self-reliance for almost three decades. The issue, therefore, is that until African leaders have the courage to challenge the chains of subservience, corruption, dependence, and domination, they cannot extricate themselves or their economies from manipulation by better organized external forces. Of course, the situation was not helped by the crass impotence and corruption of the government itself.

What is clear, however, is that deepening economic crisis pushed the masses to the wall, invigorated their political movements, increased working-class militancy, and contributed in no small way to the demands for democracy and democratization.

Notes

1. Tony Hodges, "Zambia's Autonomous Adjustment," *Africa Recovery* Vol. 2, (4) (December 1988), p. 6.
2. Ibid.
3. Fantu Cheru, *The Silent Revolution in Africa: Debt, Development and Democracy*, (London and Harare: Zed Books and Anvil, 1992), p.126.
4. Munyonzwe Hamalengwa, *Class Struggles in Zambia 1889-1989 and The Fall of Kenneth Kaunda 1990-1991*, (Lanham: University Press of America, 1992), p.22.
5. Dr. Kenneth Kaunda had become leader of the UNIP in 1960 and Prime Minister in January 1964.
6. Hamalengwa, op. cit., p.48
7. For instance, at the August 1969 UNIP National Council Meeting at Matero Hall, Kaunda insisted that mine owners must give the government 51 percent of their shares. This would of course increase state ownership even if not state control.
8. Kenneth Kaunda, Address at the occasion of the opening of the ninth national council of the United National Independence Party, 20th September, 1976.
9. Ibid.
10. Kenneth Kaunda, address to the leaders' seminar of the United National Independence Party, Mulungushi Rock, Kabwe, 14th September 1976.
11. See Kenneth Kaunda, *Communocracy: A Strategy for Constructing a People's Economy Under Humanism*, (Lusaka: Government of the Republic of Zambia, 1976).
12. Kenneth Kaunda, *Towards Complete Independence*,

speech to the UNIP National Council Meeting, Matero Hall, Lusaka, August 11, 1969, Lusaka: Zambia Information Services.

13. The ZCTU was registered in 1966 with twelve affiliated unions.

14. Kenneth Kaunda, Guidelines Issued to ZIMCO Director-General, Executive Directors, Managing Directors, Deputy Managing Directors and General Managers of all ZIMCO Subsidiaries and other Parastatal Organizations, Lusaka, 1st February, 1983.

15. Michael Bratton, "Economic Crisis and Political Realignment in Zambia," in Jennifer Widner, (ed.), *Economic Change and Political Liberalization in Sub-Saharan Africa*, (Baltimore: The Johns Hopkins Press, 1994), p. 105.

16. International Labour Office, *Narrowing the Gaps: Planning for Basic Needs and Productive Employment in Zambia*, (Addis Ababa: JASPA, 1977).

17. Michael Bratton, "Economic Crisis and Political Realignment in Zambia," op. cit., p. 106.

18. Ibid., p. 104.

19. Fantu Cheru, *The Silent Revolution in Africa*, op. cit., p.126.

20. Ibid.

21. Ibid., p. 127.

22. Ibid., p.128.

23. Ibid., p. 129. Companies like Cold Storage Board of Zambia, Nitrogen Chemicals of Zambia and the United Bus Company among others have been severely affected by these economic difficulties.

24. See "Zambia Sacks 5,000 Workers," *The Herald* (13 May 1986). Cited in Cheru, *The Silent Revolution,* op. cit., p.134.

25. See "Diplomats Recalled," *The Herald* (18 March 1986) and "Zambia Shuts Two Embassies," *The Herald* (January 1986). Cited in Ibid.

26. Hamalengwa (op. cit.), p.97.

27. Interview, Lusaka, May 1993.

28. "Third World Urged to Change Party Systems," *Times of Zambia* (April 21, 1980).

29. See "Chipimo's Views Personal," *Times of Zambia* (May 24, 1980).

30. Interview, Lusaka, May 1993.
31. Kenneth Kaunda, Address of Secretary-General on the Occasion of the Opening of the UNIP National Council at Mulungushi Hall, 1st October, 1971. In spite of this rather definitive stance, Kaunda continued in the address to comment on the advocates of multi-party democracy arguing that they had prevented the UNIP from implementing party policies, frustrated the party and "actually sabotaged the party and government authority and undermined completely our efforts to achieve our objectives."
32. "Anti-KK Men Wasting Their Time," *Times of Zambia* (May 25, 1980). "KK" which stands for Kenneth Kaunda was the president's nick name.
33. "Traders Teaming Up- KK- New Party Plot Exposed," *Times of Zambia* (September 15, 1988).
34. "Wina Heads Multiparty Drive Team," *Times of Zambia* (June 22, 1990).
35. "One Party Rule Violates Rights-Chongwe," *Times of Zambia* (July 23, 1990).
36. Ibid.
37. Ibid.
38. "MMD Accused of Lying," *Times of Zambia* (January 1, 1991).
39. "Opponents Ticked Off," *Times of Zambia* (January 30, 1991).
40. "Ex-Detainee Denounces MMD," *Times of Zambia* (January 31, 1991).
41. "MultiParty Rally Runs into a Hitch," *Times of Zambia* (August 6, 1990).
42. Chris Chitanda, "Pay MMD, Judge Tells Guilty State," *Times of Zambia* (December 20, 1990).
43. "Chiluba Claims Labour Support," *Times of Zambia* (December 24, 1990); and "MMD is Our Baby Says MUZ Chief," *Times of Zambia* (December 25, 1990).
44. "Chipata Multi-Party Advocate Fired," *Times of Zambia* (August 12, 1990).
45. "Multi-Party Drive Woos UNZA Students," *Times of Zambia* (August 20, 1990).
46. Interview, University of Zambia, Lusaka, May 1993.
47. Interview with a former Kaunda Minister, Parliamentary Motel, Lusaka, June 1993.
48. "Founder Member Quits UNIP," *Times of Zambia*

(December 29, 1990).

49. See "81 Opt for MMD," *Times of Zambia* (March 18, 1991); "2000 Party Cards Surrendered-UNIP Falls Apart in Solwezi," *Times of Zambia* (March 23, 1991); and "300 Join MMD in Choma," *Times of Zambia* (April 4, 1991).

50. "2 Bow Out of UNIP," *Times of Zambia* (January 24, 1991).

51. "Sata Quits for MMD," *Times of Zambia* (January 27, 1991).

52. Interview, Lusaka, May 1993.

53. See *Times of Zambia* (29 September, 1980); *The Workers Voice* Vol. 3 (2) (September 1980); and Speech by Frederick Chiluba to seminar of the ZCTU general council, Kabwe, September 28, 1980.

54. See Hamalengwa, (op. cit.), and Bratton, "Economic Crisis and Political Realignment in Zambia," op. cit.

55. Interview, Lusaka, July, 1993.

56. Hamalengwa (op. cit.) p.103.

57. Klaas Woldring, "Corruption and Inefficiency in Zambia: A Survey of Recent Inquiries and their Results," *Africa Today* Vol. 30 (3) (1983), p.74.

58. Interview, Lusaka, June 1993.

59. Frederick Chiluba, cited in Woldring, "Corruption and Inefficiency. . . " (op. cit.) pp.114-115.

60. Republic of Zambia, *New Economic Recovery Programme: Fourth National Development Plan 1989-1993 Volumes I and II*, (Lusaka: Office of the President: National Commission for Development Planning, January 1989), p.l.

61. Tony Hodges, "Zambia's Autonomous Adjustment," (op. cit):6.

62. Ibid.

63. Fantu Cheru, *The Silent Revolution in Africa* (op. cit.) p.131.

64. Ibid.

65. Ibid., pp.l-2.

66. Government of Zambia, *Restructuring in the Midst of Crisis*, (Lusaka: Report of the Consultative Group for Zambia, May 1984).

67. Fantu Cheru, *The Silent Revolution in Africa*, op. cit., p.132.

68. Tony Hodges, "Zambia's Autonomous Adjustment," op.

cit., p.7.

69. Fantu Cheru, *The Silent Revolution in Africa*, op. cit., p.3.
70. United National Independence Party, *Speech by His Excellency Dr Kenneth D. Kaunda* to the 9th General Conference of the UNIP, Mulungushi Rock of Authority, 22nd August 1983, p. 99.
71. Tony Hodges, "Zambia's Autonomous Adjustment," (op. cit.), p.7.
72. Ibid., p.2.
73. Kenneth Kaunda, "Forward to the Fourth National Development Plan" in Republic of Zambia, *New Economic Recovery Programme* (op. cit.) p.i
74. Ibid.
75. Ibid., p.6.
76. Fantu Cheru, *The Silent Revolution in Africa* (op. cit.) p.130.
77. The jailed officers were later released in 1990 as part of a general amnesty from the President.
78. Richard Joseph, "Zambia: A Model for Democratic change, *Current History* (May 1992), p.199. See also his "Africa: Rebirth of Political Freedom, *Journal of Democracy* 2, 4 (Fall 1991) and Michael Bratton, "The Rebirth of Political Pluralism in Zambia, *Journal of Democracy* 3, 2 (Spring 1992).
79. Michael Bratton, "Economic Crisis and Political Realignment in Zambia," op. cit., p.117.
80. Richard Joseph, "Zambia...," op. cit., p. 200.
81. Fantu Cheru, *The Silent Revolution in Africa* (op. cit.) p.133.
82. Ibid., p. 134.
83. Ibid., p. 135. Cheru also notes that "Zambia's economic fortunes deteriorated as a result of increased IMF/World Bank intervention." p.138.
84. Ibid.

CHAPTER THREE

CIVIL SOCIETY AND
DEMOCRATIZATION IN ZAMBIA

Opposition Mounts: The Hour Has Come

As soon as the Movement for Multiparty Democracy (MMD) was recognized and registered as a political party in January 1991, it was immediately regarded and treated as an enemy by Kaunda and his party, UNIP. The road to the August 1991 election was filled with acrimony and distrust. This was in some sense inevitable, given the longstanding tradition of autocracy. Until the rise of the MMD, everything was Kaunda. A young high school student interviewed in Lusaka put it this way: "I was born knowing, seeing, reading and believing in KK. I was taught that UNIP was the only party right for Zambia. I believed that without KK Zambia would simply die. In fact, I believed that all good things in this country came from KK. It was when my father joined the MMD and won the election to parliament that I knew that KK was not Zambia and was not everything."[1] Kenneth Kaunda had succeeded in domesticating, intimidating, incorporating or eliminating all opposition and did not believe that his rule over Zambia could be challenged. But the road to the MMD's victory was not new or uncharted.

The UNIP knew a long time back that the day of reckoning would dawn sooner or later. The 1980s had seen consistent challenges to Kaunda, the UNIP, and the ideology of Humanism. The economy was not improving by any standards. In every confrontation with the state through the 1980s, especially those led by labor, the challenger came away victorious or, at the least, losing nothing. But each victory also meant the demythologization of Kaunda and his ideology. It meant a delegitimization of his rule and of his government. It meant an explosion of the invincibility and popular support his party was supposed to be enjoying. It also meant the erosion of the legitimacy and viability of the one party. Labor was able to lead the struggle because of its organizational advantages, its resource base, the character of its leadership and the fact that its members were often the very first victims of the state's economic policies of adjustment and stabilization. As Munyonzwe Hamalengwa has rightly noted, labor "was the only social force that ... survived the onslaught of the state. All other would-be contenders to state monopoly...[e.g.,] opposition politicians; students; intellectuals; the media, etc...[had] been crushed. The easiness with which these possible opposition centres were crushed testifies to their weakness in the first place."[2]

By the end of May 1990, when Kaunda agreed to a national referendum on multiparty politics for October of that year, the handwriting was already on the wall. That no one, no political party, and no degree of intimidation and manipulation could halt the march towards multiparty politics in Zambia was virtually assured by the following series of events:

a) There had been a coup attempt in October 1980—of which the UNIP government accused several Zambian businessmen and the government of South Africa.

b) In March 1985, Kaunda had to adopt emergency powers to deal with increasing opposition and strikes and riots against the failure of government economic policies.

c) In December 1986, following the adoption of a policy of

desubsidization, there had been a massive, nationwide riot leading to widespread destruction, especially in the Copperbelt, forcing the government to reintroduce the subsidy.

d) Several strikes, led by the ZCTU, teachers, mineworkers, postal workers, and students had virtually paralyzed the economy by the end of 1989.

e) Efforts to amend the constitution so as to increase the size of the UNIP Central Committee as a strategy to incorporate emerging opposition elements especially in the labor movement had failed and voter turnout in the October 1988 presidential election was at a record low of 54 percent.

f) By June 1990, it had become apparent that several members of the Kaunda government, such as minister for defense Frederick Hapunda, were in support of the calls for multiparty politics in Zambia. Their dismissal from government only swelled the ranks of the opposition.

g) There was another coup attempt, led by Lieutenant Mwamba Luchembe, in June of 1990, which received wide spread support all over the country. That they were pardoned in July of the same year was general indication that Kaunda felt terribly embarrassed by the coup and the public reaction to it.

h) In August 1990, the National Assembly had proposed the introduction of multiparty politics and the need to amend the constitution in order to move Zambia away from the one-party system imposed in December 1972.

i) Developments in Eastern Europe, especially the dismantling of communist regimes and the disintegration of the Soviet Union as a nation and a superpower, gave encouragement to opponents of one-party government and to proponents of multiparty politics. Kaunda could find, at this time, very little justification and rationalization in the ideology of Humanism.

j) In June 1990, students of the University of Zambia came out openly against price increases but in reality had used the strike and riots in Lusaka as an opportunity to fight the

Kaunda government. During the riot in Lusaka, the students were "joined by ordinary people"[3] and well over 30 rioters were killed by the police.

k) In July 1991, Kenneth Kaunda's hegemony over UNIP was contested when Enoch Kavindele, a member of the Central Committee, challenged his candidacy for the leadership of the party. Though Kavindele was later to withdraw his candidature in the interest of the party and Kaunda was to be reelected President of UNIP in August 1991 to enable him contest the election against the MMD, it was clear that things had fallen apart within UNIP. People like UNIP secretary general Gray Zulu and other prominent politicians refused to contest for reelection into the Central Committee, many UNIP members began to describe Kaunda as a liability to the party.

l) The flirtations with orthodox IMF and World Bank restructuring programs had failed to resuscitate the economy. The UNIP had lost the support of the middle class on which it had heavily relied for twenty-seven years but which it could no longer continue to pamper and subsidize; the government in its insecurity had become very repressive, frequently invoking and using its emergency powers against all opposition elements; and the whole ideology of state capitalism and the pattern of accumulation through the privatization of the state and its resources could no longer be reproduced. The crisis reduced the relevance of the party and government in the eyes of the people: "most of us had reached the conclusion by the end of 1990 that KK was finished. He had failed ideologically, he had failed politically, he had failed morally, and had failed woefully economically."[4]

Given these developments, it was clear that the march towards a pluralist society was practically unstoppable.

The Rise of the MMD as a Political Force in Zambia

In May 1990, when Kaunda announced the date for a popular referendum on multiparty politics for October, he also announced that proponents of the system would be allowed to campaign, hold public meetings, and set up organizations to propagate their ideas. In July the MMD, which had till then served as an unofficial opposition and vanguard of the movement to restructure the country's political system and get the UNIP government out of power, constituted itself formally as an advocacy group, and in December 1990 it became a political party. On January 4, 1991 "the MMD transferred and registered itself as a political party...with the aim of winning the first free elections...under a Multi-party Constitution."[5] The Movement was led by former UNIP finance minister Arthur Wina and ZCTU chairman Frederick Chiluba. In the MMD's fold were also prominent political heavyweights like former solicitor general Levy Mwanawasa, former speaker of the National Assembly Robinson Nabulyato, former member of UNIP Central Committee Ludwig Sondashi, former UNIP secretary general Humphrey Mulemba, former minister for mines Andrew Kashita; and former foreign affairs minister Vernon Mwaanga. As Hamalengwa has noted, "This was an impressive collection of individuals who had at one time or another served UNIP very well."[6] The loose coalition which had become the MMD resembled in several ways the Janata Party in India, a coalition of all interest groups and persons opposed to the ruling government. It also resembled in several ways the coalition of interests against Russian president Boris Yeltsin in October 1993, a loose confederation of people whose only common bond was the desire to defeat Yeltsin:

> The MMD in Zambia is a class alliance of the urbanized working class, a segment of the comprador bourgeoisie and former bureaucratic/state bourgeoisie, urban petty bourgeoisie and the lumpen proletariat. This alliance has managed to win over the rural proletariat and its populist politics ensured that

it captured the interests of the entire population, given the aggrandizement of the Kaunda regime.[7]

To be sure, the survival of the MMD, even before it was legally registered to operate as a political party, had a lot to do with the crisis of state and economy. More importantly though, was the calibre of personalities that led the movement. These were not persons that could be eliminated through "arranged" accidents, or detained indefinitely in a world order where human rights abuses could lead to global isolation, even sanctions. As well, the leaders of the MMD and the organizations and constituencies they represented held a higher moral ground over the UNIP and Kaunda. The fact that they had fallen out with Kaunda in the past was a strong point in their favor. Chiluba for instance, was a popular union leader and was on record as having frequently challenged the government to clean up the system in the interests of nonbourgeois forces. All that the opposition had to do was announce that it had an alternative agenda for socioeconomic and political reconstruction to win popular support. Given the high degree of frustration with the incumbent government, a deep scrutiny of opposition programs hardly occurred as hundreds of thousands flocked to join in the collective effort to "take out Kaunda." The UNIP stood very little chance of contesting the legitimacy of the opposition; it was clearly the underdog early in the game.

The MMD was quick to present its program to the people of Zambia. In its *Manifesto*, the MMD argued that Zambians had become "disillusioned with the dictatorial excesses of the ONE Party System of Government imposed" on the people; that it was leading a movement for the "restoration of the multiparty political system;" and that UNIP had "embraced political and economic programmes without reference to the people, programmes which resulted in the total collapse of the country's economy"—which had been "exceptionally sound and strong at the time of political independence." It warned the people of Zambia that "if left unchallenged, UNIP would be reelected (even under a multiparty system)" and that it would simply "revert to its bad old ways of dictating to the people." The movement declared that it was "determined and committed to ensuring that basic and universally recognized human rights are enshrined in the Constitution—the right to life; privacy of property; freedom under the law; the right of movement in and out of the country; freedom of conscience and freedoms of expression, association and worship." Declaring its economic philosophy, the MMD *Manifesto* stated that:

> MMD believes that economic prosperity for all can best be created by free men and women through free enterprise; by economic and social justice involving all the productive resources—human, material and financial—and by liberalising industry, trade and commerce, with the government only creating an enabling environment whereby economic growth must follow as it has done in all the world's successful countries.[8]

In spite of its commitment to freedom, equality, and free enterprise, the MMD was conscious of the fact that:

> when it comes to power it shall inherit a totally bankrupt economy and a crippling foreign debt....MMD shall inherit an exhausted public treasury due mainly to the fact that the UNIP government during its 27 years in office wasted the national wealth, it voted itself public funds to support its own political organization, it neglected all social and economic infrastructures such as roads, schools and hospitals and reduced the nation to a starving, beggar state barely surviving on donor finance.

The movement believed that political, infrastructural, and economic recovery and rehabilitation could take place in a new Zambia with a "renewed spirit of hard work, entrepreneurship, public commitment, honesty, integrity and public accountability." It was prepared to take "bold but painful measures in order to arrest" the current decline and decay and "make a fresh start towards rebuilding a more reliable and sustainable infrastructure to promote growth."

Among the major prescriptions and hopes of the MMD as articulated in the *Manifesto* are commitment to human rights and a commitment to "upholding democracy based on multiparty system with effective checks and balances"; a revocation of the prevailing state of emergency and a control of the ability of the Executive to use emergency regulations; the separation of powers; law reform and democratization of local governments as "the only valid way of giving back power to the people"; restoration of the "traditional powers" of traditional rulers with the institution of chieftaincy "drawing support from the government"; and the depoliticization of the public service, to check inefficiency and the reorganization of the police and Zambian National Service. The MMD also promised to delink political parties from the government and ensure that "government assets which have otherwise been used by or vested in UNIP since October 24, 1964 shall be transferred to government." It promised to honor all existing international agreements and outlined a three-concentric-circle arrangement of foreign relations: The Southern African level, The African Level, and The World Level.

The socioeconomic programs outlined in the *Manifesto* begin with the movement's determination "to bring about a new era of opportunity of economic policy realism with rewards and motivate individual initiative"; and its commitment to the creation of a "stable economic environment." According to the *Manifesto*:

> The MMD is committed to creating an enabling environment for economic development in Zambia by implementing a balanced structural adjustment programme specifically suited to Zambian conditions. In order to bring about a suitable climate in which

both the private sector and public sector will flourish, the MMD will formulate and implement suitable monetary and fiscal policies; create a positive system of administering investment incentive schemes; abolish monopolies and provide a free market system; ensure free collective bargaining; institute market determined allocation policies; stimulate positive growth-oriented international trade policies; mobilize domestic savings and develop a capital market; and rationalize government regulatory measures.[9]

The movement promised to restore "investor confidence and credibility," provide appropriate incentives, and "facilitate regular institutional consultation between the Chambers of Commerce, government and labour leaders on various socio-economic matters." Privatization would be pursued vigorously in order to "optimise resource utilization, enhance productivity and profitability of the public sector and assist in the reduction of the government deficit." It specifically states that the "current economic role of government as a central participant in business undertakings shall cease. Free market and not nationalization will become the foundation stone upon which the economy under an MMD Government shall operate." Its monetary policy, budgetary agenda, public debt management, and agricultural policies all are in line with its commitment to privatization, the free market, individualism, and individual initiative, and the drastic reduction of the role of the state in the economy.

In the area of mining, the MMD promised to "steer away from the overall dependence on the copper mining industry and shall adopt mineral policies which will ensure the development of a self-sustaining mineral-based industry, exporting with a high value-added content." The power of the ZCCM was to be reviewed, small-scale enterprises are to be encouraged, the manufacturing sector is to be expanded, export base diversified, energy production, distribution, pricing, and utilization are to be rationalized, and an extensive expansion and maintenance program for railway and road transport systems is to be initiated. The MMD promised to liberalize broadcasting services; institutionalize a "modern, coherent, simplified and relevant land law code intended to ensure the fundamental right to private property and ownership of land" by reviewing the Land Acts of 1975 and 1985, the Orders-in-Council of 1928–1947, the Land Survey Act, and the Town and Country Planning Act. It will "attach economic value to undeveloped land, encourage private real estate agency business, promote the regular issuance of title deeds to productive land owners in both rural and urban areas, and clear the backlog of cadastral surveys and mapping." Housing policies shall be aimed at making it possible for all Zambians to have "access to financial resources to build a house or develop land"; foreign investors will be attracted to the tourism industry; wildlife will be protected; "wastefulness of raw materials and the destruction of the natural bases of existence" will be countered through the establishment of a "strong Environmental Protection Agency"; the rights of the trade union movement will be guaranteed and the government and party shall "open its doors to the Labour Movement as a legitimate and important partner in development"; while special attention will be paid to "the strengthening of social and welfare services and comprehensive social security."

Finally, the MMD committed itself to a complete overhaul of the educational system to make it more relevant to the needs of the society and attack the hundreds of deficiencies and contradictions in the school system; the right to information and freedom of expression will be guaranteed to the press because "journalists will have to play an important role in promoting democracy and development in an MMD-led government"; and state-owned media will serve as "vehicles to promote national unity, reconstruction, development and international cooperation." Furthermore, the

MMD promised to stop the exploitation of women by, among other things, reviewing "all discriminatory laws against women in all social and economic fields"; stop the discrimination against minority national groups; and guarantee the freedom of religion. However, the *Manifesto* which had promised to guarantee the freedom of religion and worship, declared that "The MMD government recognizes and accepts that Zambia is a Christian country which is tolerant of other religions." Noting that the MMD "does not promise a paradise on earth," the *Manifesto* asserted that its operations were guided by a firm belief in the principles and practice of democracy:

> MMD works on the basis of profound democratization of interparty relations. The MMD upholds democratic principles such as electiveness and replaceability, openness and accountability, non-subordination of the minority to the majority and the right of the minority to defend its interests publicly if these interests should be threatened.[10]

With these policies, Zambians flocked to join the MMD. Whether they were pushed by hatred for Kaunda, dislike for UNIP, frustration with the state of the economy, being members of the labor movement, or simply captivated by Frederick Chiluba's "sincerity and courage," Zambians from all walks of life flocked to join the movement. Many people read the *Manifesto* and saw in it something different from what had prevailed for 27 years. Many more agreed with one of the campaign posters of the MMD, which simply states: "Zambia needs this man as President—vote for Frederick Chiluba and set yourself free!"

The MMD *Manifesto* was more of a response to the ideological and political positions which Kenneth Kaunda had represented. The ideology of Humanism had drawn Kaunda and Zambia closer to African variants of socialism as espoused by several Afro-Marxist regimes in the continent.

The excessive intervention of the state in the economy was in line with the single-mass, one-party state prescribed by socialism. At some point in time, every member of the UNIP Central Committee and Ministers all prefixed their names with "Comrade!" For the MMD to appeal to alternative interests and show that it was a party of the future and of a "new world order" dominated by America and the capitalist ideology as determined and dictated by the World Bank and the IMF, it had to declare for capitalism, the free market, structural adjustment, privatization, and liberal democracy. The truth, however, is that Zambia was never a socialist country by any stretch of the imagination. Kaunda used a lot of populist rhetoric and erected several institutions and political structures which resembled those that existed in socialist countries. In reality, Zambia *was* a state capitalist system, where the bourgeoisie accumulated by penetrating and appropriating the state, and where, due to the weaknesses of the local bourgeois classes, the state took the place of the bourgeoisie and simply became the capitalist: a very corrupt, inefficient, and repressive one at that. As Anthony Guglielmi has noted:

> Copper in the Zambian economy has brought diminishing returns for the populace at large but an increasing concentration of power and wealth into the hands of the Zambian elites, as well as an increasing dependence on the infrastructure of international capitalism. In the past, it had been rather easy to identify the colonial powers as the chief exploiters of African labor, but with the emergence of the African national state, an African elite, capitalist class has used the cloak of nationalism to transform themselves into "champions of the people" while accruing wealth from the control of export revenues.[11]

What is more interesting is the influence labor leaders had in the MMD and the ease with which they opted for the free market, extolling the virtues of individualism and competition. Contrary to some claims as to the ideological disposition of Zambia's labor movement and of Frederick Chiluba, which both are seen as leftist in persuasion, the reality is that, just like the ZCTU, Chiluba is a conservative liberal or, at most, a social democrat who believes very firmly in the procedural elements of liberal democracy and of the so-called free market.[12] In all of his pronouncements, in his association with the UNIP, and in his politics within the MMD, Chiluba has never advocated any marxist or militantly radical political posture in Zambia. Of course, the MMD manifesto and the platform of its 1991 campaigns, as well as policies since assuming power, attest to its conservative neo-liberal ideological disposition. As Jotham Moomba noted in an interview:

> The MMD is a party of the right, in fact, the party is on the extreme right. They do not apologize for this ideological position. They do not pretend they are on the left. Their domestic and foreign policies show a clearly rightist inclination. It is as if we must all become ultra-rightists just because of developments in Eastern Europe.[13]

No doubt, the MMD document ignores Zambia's historical experience and overlooks the structural roots of the country's backwardness and underdevelopment. It ignores the inherited conditions of foreign domination and the fragility of the state. It is silent on how imperialist interests underdeveloped Zambia, ruthlessly exploited it, extracted and repatriated massive resources, and failed to assist Zambia in getting back on the path of growth, development, stability, and relative interdependence in the global system. The MMD preferred to believe that every problem, every predicament, and every contradiction was the fault of Kenneth Kaunda and the UNIP. Of course, the problem was much more than Kaunda. Kaunda was part of a class and it is essential to understand the character, weaknesses, accumulative bases, relations with foreign capital, and political convictions of that class. To what extent can we contend that the MMD does not contain persons of disposition similar to or worse than those of UNIP members? It is also important to understand the nature of the state which the UNIP operated: its degree of stability, hegemony, legitimacy, and credibility; and its ability to rationalize and mediate contradictions, extract and deploy surpluses, and generate the sort of environment that would facilitate growth and development. To what extent can we say that the MMD, as constituted, with its manifesto, will run the Zambian political economy with a different state structure? As well, it is critical to understand the location and role of Zambia in the international division of labor, the country's financial and economic relations, the role of transnational capital in the economy, and the relationship between local and foreign capitals. Will the MMD, just because it had openly and unrepentantly declared for capitalism, be treated more considerately and more compassionately by foreign capital in the search for profits, cheap labor, raw materials, and market hegemony? It is instructive that the MMD itself was formed by people who had been very much part of the UNIP as ministers, members of the Central Committee, ambassadors and the like. To what extent have they really changed in their perceptions, political attitudes, and UNIP ideological convictions? There are those who argue that "many of them have MMD membership and cards but UNIP mentality."[14]

Finally, the MMD seemed to have swallowed, hook and line, the monetarist economic prescriptions of the IMF and the World Bank. There is no doubting the fact that Zambia, like most African states, needs a comprehensive structural adjustment program. It is however wrong to assume that just by reducing the role of the state, opening up the economy, privatizing public enterprises, imposing new fees and taxes, devaluing the currency, and introducing other painful economic policies on a poor population unprotected by any welfare programs, growth and development will follow. No African state—not even that darling of the World Bank, Ghana—can claim to have reversed the processes of backwardness, economic decay, underdevelopment, dependence, foreign domination, and vulnerability in the global capitalist system through adherence to the policies of the Fund and the World Bank. The failure of structural adjustment programs all over the continent, the terrible impoverishment of nonbourgeois forces, and the tensions, violence, coups, instability, and economic and social deterioration the program has generated all over Africa were ignored by the MMD in drafting its manifesto. Of course, the open commitment to the market and to policies dictated by the Fund and the Bank endeared the movement to donors, Western powers, the Scandinavian countries, the IMF and World Bank, and other global capitalist interests.

The MMD: The Road to Victory and Power

Early 1991 witnessed the resignation of very prominent members of the UNIP, who promptly declared their support for the MMD.[15] In the same period, the Zambian Congress of Trade Unions (ZCTU) officially transferred its support and allegiance to the MMD. All trade union offices all over the country immediately became recruiting centers for the movement while trade union leaders openly campaigned for public support to defeat Kaunda and the UNIP. Towns served by railroads, provincial and district capitals, and all public institutions with trade-union branches became major organizing centers for the MMD. The leaders of the mineworkers openly declared their support for the MMD and did everything possible to discredit UNIP and Kaunda.

Violent clashes between UNIP and MMD supporters broke out in 1991 and this trend of violence led to charges and counter-charges on both sides. The already jittery Kaunda government carried out several last-minute cabinet changes

117

in the hope of demonstrating a stronger resolve to provide a democratically credible and accountable leadership. June 1991 witnessed a major struggle between the UNIP and the MMD over constitutional proposals made by the Constitutional Commission (CC). Among other recommendations, the CC had recommended the creation of the post of vice-president, expansion of the National Assembly from 135 seats to 150 seats, and the establishment of a constitutional court. Though Kaunda had accepted most of the CC's proposals and had them submitted to the National Assembly for ratification, the MMD opposed them because the proposed changes vested too much authority in the president and too little in the National Assembly. It also opposed the recommendation which allowed ministers to be appointed outside the National Assembly, as that would only create opportunities for patronage and for rewarding vested interests. The MMD threatened to boycott the elections if the Assembly ratified the recommendations and, to demonstrate its resolve on this matter, it refused to attend an interparty conference chaired by Kaunda in July 1991 to discuss the draft constitution. Representatives of the UNIP, MMD, and seven other political associations were later to meet on the issue under the chairmanship of Zambia's deputy chief justice, Matthew Ngulube. Following this meeting, Kaunda suspended the draft constitution and agreed to further negotiations. With the intervention of church leaders, a joint commission was set up to review the constitutional proposals, and in July Kaunda agreed to MMD demands to abandon the idea of a constitutional court and not to appoint ministers from outside the National Assembly. The power to impose martial law previously recommended for the president was abandoned, and any imposition of a state of emergency beyond seven days was to be approved by the National Assembly. The new proposals were approved by the National Assembly on August 2, 1991.

This was a major victory for the MMD. It signaled the end

of the UNIP government even before the elections. The powerful Kaunda had been forced to give in once again to the opposition on practically all their demands. This was followed in quick succession by agreement to allow international observers into the country to monitor the elections, a position Kaunda had previously opposed. Kaunda also agreed to grant state subsidies to all registered political parties. As noted earlier, Kaunda's leadership of UNIP was challenged partly as a result of frustration over his declining political credibility and influence in the country. As far back as september 1990, Kaunda had urged so-called UNIP militants to revamp the party and, "to rejuvenate" it "into a formidable political organ if it is to win the 1991 elections."[16] Of course, he managed to retain control and get nominated to lead UNIP into the struggle for the presidency. He tried as much as possible to convince the opposition that the election would be free and fair; he disassociated the armed forces from UNIP, and senior officers were required to retire from the UNIP Central Committee.

It was obvious to all observers that the electoral battle was going to be between UNIP and MMD. The few fringe political parties that emerged on the national scene lacked the organizational structure, resources, credible leadership and programs, as well as the experience and ability to mount effective political campaigns. Yet, they were part of the growing civil society and evidence of the demise of the one-party state; and they signified the enthronement of multiparty politics. The Movement for Democratic Process (MDP) paid the K20,000 registration fee but "failed to raise the 200 registered voters in support" of Chama Chakonmmoka's presidential ambitions. The Christian Alliance for the Kingdom of Africa (CHAKA), led by Jairus Kalisirila, withdrew from the electoral race for the presidency on "technical grounds." Emmanuel Mubanbga Mwamba of the Democratic Process (DP) "never even pitched up to file his nomination" to run for the presidency.[17] Early efforts by the DP to organize a rally in April 1991 flopped very badly as "only 15 children aged between 5 and 10 gathered at Kampenba Welfare Hall in Twapia township" to listen to what the party had to say.[18] There were other fringe parties like the Multi-Racial Party of Zambia (MP), The Theoretical Spiritual Political Party (TSPP), the Peoples Liberation Party (PLP), and the National Democratic Alliance (NADA).[19]

Following the dissolution of the National Assembly in September 1991 in preparation for the October elections, Kaunda tried to demonstrate that a new UNIP would emerge from the election to lead a reinvigorated and more democratic government: UNIP was disassociated from the state and workers in the public sector were banned from participating in political activity. Of course, Kaunda knew that it would take more than one month for people to unlearn what it had taken them 27 years to learn. In any case, the state-controlled media houses continued to campaign for UNIP and Kaunda and to discriminate openly against the MMD. Kaunda directed the *Zambia Daily Mail*, the *Times of Zambia*, and the Zambia National Broadcasting Corporation (ZNBC) not to cover the activities of the MMD. Even without such directives, some over-zealous bureaucrats had gone beyond the call of duty to discriminate against the MMD in their news coverage and to play up the popularity of Kaunda and the UNIP. The MMD challenged this order in court and won a victory over the government. The UNIP secretary-general, Grey Zulu, also challenged the MMD's use of certain political symbols in court. As well, the state of emergency which had allowed Kaunda to suppress the opposition was still very much in force.

Kaunda made threats against "anarchists" and warned the nation that he would "brook no nonsense from opposition elements who might try to disrupt" the political system. He then ordered the police to "arrest multiparty advocates who might have issued insulting utterances to the leadership."[20] Of course, support for UNIP and Kaunda was not in short supply, mostly "out of loyalty to the old man rather than any serious commitment to the party which was already withering away."[21] Area governors like Imasiku Lyamunga campaigned for Kaunda, district governors like Shiyenge Kapriri supported Kaunda, and traditional rulers from Luampula Province and several chiefs who had actually been maintained in office by Kaunda, threw their weight behind Kaunda and UNIP.[22] Because workers and urban residents who bore the brunt of inflation, unemployment, crime, and deteriorating social services had turned to the MMD, Kaunda had concentrated his campaigns in the rural areas, relying on traditional chiefs, making promises, and hoping the rural dwellers had remained insulated from the campaigns of the MMD and the pains of a failed adjustment program. With this, the reports from his security forces and the scores of sycophants surrounding him, and his personal confidence that there was no way a person like him could lose an election in Zambia, Kaunda predicted several times, even on election day that UNIP would not only sweep the polls, but "Will continue winning any polls."[23] Unfortunately, such predications were completely out of tune with reality. Bitter ethnic and regional divisions, and a badly eroded legitimacy had pushed most Zambians in and beyond the urban areas to the MMD's camp, except perhaps in the Eastern Province, Kaunda's home base.

There were several reports of violence, especially against MMD supporters by ardent UNIP supporters. The MMD revealed that UNIP members, probably in anticipation of losing the election, were looting state monies and property. In January 1991, the UNIP Parliament granted "K1.3 billion to members for various party schemes" while government properties "were being taken over locally and abroad."[24] The MMD urged their supporters to "expose the cash grabbers." Vernon Mwaanga accused UNIP of using the government printer to print party membership cards and of misusing public funds. As well, Kaunda was very direct in his threats against the MMD and warnings to Zambians that a vote for the opposition was a vote for anarchy. This was because the MMD was bound to sink the economy further into crisis: "The campaign against our party was terrible. Zambians were told that we lacked experience, that we had no international support, that we were going to destroy the economy and make life unbearable for all. In fact, the picture that was painted was one of total disaster without the UNIP and KK."[25]

Kaunda accused the international observers of meddling in Zambian affairs by trying to influence the content and direction of politics in favor of the MMD. According to Hamalengwa (and this was confirmed in several interviews in Zambia), Kaunda "repeatedly accused the MMD advocates of inciting the army and mineworkers to disrupt the country in order to weaken the power of UNIP. He also accused them of soliciting military support from the rebel leader in neighboring Angola."[26] In addition, Chiluba, the presidential candidate of the MMD, accused Kaunda of amassing troops on the Malawi border to fight the MMD if the UNIP lost the election; and he called on the Organization of African Unity (OAU) to send peace-keeping forces to Zambia because a plot to assassinate him had been hatched by the UNIP. As Michael Bratton has noted, the campaign "was highly vituperative and centered on personalities rather than issues. Perhaps unsurprisingly after thirty years of one-man rule, the election became a referendum on the performance of Kaunda himself. All candidates resorted to character assassination, most often involving charges and countercharges about dishonesty in the use of public funds."[27]

It is interesting to note that both political parties relied on and used virtually similar political campaign strategies relying mostly on patronage. The UNIP in classic display of traditional political tactics, aligned itself with conservative political forces. It promised to give chiefs more powers and very prominent roles in the National Assembly and did allow some chiefs to contest the parliamentary elections. It also increased their salaries and distributed very expensive Toyota Land Cruisers to senior chiefs, especially in the Eastern Province where it was to win its few parliamentary seats and defeat the MMD in the presidential election. UNIP chose the hoe as its ballot symbol in order to reassert its commitment to agriculture, peasants, traditional constituencies, and the poor. For whatever it was worth, such actions simply contributed to discrediting the party and Kaunda. For a government that was practically bankrupt, such a distribution of largesse, including the widespread use of money, only demonstrated to the MMD that the party had learnt nothing from its past experiences. As well, after neglecting the rural areas and poor peasants for almost twenty-seven years, the symbol of the hoe meant absolutely nothing to this constituency: they wanted change and a better life.

The UNIP had grossly miscalculated the spread of the MMD's influence. It was shocked to be confronted in the villages with shouts of "The Hour Has Come." Villagers had felt the brunt of the government's failed economic policies. They were still neglected. More importantly, village dwellers had seen a drastic fall in monetary remittances from urban relatives and had to welcome frustrated and destitute relatives who had been forced out of the cities by poverty, unemployment, and other pressures. According to Frederick Hapunda, MMD MP for Siavonga, "the Unions, churches, schools, and businesses helped to spread the message of the MMD to the remotest parts of Zambia. We knew that the challenge, being quite new, would attract a lot of interest. Once we were able to show that UNIP had outlived its usefulness and publicized our message, the people, irrespective of location would rally to our support. In the Eastern province, it was mostly a case of harassment and shameless bribing of people."[28] Yet, the MMD was not discriminatory as to whom to accept campaign contributions from, just as it had not discriminated as to who could join or even lead the party. Hence, several persons with "unknown" sources of wealth contributed to the campaign purse of the party, thus raising credibility issues. As Bratton has noted, "during the selection of parliamentary candidates, MMD headquarters often pushed local preferences aside, creating an unfortunate precedent of arbitrary, patrimonial decision-making. Top MMD bosses grabbed safe seats in Copperbelt Province, and regional MMD bosses allegedly bought party cards en masse to boost their own local followings."[29] In the campaigns, the MMD relied heavily on foreign sources for financial and other support to counter the advantage of incumbency which the UNIP enjoyed. It also made outlandish promises and distributed T-shirts as the UNIP had done, its supporters were equally unruly, and the use of money was not completely out of the question. As an MMD stalwart explained in an interview, "actually many of our supporters, especially the younger ones who had known nothing but poverty and hunger were over-enthusiastic in several ways. But that is exactly what the politics of change is all about. As soon as it became necessary, the party brought such persons under control. Since the UNIP denied us several opportunities to publicize our message, it was a big battle fighting Kaunda and his money."

The October 31st election in Zambia witnessed the monumental routing of UNIP, ushering in the very first democratic transition from authoritarian rule in Anglophone Africa. The election also set the record for being the very first to unseat a founding father of the nationalist struggle in the entire continent. As Zambians flocked to the polls, courts and businesses were shut, and acts of violence and intimidation were few and far between on election day.[30] Chiluba received 75.79% of the votes cast in the presidential election, soundly defeating Kaunda who received a mere

24.21% of the vote. In the election to the National Assembly, the MMD won 125 seats, leaving the remaining 25 to UNIP. The MMD won well over 70 percent of the parliamentary votes in all the provinces except in the Eastern Province, where it won only 26.08 percent to UNIP's 73.92 percent. In the Copperbelt, the MMD won 89.77 percent, 73.07 percent in Central, 86.27 percent in Luapula, 77.03 percent in Lusaka, 85.97 percent in Northern, 70.33 percent in Northwestern, 84.10 percent in Southern, and 80.56 percent in Western. Except for the Eastern Province, therefore, the MMD's support was widespread, rural *and* urban, and did cut across ethnic groups.

It was a crushing defeat for UNIP, and many reached the conclusion that the party had been "wiped out."[31] All but four of the members of the previous government were defeated in the election. A UNIP candidate for Nkana Constituency Noel Mvila was crushed by an unknown MMD candidate Barney Bungoni with a "big margin." Mvila quickly announced that the polls had been rigged because his opponent was "so old."[32] In Livingstone Constituency, MMD candidate Peter Muunga defeated two former members of parliament, Kebby Musokotwane and Daniel Lisulo, who ran as independents.[33]

Many members of UNIP put the blame for the party's humiliation on Kenneth Kaunda. Enoch Kavindele a former member of the UNIP Central Committee argued that Kaunda was "responsible for the party's humiliating defeat in (the) elections because by clinging to leadership despite apparent unpopularity from the masses," he made it easy for alienated and disaffected supporters to switch to the MMD.[34] A loyal UNIP supporter interviewed in Lusaka supported this view when he noted that "KK was just stubborn. You see, he is a very stubborn man. He did not want to believe that the people were fed up with him, that his government (had) failed and that the MMD was popular. If he had stepped aside, the defeat might have been less."[35] The parliamentary election had been contested by 330 candidates from six political parties. It was indeed a new dawn in Zambian politics as Frederick Chiluba, former chairman of the ZCTU, leading an amalgam of political interests known as the MMD, was inaugurated as president on November 2nd, 1991.[36]

Beyond KK: The Politics of Election Monitoring in Zambia

It is true that Kenneth Kaunda, the UNIP, and the deepening crisis of the economy, as well as unfavorable global conditions combined to see power snatched from the UNIP government by the MMD. Yet, it is not as straightforward as it is often presented: a multiparty democracy movement, led by a trade unionist, defeated one of the early nationalists in Africa who had bestrode the political landscape of Zambia for almost three decades like a colossus. It is important to go beyond the aforementioned forces and factors, beyond the disillusionment of the people (which had a bandwagon effect during the election) and beyond the new desire for freedom and democracy. It is important to see the role of Western nations, donors, and other external interests in the establishment of liberal democratic politics, institutions, and relations of power. With the end of the Cold War, there seems to be an increasing "internationalization of domestic politics," with the developed nations, donors, and lenders as well as investors taking a keener interest in the domestic political affairs of other nations. As Larry Diamond has noted, this interest is—or at least ought to be—part of a larger political agenda of the developed nations:

> Just as economic development can be aided by timely and well crafted international assistance, so can political development. In fact, political development is a much more flexible process than economic development and it is also cheaper financially. By helping to train legislators and their staffs, party officials, lawyers, judges, journalists, civic groups and trade union organizers, and election adminis-

trators, we can help to "jumpstart" the process of democratic development....[37]

The Polish experience was perhaps the very first recent experiment at joining hands and resources with opposition elements in order to defeat an incumbent regime and to "jumpstart" the "process of democratic development."

In the case of Poland, U.S. President Ronald Reagan and Pope John Paul II forged a so called "Holy Alliance" to "keep the Solidarity union alive" in the hope "not only to pressure Warsaw but to free all of Eastern Europe."[38] Both leaders agreed at a June 7, 1982 meeting at the Vatican, to "undertake a clandestine campaign to hasten the dissolution of the communist empire" and they "committed their resources to destabilizing the Polish government and keeping the outlawed Solidarity movement alive after the declaration of martial law in 1981."[39] As part of the support for this project of forcing Poland onto the path of capitalism which Solidarity stood for, Solidarity "flourished underground, supplied, nurtured and advised largely by the network established under the auspices of Reagan and the Pope. Tons of equipment—fax machines (the first in Poland), printing presses, transmitters, telephones, shortwave radios, video cameras, photocopiers, telex machines, computers, word processors—were smuggled into Poland via channels established by priests and American agents and representatives of the AFL-CIO and European labor movements. Money for the banned union came from CIA funds, the National Endowment for Democracy, secret accounts in the Vatican and Western trade unions."[40] As well, spies were recruited from within the Polish government, including a deputy minister of defense "who was secretly reporting to the CIA."[41] The Zambian experience was not as elaborate only because Zambia was a smaller prize and the transition to multiparty politics in Zambia would not have the sort of impact that the "fall" of Poland was to have in Eastern Europe.

Though Kaunda dropped his opposition to having international observer groups monitor the 1991 elections, he remained suspicious of their role.[42] This fear was not unfounded, as the general feeling is that these monitoring bodies tend to favor prodemocracy movements and have been known to dislike sit-tight leaders in developing countries. To allay such fears, though, the Commonwealth Secretariat set broad guidelines on its election-monitoring activities: "missions are undertaken only at the invitation of a member government and if all contesting political parties agree; observers have no executive or supervisory role in the election process; though appointed by the Secretary-General, observers are independent individuals representing only themselves; and their task generally is to observe all aspects of the organization and conduct of an election according to that country's law and to come to judgement as to whether that process has been free and fair."[43] The Commonwealth also has what it describes as the "essentials" for the "practical expression of democracy": "the participation of the adult population in the selection of government through free and fair elections; freedom of association and expression, including freedom of the press; the transparency of the process of government, and...the rule of law with guarantees for equality under the law."[44] Not all monitoring bodies have laid down conditions for participation, and some representatives have been carried away with their personal views or biases. These happened in the Zambian situation, though not to a degree capable of marring the contribution of these bodies to effective monitoring of the elections.

Fears existed within both parties that the election would be rigged. This is largely a precipitate of the importance of state power in politics. Without capturing the state, the interests which political parties represented could not be incorporated into policy and expressed in actions. Failure to capture power (in the context of a weak civil society) and the lack of institutions to protect the disadvantaged could mean intimidation, elimination, or marginalization in the political process. Hence, political parties and their candidates do everything possible to rig or ensure that opponents do not rig elections. This, of course, is not peculiar to Africa. The UNIP was of the view that the MMD was so desperate to unseat it from power, that it would do anything to rig the elections. At that point in the competition, it was difficult for the UNIP to determine how many of its remaining supporters actually sympathized with the MMD even though they had held on to their UNIP membership cards. The MMD, on the other hand, believed that UNIP was so used to power and had an overblown image of its continuing influence that it would do anything to remain in power. It was only natural therefore that monitoring groups from within and outside the country be allowed to observe the conduct of the election in order to promote an environment of fair play, tolerance, and democracy.[45] Both parties tried to assure the nation that the election would not be rigged. UNIP also declared its opposition to calls for an early poll. According to Joseph Mutale, UNIP Chairman for Publicity and Elections, the "MMD statements were the usual rubbish which should be dismissed with the contempt it deserves."[46] It was felt that the calls for an early poll by some MMD leaders was an attempt to capitalize on or maximize the widespread support and enthusiasm which the party was enjoying and a "sign of fear that by election day, UNIP would have regained all lost ground."[47] In June, Kanyama MP Donald Chilutya "hoisted a small black coffin with 'MMD is Dead' written on it in white in a mock burial" to demonstrate how UNIP was going to destroy the opposition.[48] Such open display of hostility towards the MMD convinced the party of the need to have neutral actors on the scene, especially as Kaunda still had control of the state, its resources, and its coercive power.

The MMD benefitted extensively from foreign support at

a level which might not be replicated in any other African country. In fact, information available shows that no other African prodemocracy movement or political party in the post–Cold War era has enjoyed such extensive financial, logistical, political, moral, and financial support as the MMD. In June 1991, the governments of Denmark, Finland, Norway, and Sweden offered to "help run the elections" in Zambia. They announced that the Zambian government had made a request for "transport, publicity and provision of stationery for the government printer"—which had been turned down.[49] This meant that the offer to help was not aimed at helping the government remain in power. In the same month, Kaunda himself surprised the opposition by personally inviting the Carter Center at Emory University in Atlanta and the Ford Foundation to Zambia to monitor the elections.[50] UNIP itself started seeking "international aid to help it to organize...[the] presidential and parliamentary elections."[51] This was a public demonstration of financial weakness and vulnerability of the party which had dominated Zambian politics and had control of the national wealth for twenty-seven years.

Within a short time, several independent monitoring organizations emerged in Zambia. The Independent Zambian Poll Monitoring Team (ZIMT), led by former Bank of Zambia governor David Phiri, was created in July 1991.[52] It received support from the American National Democratic Institute (NDI) and other prominent Zambians like former Law Association of Zambia chairman Ali Hamir, and Chaloka Beyani, a prominent legal figure. With the increasing enthusiasm for foreign observers and the growing influence which foreign NGOs and ambassadors accredited to Zambia were having on the election process, Kaunda began to have second thoughts about their presence in Zambia. In August he alleged that "foreign and local agents are working to disrupt the polls." He specifically alleged that three ambassadors "from otherwise friendly countries" were working with the opposition to subvert the polls in favor of the MMD.[53] Such allegations did not discourage Zambians from going ahead to form new monitoring bodies.

In August the Zambian Voter Observation Team (ZVote) was formed by the Carter Center and the National Democratic Institute for International Affairs, with Karen Jenkins as its director. ZVote also included "experts from Europe, America and Benin. Part of its mission in Zambia was to advise ZIMT on a nonpartisan basis and independently monitor the electoral process." In the same month, the Canadian Government donated $50 million to ZIMT. With this money ZIMT, which had emerged as the most credible independent Zambian monitoring agency, embarked on a mass training program for volunteers who were mostly students from the University of Zambia. The National Democratic Institute and ZVote assisted with the training of the volunteers. By the end of August other monitoring bodies had joined ZVote and ZIMT: Elections Canada represented by Ronald Gould; Namibian Council of Churches represented by Vero Mbahuurua; Philippines National Movement for Free Elections represented by Martino Queseda; the British Council; University of Zambia Students; the National Women's Lobby Group of Zambia and a monitoring group from Chile.[54] In less than a month, over a hundred and fifty volunteers had been trained by ZIMT.[55] Based on recommendations from other international bodies active in Zambia, the ZIMT received more donations from foreign governments. The British government donated £7,000 worth of vehicles and £3,000 worth of communications equipment.[56] Denmark donated K1 million, which was used to pay the rent for ZIMT's Headquarters on Lumumba Road in Lusaka; Sweden pledged $40,000 while the United States and Norway promised further assistance. Former American President Jimmy Carter also arrived in Zambia, accompanied by the senior political officer of the Organization of African Unity (OAU), Mr. Chriss Bak

Wesegha; Michelle Kourouma of the National Conference of Black Mayors; and a top member of Nigeria's National Electoral Commission (NEC), Dr. Adele Jinadu. It was as if a miracle were about to take place in Zambia and as if the whole world had descended on the country to watch every move made by both parties—or, more fascinatingly, to watch the MMD snatch political power from Kenneth Kaunda and UNIP.

With this sort of support, ZIMT was able to intensify its campaign, set up a twenty member board of directors and recruit an additional 1,500 University of Zambia students as volunteers.[57] Though the ZIMT had started out forging a strong alliance with the church and church premises had been used for some of the training programs, the heavy presence of UNZA students in ZIMT began to cast shadows on its neutrality. Students at the UNZA have traditionally been opposed to the Kaunda government. Many of the young MMD candidates had been victims of Kaunda's high-handedness when they were students at UNZA. Throughout the seventies and eighties, the university had been closed several times for opposing government policies, hundreds of students had been rusticated or suspended for speaking out against Kaunda and his policies.[58] The Church began to accuse ZIMT of being partial and UNZA students of being clearly partisan towards the MMD.[59] In protest against ZIMT, representatives of the Church pulled out of ZIMT "after they voiced strong opposition to the presence of officials with 'links' to the state in the group."[60] Father Ives Bantungwa (secretary general of the Catholic Secretariat) and overseer of the Church of God Bishop John Mambo announced that they were starting their own independent monitoring team. The churches eventually set up a new monitoring group, the Christian Churches Monitoring Group (CCMG), to educate Christians on the electoral process. The CCMG had representatives from the Christian Council of Zambia (CCZ), Evangelical Fellowship of Zambia, and Zambia Episcopal

Conference. Its 12-man board was chaired by Reverend Foston Sakala of the Reformed Church of Zambia and they pledged to work with ZVote and ZIMT.[61] UNIP seized the opportunity of this disagreement to accuse ZIMT of being "70 per cent MMD." Ironically, the UNZA Students Union (UNZASU) also called for a "new look at ZIMT," arguing that it was a partial body which had co-opted two students, Edward Sefuke and James Lungu without clearance or consultation with the union. The two students were disowned by the students union as representing themselves and not the students of the university.

With the developments sketched above, ZIMT came under heavy pressure. It was "clear that antidemocratic forces were at work. They had succeeded in sponsoring confusionists and trouble makers into ZIMT. The plan was to weaken it, discredit it and harass the foreign observers who would now be left open without any indigenous group to work with."[62] The media in Zambia orchestrated the crisis and pronounced the ZIMT dead. The *Times of Zambia* reminded its readers that the ZIMT was actually conceived by Africa Bar Association Chairman Roger Chongwe, who was a member of the MMD,[63] and towards the end of September the paper gleefully announced that ZIMT was no more, that it had "been dismantled and a new coordinating body formed in its place."[64] At a meeting of some NGOs, churches, the Law Association of Zambia, and UNZASU a new monitoring body—Zambia Elections Monitoring Coordinating Committee (ZEMECC)—was created with representatives from each group and with a commitment to go beyond the limitations which had plagued ZIMT. What happened in ZIMT was actually a very deep ideological and power struggle between those who wanted to use the group to support either the MMD or UNIP. As well, as "soon as money started coming in, especially in foreign exchange, some people got greedy. They wanted to lay their hands on the money for personal use. When they could not do so, they decided to destroy the group. There were also those who saw that money could be made by networking with the foreign observers. To create their own monitoring group and gain some legitimacy, they had to first, discredit and destroy, or at the very least weaken ZIMT. They did just that."[65] ZIMT continued to exist in Zambia though the political attacks were now shifted in some sense to ZEMCC. In fact, donor agencies which had supported ZIMT from the beginning reaffirmed their support for and confidence in the body when Peter Faxell, representing the Scandinavian countries and donors, "expressed displeasure at the mudslinging levelled against ZIMT and declared their support for the body by donating $1.7 million to be shared with ZVote and the electoral commission."[66]

ZEMCC began its foray into the political terrain by setting up a fourteen-member executive board and dedicating itself to its motto: "Setting Standards for Africa. Free and Fair Elections." It advocated the need to count votes at the polls rather than moving them to other locations in order to avoid switching and stuffing of ballot boxes; the need to provide tilley lamps at polling stations to avoid irregularities in the dark; that those who had lost their voter registration cards should be allowed to vote with their national registration cards; that Kaunda should lift the state of emergency immediately; that security forces who were obviously loyal to UNIP should not be deployed to polling stations; and that continuing acts of intimidation and harassment of ordinary people was creating fear among the people and threatening possibilities for a free and fair election. ZEMCC declared that its operations would be completely nonpartisan and went on to attack the composition of the national electoral commission, arguing that it was incomplete. The organization contended that having a chairman and one other person did not leave room for checks and balances, that a third member was needed.[67] ZEMCC also condemned what it described as "the use of scares of violence and civil strife in

TV campaign advertisements" and advised donor countries not to "decide which monitoring group was right for Zambia."[68] This statement was directed at the intensification of negative and dirty campaigns, especially by UNIP members warning Zambians not to tolerate—much less, vote for—the MMD because it would plunge the nation into "war and untold pain." It was also a response to the statements by Peter Faxell above, reaffirming the confidence of the donors in ZIMT.

Within a week of being registered, ZEMCC had set up monitoring centers across the country using several church buildings; trained 250 monitors "from all parts of the country who were asked to recruit 3000 to be stationed at polling booths;" provided bicycles to its monitors and deemphasized the use of money in politics; had attracted over 700 UNZASU members and emphasized free and fair elections as "intimidation, coercion, corruption, violence and anything intended to subvert the will of the people" will be resisted.[69] ZEMCC announced, a day before elections, through its provincial chairman Pastor Kabila, that it had uncovered a plot in Livingstone where UNIP supporters were misleading the people that "voting symbol 'X' was meant for candidates they did not favour."[70]

Meanwhile, UNIP and other opponents of the MMD intensified their attacks against foreign and local observer groups. The outgoing UNIP Chairman for Social and Cultural Committee Joshua Manuwele described ZEMCC as a "body of stooges allegedly designed to cause confusion to the electorates" and pointed out that the bodies which make up ZEMCC, including students, the law association, and churches were actually pro-MMD and opposed to UNIP."[71] According to Hon. Samuel Miyanda, "the renewed attacks convinced us that it was good to have them (the election monitors) here. They were disturbing no one. In fact, they brought in a lot of foreign exchange to the cash-starved government. The UNIP was just scared that it could not go all out to intimidate the opposition without international con-demnation."[72] For instance, minister for mines Mulondwe Muzungu contended that the groups "appeared to have come to dictate election policy to Zambia."[73] According to the minister,

> They give the impression that they are not here to observe but to dictate to us what should be done as if we do not have election procedures.[74]

Kenneth Kaunda himself showed a great deal of anger and disillusionment with the alleged activities of the observers. He alleged that a foreign observer questioned a Mazabuka UNIP businessman why he had not defected to the MMD like others had done. He reached the conclusion that "all these things are showing that there is a plan somewhere to get Zambia into turmoil."[75] Finally, a group calling itself Lusaka Concerned Citizens also launched an attack against the observers:

> It is very sad to note that we have invited outside countries to observe our first plural presidential and party elections. Sad in that Zambian tax payers money is so good to waste to entertain Americans, Nigerians, Europeans etc to come and tell us that we have voted correctly....No body came to verify the fairness of colonial elections in 1964....We have our professional lawyers and judges in this country to do the job....Most of the observers who have been invited come from countries with bad reputations and also countries where assassinations take place during elections. Who decides the fairness of an elec-tion in America? How democratic are American elections?[76]

Such nationalistic positions cannot be dismissed as mere signs of "frustration." Foreign election monitoring bodies give the impression that Africans are incapable of conduct-ing elections and behaving themselves. They give the impression that even an issue like conducting elections can only be carried out with the support and direction of foreigners, without whose pronouncement as to the fairness of the exercise it would not receive recognition from abroad.

Another group, which called itself Concerned Zambians Abroad, also warned Zambians to beware of observer groups from other countries. In a letter to all media houses, it argued that the ultimate objective of these observer groups is to replace governments with puppets "that will pledge allegiance to western ideals."[77] In spite of these attacks on the foreign and domestic observer groups, donors and Western governments continued to provide support to the NGOs to enable them monitor the elections and contain acts of violence and fraud. In early October, just a few weeks before election day, the Canadian government donated office equipment worth K2.8 million to ZIMT. The acting Canadian high commissioner, Bob Pim, announced that the equipments included fax machines, hard disk computers, rank xerox copier with accessories, and a desk computer. The Government of Denmark also donated K1 million.

While these donations might have been well intentioned, they certainly invoked in the minds of many Zambians a feeling of loss of autonomy. Many of the donors and ambassadors actually behaved like "godfathers," appearing on television regularly and often making press statements, and commenting on local politics; an action African ambassadors to Western nations will hardly contemplate. As well, by giving them these monies and materials, they "discouraged indigenous bodies from raising resources locally, an effort which would have brought them closer to the people and forced them to educate the people."[78] Such a development of contact and work with local constituencies would have contributed significantly to expanding and strengthening civil society. Finally, one critical question which many Zambians asked was "Will these countries and organizations continue to give us money any time we have elections? Will they invite us to monitor elections in their home countries if *we* feel that their elections will not be free and fair?"[79] These might sound simplistic or rhetorical, but they reflect a genuine concern for the way and manner in which foreign observers and donors and Western governments invade African countries, as if their presence is enough to encourage and sustain the democratic process long after they depart. As Salim A. Salim, Secretary-General of the Organization of African Unity (OAU) has noted: "...before a country is democratized, there is a lot of interest, a lot of concern by the world community, including the imposition of conditionalities to insure that there is a democratic setup, when are you going to hold elections, when are you going to do that and the other, which is fine. But when the process of democratization has set in, the interest diminishes. And so you have situations in which people have great expectations, and what is happening?"[80] Pronouncing an election as "free and fair" does not in any way guarantee the survival and strengthening of the democratic process. It might buy some foreign recognition, demonstrate growing political maturity and sophistication, but it does not guarantee that the contradictions which inhibit democracy and democratization will disappear. The Nigerian experience after the annulment of the June 12, 1993 presidential election and the Sani Abacha coup of November 1993 are clear evidence of the limitations of foreign election monitoring which is not part of a broader strategy to protect democracy. Ironically, after Abacha dismantled political institutions, terminated the march towards a third republic, closed media houses and threw many politicians and activists (including the secretary of the oil workers union and the winner of the June 12, 1993 presidential election) into jail, Jimmy Carter went to Nigeria in 1995 to endorse military rule till 1997! This was at a time when even the military created Constitutional Conference had asked it to leave on January 1, 1996. Jimmy Carter's action now encouraged a reversal of the Conference position which now endorsed military rule for as long as general Abacha wished to remain in office. Yet, the Carter Center is one of the largest and most active election monitoring bodies in the world!

There is no doubt that foreign observers make substantial ideological inputs into the political process by emphasizing Western liberal ideological and political models and traditions which might have in reality been overtaken or rendered irrelevant by concrete objective "conditions on the ground" (i.e., conditions which seek to go beyond the mere procedural features of democracy to emphasize the issues of empowerment and *democratization* through the gradual strengthening of the people and their communities and organizations on terms determined and dictated by the people themselves). In other instances, the observer groups tend to be very domineering, patronizing, even dictatorial in their pronouncements. For instance, the Commonwealth Observer Group led by Justice Telford Georges arrived in Zambia only on the 23rd of October, about a week before election day, and immediately called for the lifting of the state of emergency, and for the police to not deny political parties permits to hold rallies.[81] Yet the Commonwealth Observer Group had very limited experience in the monitoring of elections in Africa: prior to the 1991 Zambian elections, it had monitored elections in Zimbabwe and Uganda in 1980, Namibia in 1989, and Malaysia in 1990.[82]

Another interesting development was Frederick Chiluba's trip overseas in April 1991 at the heat of the campaigns. The MMD National Convention was February 27 to March 5, 1991. Following his election at the convention as MMD flag bearer in the elections, Chiluba declared that the movement was a "shadow cabinet."[83] Rather than stay to put the party together, he embarked on an overseas trip to the United States and the United Kingdom to honor "invitations from organizations" in these countries. He was to meet with officials of the National Endowment for Democracy (NED) because the NED was honoring Violeta Chamorro of Nicaragua and Vaclav Havel of Czechoslovakia. He was also to meet with Herman Cohen at the State Department and with the Foreign Affairs Committee of the U.S. Senate. Chiluba was also to meet with Linda Chalker in the United Kingdom.[84] It is possible to question the necessity for such a trip at a critical moment in the history of the MMD and of Zambia. Why were these Western agencies so interested in treating Chiluba, who was yet to be elected president of Zambia, as a head of state? This was exactly the way the United States treated Boris Yeltsin even while Gorbachev was still in power, and no one was amazed when Yeltsin eased the former out of power. It is precisely such "inability to determine priorities that will preserve the dignity of our leaders that have turned them into errand boys of the West."[85] Whatever our judgements, Chiluba certainly made some error in judgement and opened up his relations with Western interests to question.

Without doubt, observer groups are very important. There is a need, however, for them not to take the place of indigenous efforts and not to dictate the content of political discourse. Otherwise, they can be accused of installing governments directly and/or indirectly. In the Zambian situation they played a major role in the survival of indigenous groups which were unprepared for such a role. They were, however, too visible and the infusion of money was too heavy and too obvious. Such actions mortgage the ability and desire of local political actors from working hard, reaching out to rural and disadvantaged communities, learning to be self-reliant, and building their power bases in the people and their communities. More often than not, African prodemocracy movements begin to see themselves as branches of the NED! Can the donors replicate this degree of support in other African states, or was Zambia a special case?

Notes

1. Interview, Lusaka, June 1993. The respondent is the son of a young and militant MMD member of parliament.
2. Munyonzwe Hamalengwa, *Class Struggles in Zambia 1889-1989 & The Fall of Kenneth Kaunda 1990-1991* (Lanham: University Press of America, 1992), p.130.
3. Ibid., p.135.
4. Interview with Honorable Samuel Miyanda, Member of Parliament for Matero, Lusaka, July 1993. Miyanda was elected Chairman of the MMD's Lusaka Central District while the field work for this project was going on in Zambia.
5. Movement for Multi-Party Democracy, *Manifesto* (Campaign Committee: MMD, Lusaka, n.d.), p.2. Hereafter cited as MMD Manifesto.
6. Hamalengwa, *Class Struggles in Zambia...* op. cit., p.149.
7. Ibid., p. 160.
8. Ibid.
9. Ibid., p.4.
10. Ibid., p.11.
11. Anthony Guglielmi, "The Crisis of Plenty: Africa," in Gerald Epstein, Julie Graham and Jessica Nembhasrd, eds., *Creating a New World Economy: Forces of Change and Plans for Action* (Philadelphia: Temple University Press, 1993), p. 341.
12. See Bill Schiller, "Zambian Opposition Seems Unstoppable," *Toronto Star* (October 30, 1991).
13. Interview with Dr. Jotham Moomba, Department of Political Science, University of Zambia, Lusaka, Zambia, May, 1993.
14. Interview with a member of Parliament, Lusaka, May 1993.
15. See Melinda Ham, "An Outspoken Opposition," *Africa Report* (November-December 1993).
16. "Revamp UNIP, Militants Prodded," *Times of Zambia* (September 25, 1990).
17. Isaac Malambo, Agnes Banda and Victor Kayira, "Three Bow Out of Presidential Race- Its Now KK Vs Chiluba," *Times of Zambia* (October 2, 1991).
18. "DP Ndola Rally Flops." *Times of Zambia* (April 8, 1991).
19. When NADA tried to organize a rally at Kamanga Township in March 1991, not a single person showed up.

See "NADA Rally Flops," *Times of Zambia* (April 1, 1991).

20. "Don't Spare Anarchists," *Times of Zambia* (September 28, 1990).

21. Interview with Hon. Samuel Miyanda, Lusaka, May 1993.

22. See "Campaign for Kaunda- DG," *Times of Zambia* (November 16, 1990); "Campaign for Kaunda," *Times of Zambia* (December 4, 1990); and "Chiefs Throw Weight Behind Kaunda," *Times of Zambia* (September 28, 1990).

23. "UNIP to Sweep Polls- KK Tells Press," *Times of Zambia* (October 5, 1990).

24. "Leaders Scramble for Wealth." *Times of Zambia* (January 13, 1991).

25. Interview, Lusaka June 1993.

26. Hamalengwa, *Class Struggles in Zambia* (op. cit.), p.149.

27. Michael Bratton, "Economic Crisis and Political Realignment in Zambia," in Jennifer Widner, ed., *Economic Change and Political Liberalization in Sub-Saharan Africa* (Baltimore: The Johns Hopkins Press, 1994), p. 120.

28. Interview, Lusaka, June, 1993.

29. Bratton, "Economic Crisis and Political Realignment" (op. cit.), p. 118.

30. See "Courts Shut as Workers Vote," *Times of Zambia* (November 1, 1991); "Zambians Flock to Polls," *Times of Zambia* (November 1, 1991).

31. Hicks Sikazwe and Davis Mulenga, "UNIP Wiped Out—Zambians Reject Kaunda's Rule as MMD Heads for Landslide," *Times of Zambia* (November 2, 1991); and Kondwani Chirambo, "Zambia Goes Agog," *Times of Zambia* (November 3, 1991)

32. "Polls Rigged Says Mvila," *Times of Zambia* (November 2, 1991).

33. "Ex-Premiers Routed," *Times of Zambia* (November 3, 1991). While Muunga received 14,711 votes, Musokotwane received a mere 3,246 votes and Lisulo got only 881 votes.

34. Davis Mulenga and Victor Kayora, "KK was a big liability," *Times of Zambia* (November 4, 1991).

35. Interview, Lusaka May 1993.

36. At the formal swearing in of Chiluba as President, the Zambian National Broadcasting Corporation blacked out the event probably as their last demonstration of power

given their open support for Kaunda and UNIP before and during the election. See "TV Blackout Shocks Nation," *Times of Zambia* (November 3, 1991).

37. Larry Diamond, *An American Foreign Policy for Democracy* (Washington, D.C.: Progressive Policy Institute, Policy Report No. 11, July 1991), p. 12.

38. See Carl Bernstein, "The Holy Alliance," *TIME* (February 24, 1992).

39. Ibid.

40. Ibid.

41. Ibid.

42. "Observers Welcome," *Times of Zambia* (April 24, 1991).

43. "Breathing New Life Into Democratic Hopes," *Commonwealth Currents* (December 1992– January 1993), p.2.

44. Ibid.

45. See "Election Rigging Danger Exists," *Times of Zambia* (April 27, 1991); and "Ngulube Dispels Vote Rigging," *Times of Zambia* (May 15, 1991).

46. "UNIP Dismisses Early Polls Call," *Times of Zambia* (May 21, 1991).

47. Interview with a UNIP Member, Lusaka, Zambia, May 1993.

48. John Phiri, "Campaign Drive in Top Gear," *Times of Zambia* (June 16, 1991).

49. "October Polls: Nordic States Offer Help," *Times of Zambia* (June 12, 1991).

50. Geoffrey Zulu, "Foreign Observers Coming," *Times of Zambia* (June 16, 1991).

51. "UNIP seeks foreign aid," *Times of Zambia* (June 19, 1991).

52. "Phiri Heads Watchdog," *Times of Zambia* (July 27, 1991).

53. "Poll Plot Laid Bare," *Times of Zambia* (August 7, 1991).

54. "Polls Monitors Under Training," *Times of Zambia* (August 25, 1991).

55. See "Election Volunteers Trained," *Times of Zambia* (August 26, 1991); "Get ZIMT Moving-Mambo," *Times of Zambia* (September 1, 1991); and "Have Observers at Booths-Expert," *Times of Zambia* (August 29, 1991).

56. "ZIMT Gets Shot in the Arm," *Times of Zambia* (September 6, 1991).

57. It should be noted that all donations to ZIMT were received by the accounting firm of Peak Marwick and Co. in Lusaka.

58. See Hamalengwa, *Class Struggles in Zambia* (op. cit.) and his *Thoughts Are Free: Prison Experience and Reflections on Law and Politics in General* (Don Mills, Ontario: Africa in Canada Press, 1991).

59. "Church Doubts ZIMT Fairness," *Times of Zambia* (September 15, 1991).

60. "Church Quits Monitoring Group," *Times of Zambia* (September 20, 1991).

61. See "Churches Set up Own Polls Watchdog," *Times of Zambia* (September 21, 1991) and "Church to Monitor October Election," *Times of Zambia* (September 21, 1991).

62. Interview with Hon. Samuel Miyanda, Lusaka, June 1993.

63. "ZIMT Under Fire," *Times of Zambia* (September 23, 1991).

64. "ZIMT is no More," *Times of Zambia* (September 24, 1991).

65. Interview with a former ZIMT official, Lusaka, June 1993.

66. "Squabbling Irks Donor Agencies," *Times of Zambia* (October 10, 1991).

67. See "ZEMCC Pledges Fight for Fair Polls," *Times of Zambia* (October 3, 1991); and "Elections Body Not Complete," *Times of Zambia* (October 3, 1991). The Chairman of the electoral commission was Deputy Chief Justice of Zambia Matthew Ngulube.

68. "Monitors Slam Scary Ads," *Times of Zambia* (October 11, 1991).

69. Sam Phiri, "Is ZEMCC Mature Enough to Judge Polls?" *Times of Zambia* (October 12, 1991).

70. "Voters Misled," *Times of Zambia* (October 30, 1991).

71. "Manuwele Ticks Off ZEMCC," *Times of Zambia* (October 21, 1991).

72. Interview with Hon. Miyanda, Lusaka, May 1991.

73. "Observers Off Mark, Says Muzungu," *Times of Zambia* (September 26, 1991).

74. Ibid.

75. "Observer Irks Kaunda," *Times of Zambia* (September 27, 1991).

76. Lusaka Concerned Citizens, "We Don't Need Americans

to Monitor Elections," *Times of Zambia* (September 29, 1991).

77. Concerned Zambians Abroad, "Beware of Observer Groups- Zambians Warned," *Times of Zambia* (October 12, 1991).

78. Interview with Mr. Johnson Kanduza, Mamba Collieries Guest House, Lusaka, June 1993.

79. Ibid.

80. Salim A. Salim, "Transition in Africa," in William Minter, (ed.), *U.S. Foreign Policy: An Africa Agenda* (Washington, D.C.: Africa Policy Information Center, 1994), p. 4.

81. "Ban Must Go-Commonwealth Observer Group," *Times of Zambia* (October 26, 1991). This group was in existence all the while UNIP had the state of emergency in place. It did not work for sanctions against Zambia for that reason. It is equally doubtful if it had sufficient information and ground experience to understand how and why the Zambian police denied permits to some political parties.

82. "Breathing New Life into Democratic Hopes," *Commonwealth Currents* (December 1992–January 1993), pp.2-3.

83. "We are a Shadow Cabinet," *Times of Zambia* (April 4, 1991).

84. "Chiluba Off on Overseas Trips," *Times of Zambia* (April 10, 1991).

85. Interview with a UNIP official, Lusaka, June 1993.

CHAPTER FOUR

FROM MOVEMENT TO GOVERNMENT: THE RISE AND CONSOLIDATION OF THE MMD REGIME

The Dawn of a New Era: The MMD in Power

When the MMD was sworn-in to govern Zambia on 1 November 1991, it had no illusions as to the difficult challenges ahead. Many observers were taken aback by the peaceful nature of the transition from one-party rule dominated by the personality of Kaunda to a multiparty political dispensation controlled by the MMD.[1] The country had been terribly run down. The overwhelming victory was just part of the required responses to tackle the numerous problems of the political economy. Zambians had never had it so bad. Many just could not believe that it was the same country which a decade earlier had held out great promise for the young and hardworking. According to Samuel Miyanda, MP for Matero, "our children were going hungry. Unemployment had reached new proportions, schools lacked amenities and had become a national disgrace. Inflation was out of control, crime was on the rise and people were getting desperate. Our future had been simply mortgaged by KK and UNIP."[2] In addition, food riots had become commonplace as malnutrition and disease ravaged the countryside. There was no clear program for recovery, and the government seemed to have been rendered completely impotent by a combination of falling copper prices, external indebtedness, mounting internal opposition, rising corruption, and delegitimization of the state. The Managing Director of the IMF noted in February 1991 that the Zambian economy "nearly reached rock bottom because of state protection which did not allow any competition as exercised in a free market economy."[3] Of course, the IMF was trying to sell itself and provide support for the MMD, which had declared a total commitment to its policies and the free market. As discussed earlier, the MMD manifesto placed its hopes for recovery on privatization, the free market, and structural adjustment. During the campaigns, Chiluba, the MMD flag bearer, stated that "privatization will play a major role in the economic development process of Zambia when the MMD is elected into power." He promised to leave the running of the economy to local and international entrepreneurs and that "our government will not interfere with the economy. There will be no nationalization of companies."[4] Lewanika, the chairman of the party's finance committee, also announced that the MMD "will continue with the current government's economic restructuring programme" but would achieve better results and avoid the errors of the past because the MMD "would correct those flaws and continue with the long term programme which held the future of the country's economy."[5] At the end of 1990 Zambia's foreign debt stood at $7 billion, its foreign reserves at the end of 1989 were $130 million, and inflation reached 100 percent.

The challenges that confronted the new democratic government therefore were quite enormous. First, restoring the confidence of the people in the government and nation. Second, making visible improvements in the living conditions of the majority who had been severely impoverished. Third, promoting economic recovery especially through the control of inflation and the revitalization of agriculture and industry. Fourth, restoring investor and donor confidence in the economy in order to attract required foreign aid, foreign investment, and foreign exchange. Fifth, bringing the various ethnic, regional, and religious groupings and tendencies together in the spirit of reconciliation and peace. Finally, sixth, the new government had to find ways of appeasing alienated communities, bringing realism to the expectations of its members, and making the defeated party accept the reality of defeat, and to contribute its quota to the process of recovery. These challenges, and more, were certainly not going to be easy, especially against the background of a bankrupt economy.

In his speech at the opening of Parliament on 29 November 1991, the new president drew attention to the "country's devastation." He noted that Zambia was only "at the start of (its) democratic journey. And have no illusions; the road ahead is still dark and dangerous." He noted that the battle ahead would not have been won until Zambians "have food, clothes, medicine, education, jobs and money;" urged parliament to "use power to help people;" and all Zambians must be prepared to "heal the wounds of destruction and rebuild a tattered and battered nation." Chiluba warned Zambians that the government would have to "make some hard choices" and promised to restructure the civil service: "Civil servants are not politicians, they should refrain from usurping the political role. Be reminded that there is now a clear division between party and state, between politics and administration." Finally, Chiluba stated that "the people of Zambia is the rock upon which we build our government...we are a government of the people for the people;" and the people could get on with their lives "without fear of harassment, without government interference, without excuses":

> For too long the mandarins of one-party rule have pounded the souls of ordinary citizens with contempt, with lawlessness and with suppression. They have bombarded them with high-handedness and ineptitude beyond forbearance, damaging the fabric of our society with more devastating effect than any bombing in wars of recent memory. This is an era of rights and accountability in Africa.[6]

Chiluba's postures, pronouncements, and addresses were deliberately designed to gradually let Zambians know that the victory of the MMD did not mean an immediate end to the predicaments of the country. With a mixture of populism and determined responses to inherited and new demands and pressures, Chiluba tried to lay a foundation for a new socio-economic and political agenda in Zambia: he was to be called simply "Mr. President" rather than "His/Your Excellency," as Kaunda had insisted upon. Ministers were going to work for the people, make sacrifices, and not treat their positions as avenues to get filthy rich at the expense of the nation. All denominations of Zambia's currency were to be reminted without the portrait of Kenneth Kaunda—or Chiluba's—in keeping with the strategy of depersonalizing Zambian politics. Immediate steps were to be taken to revive investor confidence in the economy, attract foreign aid, and recapture the attention, sympathy, and interest of donors and lenders.

The new president's assessment of the economic situation in his address to parliament was chilling. He noted that Zambia was "in a grave situation"; that he had been careful not to "encourage false hopes or prophesy smooth and easy times ahead"; and that there was a "darker, more dangerous and more serious" aspect of the affairs of state the MMD inherited: "In the limited time- available we have at least managed to shine a torch in the cupboard of state. Regretfully I must inform you that the cupboard is bare. Even the crumbs are few." According to the president,

We have found the economy in ruins: This year, as before, Zambia's economy has declined. The decline of three per cent, linked to the one per cent of the year before means, ... that the standard of living of our people has actually fallen by some ten per cent over the last two years....It is no exaggeration to say that the present living standard of our people measure at far less than half of what they were twenty years ago. The aggravating situation effect of the previous government's incompetence is eloquently explained by inflation levels exceeding 100 per cent per year. Adding insult to injury, they have contracted external indebtedness to the point where we owe something like one thousand United States dollars to the rest of the world for every Zambian. Our economy is in ruins and even the ruins are in danger.

In response to these predicaments, the MMD president outlined a series of policy measures and programs designed to put the country back on the path to recovery. These will be discussed later.

It is important to point out that the magnitude of the problems inherited by the government posed the very first challenge to its survival. On coming to power, "the party discovered that it was easier to be in the opposition, to criticize and to be a 'movement' than to be a government. So many demands were being made and expectations were much higher than we could deliver. Unfortunately, any attempt to draw a realistic picture of the situation was interpreted by the opposition as a sign of weakness and evidence that the MMD had tricked the people to get elected."[7] In its efforts to move in an opposite direction from the UNIP government, the MMD made very open overtures to Western nations, donors, investors, and finance agencies. At one point it was as if the Zambian government had become a truly beggar government asking for and receiving aid from all sorts of sources, almost without regard to the strings attached. But this was clearly evidence of the degree of desperation and the dire need for foreign exchange. It made unmediated statements as to how it was going to free the market, empower the private sector, attract investors and so on. It was clear that the MMD had given very limited thought to the contradictions, coalitions, conflicts, and crises which combine at different levels to reproduce Zambia's underdevelopment and marginalization in the global system.

The global system is structured in such a way that mere declarations of economic openness are often not enough to attract foreign aid, sympathy, investors, and support; at least, not on a permanent basis. As the Catholic Bishops of Zambia rightly warned, "liberalization, privatization and a free market system are laws which should not be blindly obeyed in running the economy."[8] It is an irony that the very powerful institutions and nations of the world also have several geostrategic and political considerations in the disbursement of aid and in their patterns of guaranteeing investments. The fact that Russia and the Ukraine are the most visible countries with which the West appears to be concerned in the former Eastern bloc is reflective of the power, potential, and military importance of the two countries. The response to Kuwait following the Iraqi invasion as compared to initial responses to Somalia, Liberia, the Sudan, and Bosnia also show that all nations are not equal and that, at times, democracy or open commitment to the market is not enough to attract aid and investment. It is on record that the response of the developed nations to the political and economic restructuring programs, which have at times been based on blue-prints supplied by aid and other western agencies, have been very weak or really poor. Zambia and the MMD were to learn this very quickly.

The MMD Agenda for Economic Recovery in Zambia

The first public insight into the comprehensive MMD agenda was from Chiluba's address to the new MMD-dominated parliament in November 1991. In the address he stressed that the "economic heritage" of Zambia was the need to launch a "major programme for reconstruction and development without capital, without credit-worthiness." Immediate tasks included:

a) putting the economy on the path of growth;

b) raising the standard of living for all Zambians;

c) creating jobs and generating income;

d) generating foreign exchange by all possible means;

e) reducing the country's debt-stock as much as possible by immediately trying to reach some understanding with creditors and developing the "capacity to repay at least part of our debt";

f) avoid being "banished to the dark dungeons of international disrepute and perpetual internal decline";

g) initiating joint ventures on major projects with the private sector, farmers, exporters, industrialists, and workers;

h) reaching out to "our friends abroad" because only "donors and patient creditors stand between us and calamity";

i) cutting the cost of government drastically by "reducing and eliminating those sectors that are not contributing to ... reconstruction efforts";

j) balancing the national budget over a two-year period and controlling inflation;

k) directing funding only to "priority programmes which include programmes for the rehabilitation of our schools and hospitals, and the repair of our road network";

l) revamping the industrial, commercial, trade and agricultural infrastructure of the country from afresh because "the previous government left us with nothing to build on." This will involve promotion of the growth of the private sector; restructuring incentives in favor of export-based and export substitution activities; encouraging local and foreign investment by streamlining regulations and procedures; and removing barriers to foreign trade and investment;

m) simplifying licensing and registration procedures, and creating a "strong information and data base to serve the business community and government," increased openness in all business and commercial activities;

n) improving and increasing the capacity of the government to collect revenue rightfully due it;

o) rationalization of public enterprises, which "inevitably means sacrifices" to which the country has no alternative;

p) creation of a consultative mechanism with representatives from government, industrial, and farming communities and the labor movement to "discuss and solve problems of mutual interests";

q) normalizing strained relations with the donor community, reaching an agreement with the IMF and World Bank, and sticking to these agreements, unlike the cases in the past;

r) diversifying the economic base of Zambia by reducing the heavy dependence on copper and reversing "the decline in ...non traditional exports";

s) creating an "enabling environment for all partners in Zambia's reconstruction efforts;"

t) "avert imminent disaster" in the agricultural sector by privatizing the agricultural sector and putting "many parastatal farms...under private management and ownership," expanding small scale farming communities, concentrating on production for export, and "divest[ing] government of the responsibility of running" cooperatives "as if they were parastatals." Farmers would receive financial incentives and fair prices for their produce, and marketing networks would be streamlined while improvements in storage and infrastructure will take place;

u) recognizing the changes in the global system, which have in fact created the MMD government, foreign relations would be deigned to improve the living conditions of Zambians and the MMD government will be a "catalyst for all changes that will make this planet a better place for all its inhabitants. Even in pursuing our foreign policy we shall put Zambia first." Relations with Israel will be reestablished and a trade mission will be opened in South Africa immediately, while a permanent diplomatic mission will follow later and appointments to these missions shall be based on merit, professionalism, and experience;

v) promoting a "new efficient work culture and ethic," reviewing existing laws and procedures which breed inefficiency in the bureaucracy, and reappraising laws which have tended to reduce investor confidence in Zambia; and

w) respecting human rights in all its ramifications, guaranteeing basic and fundamental freedoms and liberties; revision of local laws to make them more humane and democratic, ratification of all international covenants on human rights and incorporating them into domestic laws, and guarantee the independence of the judiciary.[9]

Though the programs listed above sound more like a chapter from a World Bank/IMF document, they were nonetheless a response to the realities of the situation. Zambia was already down and almost out. As Chiluba himself admitted, the MMD government is a creation of global changes and foreign interests have—directly and/or indirectly—played a major part in putting it in power. The Kaunda government had squandered all national resources and the economy was on its knees. There was no way the MMD government was going to receive more aid, loans, credit, rescheduling agreements or any form of sympathy in a global system dominated by the IMF, the World Bank, creditors, and Western ideological influences without openly declaring for capitalism and the market in every possible way. The real issue was not the declaration for capitalism and the forces of international finance capital. The real issue was the very simplistic and rather naive understanding and appreciation of the dangers of an unmediated surrender to the ideological, economic, and political values and dictates of donors and lenders, and the lack of a sophisticated appreciation of the complex dynamics of class coalitions, contradictions, and struggles within Zambia. In spite of reliance on populist rhetoric and the constant declaration of commitment to the people, the truth is that the people would be the first victims of the MMD's capitalist ideology.[10] There is no way it can generate surpluses without exploiting the working classes and the peasantry.

As a rightist movement, its ultimate agenda would be the extraction of surpluses from nonbourgeois forces to subsidize the accumulation of capital by the bourgeoisie. We must bear in mind that Zambia has a very weak economic base, even without taking corruption and mismanagement into consideration. As of March 31, 1990, there were only 77 foreign investors in the country. According to Mr. Muzungu, the minister for mines, there were 14 in the agricultural sector with a total investment of $148,782,980; 20 in transport with a total investment of $44,607,152; two in Mining worth $1,871,725; two in fishing with investment totalling $80,000; 12 in industry with total investment of $1,290,513; and 27 in manufacturing with investment worth $21,205,269. Thus, compared with many African states, the Zambian economy is pretty weak.

Though it had a strong political mandate to carry out reforms, if any lessons are to be gleaned from the experience of Boris Yeltsin in Russia it is that the initial enthusiasm for liberal democracy and support for reforming governments can evaporate rapidly if visible changes in living standards are not evident in a relatively short period. This is the more so where the vast majority has been severely impoverished for a long period of time and the elasticity of hope and patience has become rather weak. Carol Graham might not be exactly right in contending that the MMD did not make any "false promises in its electoral campaign," and that Chiluba's "labor background guaranteed him a certain amount of union support."[11] The

MMD did make a lot of promises, many of which it lacked the resources and capacity to fulfil. It promised a new era, and announced that the *hour* for change, for a better, stronger, peaceful, and more productive Zambia had come. It did not inform Zambians that the hour which had come was only the beginning of a long and very painful hour, day, week, year or decade. By distancing itself from UNIP and capitalizing on the incumbent government's economic failure, the MMD made it clear that it was in a position to do better. Millions flocked to the MMD because they wanted jobs, food, security, health services, education for their children, and freedom. In any case, as events have shown, Chiluba's labor background has not made any difference. The trade unions, including the ZCTU, which he led for almost two decades, have organized scores of strikes against the government and its policies. How the party will play the very complex and difficult game of populism and rightist ideology, the encapsulation of its programs by monetarist policies from the World Bank and IMF, and the need to meet the basic needs of the people, will be the challenge of the 1990s.

The First Two Years in Power, 1992-1993: An Evaluation of the MMD's Economic Record

Without doubt, the MMD was very optimistic as to how it would turn the devastated Zambian economy around. In spite of the fact that the economy is a distorted, foreign-dominated, monocultural, disarticulated, peripheral one with a weak and unsteady state and a largely unproductive and very corrupt dominant class, Chiluba was convinced that,

> The MMD government is as committed to freeing the economy, as to freeing the people. In this way we shall optimise resources, increase local value added, create employment opportunities, promote competition and create a more realistic environment for

foreign investment. We have our work cut out indeed.[12]

The new party and government promised all Zambians an "equitable distribution of the burdens that will come with the reconstruction efforts" through a "democratic way." However, such hopes were dashed against the background of the damage the UNIP government had done to Zambia and Zambians: "Once again I can only report decline and devastation. The UNIP government bequeathed us insufficient stocks, a shortage of agricultural imports and an almost nonexisting marketing system."[13] Under the UNIP administration "extremely inefficient, costly and unproductive agriculture and particularly maize" became "the biggest drain on the nation's resources." Subsidies to the agricultural sector—transport, fertilizer, maize and losses by parastatal firms and cooperatives in the agricultural sector—cost the government K20 billion annually.[14] Prior to the October 1991 elections, cabinet ministers enjoyed free fuel supply and all sorts of allowances and privileges; Kaunda had ordered parastatals to provide him and the UNIP with large sums of money without accountability; and the bureaucracy was plagued with corruption from top to bottom. In November 1990, Kaunda embarked on one of his most reckless policies in the midst of an economic crisis: he organized a so-called National Prayer Breakfast at the Inter-Continental Hotel in Lusaka at a cost of K5,733,040. He had invited foreign leaders, ambassadors, and other dignitaries, as well as liberation movements. Though no Zambian took this very seriously, as "the situation could no longer be helped with prayers, even if he prayed from Lusaka to Jericho,"[15] it was a very irresponsible and irrational expenditure at that time. Why the Inter-Continental for a government that owned several guest houses and one of the largest Government Houses in Africa? When Mr. Sekuila, a member of Parliament,

Parliament, raised this issue and wanted to know why the prayer was not held at the huge Holy Cross Cathedral in Lusaka, he was ruled out of order.[16] In January 1990 alone, the UNIP government had spent K52.2 million on mealie meal subsidies for police officers and in the National Assembly, Mr. Miyato, the minister of state for finance, argued that the subsidy constituted part of "the conditions of service till further notice."[17] Finally, in the last months of the UNIP government, largely as a strategy for bribing the working classes, the Kaunda government had granted a 100 percent pay increase to the 150,000 strong civil servants, with the agreement that another similar increase would be granted in June 1992! These and other worrying reports of financial recklessness in the 1990–91 period confirmed allegations that the UNIP leadership was bent on destroying the economy to make recovery impossible under the MMD. The MMD clearly inherited a country and economy that was in free fall. It is important to have this brief background in order to appreciate the poor results of the MMD's recovery program in spite of massive foreign assistance.

1992: The New Economic Recovery Programme

The long-term goals of the New Economic Recovery Programme (NERP), introduced in 1992 were: *a)* economic stabilization through the implementation of IMF/World Bank prescriptions; *b)* economic efficiency and growth through local restructurings and encouragement to private initiative and a reduction in the size and role of the state; and *c)* alleviation of the sufferings of the poor through improvement in the standards of living. The program also envisaged a real GDP growth rate of two percent; reduction of inflation from 100 percent in 1991 to 45 percent at the end of 1992; privatization of state parastatals; rehabilitation of productive and social infrastructure; debt servicing and rescheduling, and employment generation.[18] In all these areas the MMD government failed to record any success. A combination of natural disaster, continuing mismanagement, inefficiency, policy confusion, inexperience within the movement, and crisis overhang from the UNIP years combined to worsen the state of the nation and economy. According to the National Commission for Development Planning,

> The performance of the Zambian economy in 1992 was unsatisfactory. A decline in real Gross Domestic Product of 2.8 percent was recorded. The inherent negative factors including the deterioration in terms of trade, low investment rates, high inflation and heavy external debt burden continued to inhibit the growth prospects. Economic growth in 1992 was particularly limited by the severe drought that affected the whole of Southern Africa.[19]

Efforts to limit the growth of money supply to 25 percent for 1992 also failed, since interest rates had gotten out of control with the liberalization policies and the government itself had a more than usual or more than anticipated "recourse to the banking system...to finance the rising drought and non-drought budget deficits and failure to sterilise in a timely manner ZCCM's excess copper earnings during the year."[20] According to finance minister Emmanuel Kasonde, "with output falling and money supply increasing, inflation accelerated. Prices in December 1992 were 207 per cent higher than in December 1991.... Our performance in this area is totally unsatisfactory."[21] Value-added in the agricultural sector declined by 39.3 percent in 1992, negating the modest 5.6-percent growth rate in 1991. The sector's share in the GDP fell from 11.6 percent in 1991 to 7.2 percent in 1992. Output in the manufacturing sector declined 4.2 percent in 1992, and its share in GDP declined from 20 percent in 1991 to 18 percent in 1992. According to the National Commission, this sector "lacked infusion of fresh capital while existing capacity has not been fully utilized for lack of inputs."[22]

The same fate befell construction, electricity, water, real estate, retail and wholesale trade, hotels and restaurants, transport and communications, and social services where performance was "sluggish." For instance, output of electricity and water declined by 4.2 percent in 1992 while poor power supply and scarcity of raw materials and spare parts severely constrained output in the industrial and manufacturing sectors. Merchandise export for 1992 was estimated at US$1,072 million while imports were US$1,286 million. Thus Zambia imported more than it exported leaving a deficit of US$519 million. Employment declined from 485,000 in 1991 to 474,00 in 1992, leading to a net loss of 11,000 jobs. Some 15,000 employees were retrenched from the public service, with very few new job openings or programs to protect them in the unemployment market. Summarizing the tale of economic woes to parliament, finance minister Kasonde noted soberly that:

> When I presented the 1992 budget to this Honourable House, the government's intention was to fully finance the budget without borrowing from the banking system. Events did not turn out as we intended. Non-drought expenditures for the year amounted to K106.4 billion, as against the original estimate of K90 billion. There were several unanticipated developments. The wage increase added K15.5 billion to personal emoluments. The subvention to Zambian Airways cost K3.2 billion. And due to inflation and the depreciation of the Kwacha, the cost of local purchases and foreign missions abroad rose...the problem we face is that the economy is now hypersensitive to *any* deficit spending by Government. The general public and business community have given up trying to keep up with inflation; most pricing decisions are now made so as to get ahead of inflation....This situation is highly unstable.[23]

With no visible progress on virtually all economic fronts, tensions began to mount. The MMD's campaign, in spite of strenuous efforts by its flag bearers, had raised the hopes of the average Zambian. The party's campaign slogan, "The Hour Has Come" meant to many that the "days of milk and honey had arrived. As soon as Kaunda was defeated, every one would begin to enjoy life more abundant."[24] The last thing that Zambians expected were lamentations about economic failure and the inability to meet the needs of the people. The policies initiated in the first three quarters sent mixed signals and different to popular expectations: devaluation of the Kwacha, removal of subsidy from mealie meal, massive retrenchment in the public services, liberalization of interest rates which made it practically impossible for any one to borrow; removal of fertilizer subsidies; and general subservience to dictates from the IMF and the World Bank. People started grumbling about the "slow pace of change," about continuing corruption in the system, about nepotism in the MMD, and about the continuing influence of UNIP in the party!

> I just can not believe these people. All the promises about a better future. Did they not know we had no money? KK said so before he left office. But Chiluba said we had friends abroad. We were told that food would come from America. Now, look at me. I cannot even pay my rent and take care of my children. Maybe we should try running the country without a government for a while.[25]

There were also complaints about continuing brain drain to other countries in the region as well as overseas, and there were predictions of social unrest.[26] It was clear to observers that political pluralism was being conditioned and contained by deepening economic crisis in Zambia.

In spite of the rather poor results, the MMD took solace in its continuing popularity within and outside the country and the massive support it had received from donors. The

British government forgave 60 percent of the debt owed it by Zambia after the election. The United States forgave $110 million in debt provided the MMD reached agreement with the multilaterals. (The MMD immediately fulfilled this condition.) In early 1992 the Chiluba government was able to work out an arrangement with bilateral donors to pay $50 million, which had led to Zambia's suspension from Bank operations. During the drought, donors and relief agencies responded rapidly to the situation, thus producing one of the best drought-management programs in the region.[27] The Scandinavian countries, France, and Canada also assisted the new democratic government. Obviously the commitment to market reforms, irrespective of the pains it was inflicting on vulnerable groups, had retained the support of donors and lenders than from the Zambian constituency. As Kasonde noted, "our commitment to policy reform has yielded substantial benefits already. For example, we have been able to reactivate our Rights Accumulation Programme with the International Monetary Fund which paved the way for external assistance amounting to US$1.5 billion. This amount is unprecedented in our history."[28] It is more the support from the donors and lenders that gave the MMD the courage to proceed with its 1993 recovery plans.

1993 and Beyond: Still No Recovery in Sight

The National Commission for Development Planning noted in its 1992 report that the "prospects for employment in 1993 are not very promising due to envisaged loss of jobs because of factors such as: privatization; retrenchment in the public sector; continued credit squeeze which is likely to restrict investments; and measures to control inflation are likely to cause a contraction in the economy and hence inhibit expansion in employment."[29] Kasonde made it clear to Parliament that in spite of the NERP and support from donors and lenders, "some major challenges remain. Our main problem is inflation. Unless we drastically reduce the rate of inflation, the economy will not stabilise, confidence will not return, investment will remain depressed, and we will fail in our attempt to regenerate economic growth."[30]

For 1993, therefore, the primary objective of government recovery programs focused on tighter fiscal policies; reduction in domestic borrowing by government and the parastatals; bringing inflation down to 10 percent; abolishing supplementary appropriations to government ministries; repaying much of government's outstanding debt to the banking system; freeing up resources for private sector expansion, and running the government on a cash basis. The Bank of Zambia was instructed to "deny any government transaction unless there are adequate funds in the appropriate accounts."[31] An extensive tax review, administration, evaluation, and collection system was introduced; a Special Fund was created for revenues from the privatization of government companies; K2 billion was earmarked for rehabilitating Zambia's terrible road network; tax relief for the handicapped and low-wage-earners was introduced and along with other tax measures the government expected to raise K15 billion in 1993. Proposed expenditure for 1993 was put at K231.9 billion: K197.1 billion was designated as non-drought expenditure, K34.8 billion as drought related. Of the K231.9 billion proposed expenditure, K19.8 billion was expected from the sale of donated maize and K212.1 billion from other domestic sources. Noting that "tax incentives are not the foremost considerations among serious investors," the MMD government contended that investors would consider "favourable macroeconomic policies, political stability, security, the availability of resources and markets, and liberal provisions for the repatriation of profits." As a measure of the degree of openness of the economy and in addition to the "package of tax measures" which should "attract investors and stimulate investment," the MMD government announced that it "will allow the repatriation of 100 percent of after tax profits, with no restrictions, and no bureaucratic screening."[32] This new posture in itself generated heated debates on the steady recolonization of the Zambian economy. However, except for UNIP members (and until the recent emergence of several opposition parties), it was not politically wise to oppose the MMD. The debates were hardly conducted in public.

As of the middle of 1995, the government had not recorded much success in its recovery program. In May 1995, it faced another severe drought. As in the 1992 experience, the government was ready and made plans well beyond the traditional reliance on foreign sources to assist affected communities. The level of indignation had reached worrisome proportions. Infrastructures were still in very bad shape. Inflation had practically destroyed the social fabric of the nation though it had been brought down somewhat. Workers found it very difficult to make ends meet and unemployment remained a major problem. The bureaucracy was still riddled with corruption and mismanagement. Transportation was still in disarray, as spare parts could not be imported and, with the devaluation of the Kwacha, the cost of vehicles had become prohibitive. Crime had become rampant and armed robbers were daring to operate in broad daylight. As one respondent put it:

> We now know that politicians are all the same. UNIP or no UNIP, I not only lost my job under the MMD but I also lost my house. I cannot pay rent and life has become unbearable. It is clear that these MMD boys do not know what they are doing. They do not know how to govern. They make conflicting statements and the Ministers are very corrupt. All they know how to do is ride mercedes benz cars on bad roads like the Kaunda people. Only God will save the poor in this country.[33]

Regardless of the negative social pressures which the reform program was generating, the MMD has pressed on with its economic reform program with lender and donor support. At the end of 1994, it was still difficult to point at any real signs of change and recovery. Scandals in the cabinet, inefficiency, contradictory pronouncements, and sycophancy *á la* Kaunda have come to dominate MMD politics in Zambia. Though the political terrain has changed significantly, living standards are still as bad as ever and for many Zambians the nightmare has returned, except that this time, "it is wiser, more beautiful, younger, and more ruthless."[34]

Notes

1. See Carol Graham, *Safety Nets, Politics, and the Poor-Transitions to Market Economies* (Washington, D.C.: The Brookings Institution, 1994), pp. 156-158.
2. Interview, Lusaka, June 1993.
3. "Zambia's Economy Nearly Collapsed," *Times of Zambia* (February 23, 1991).
4. "MMD Wants Open Economy Says Chiluba," *Times of Zambia* (May 26, 1991).
5. "MMD to Pursue Growth Plan- Lewanika," *Times of Zambia* (June 4, 1991).
6. Ibid.
7. Interview with Hon. Frederick Hapunda, Lusaka, Zambia, June 1993.
8. "Evaluate Economic Policies, Bishops," *Times of Zambia* (March 18, 1992).
9. These programs are all drawn from F. J. T. Chiluba, *Opening of Parliament: Speech by President F. J. T. Chiluba on 29th November 1991*, (Lusaka: Government Printer, 1991).
10. See David Kabenda, "Market Forces May Lead to Unknown Destination," *Times of Zambia* (March 14, 1992); Sherman Drake, "Social Unrest Looms," *Times of Zambia* (February 4, 1992); and David Bantu, "People Want Results, Not Promises," *Times of Zambia* (February 8, 1992).
11. Carol Graham, *Safety Nets, Politics, and the Poor* (op. cit.), pp. 159.
12. Ibid.
13. Ibid.

14. Ibid.
15. Interview with Ms. Loveness Malambo, Lusaka, June 1993.
16. Government of Zambia, Third Session (Resumed) of the Sixth National Assembly: No 87 *Official Verbatim Report of the Parliamentary Debates 25th June-2nd August 1991*, (Lusaka, 1991).
17. Ibid.
18. See Republic Of Zambia, *Economic Report 1992* (Lusaka: Office of the President, National Commission for Development Planning, January 1993), and The Hon. E. G. Kasonde, MP, *Budget Address by the Minister of Finance* (Lusaka: Government Printer, 29th January, 1993).
19. National Commission for Development Planning, *Economic Report 1992* op. cit., p. 15.
20. Ibid., pp. 15-16.
21. E. G. Kasonde, *Budget Address* op. cit., p. 3.
22. National Commission for Development Planning, *Economic Report 1992* (op. cit.), p.18.
23. Kasonde, *Budget Address* (op. cit.), p.6.
24. Interview with Samuel Bandu, Lusaka, June, 1993.
25. Interview with a female public servant, Lusaka, June 1993.
26. See George Sunguh, "Braindrain Persists," *Times of Zambia*, (September 10, 1991); and Sherman Drake, "Social Unrest Looms," *Times of Zambia* (February 4, 1992).
27. See Carol Graham, *Safety Nets, Politics, and the Poor* (op. cit.), pp. 158-160; "UK to Cancel Zambia's Debt," *Zambia Daily Mail* (November 9, 1991); and "US to Scrap $270 Million Debt," *Times of Zambia* (November 18, 1991).
28. Kasonde, *Budget Address* (op. cit.), p.4. This statement shows clearly how the IMF strangles poor developing countries by closing off all sources of foreign aid if governments do not toe their line as dictated.
29. National Commission for Development Planning, *Economic Report 1992* (op. cit.), p. 21.
30. Kasonde, *Budget Address* (op. cit.), p.9.
31. Ibid., p. 19
32. Ibid.
33. Interview with a laid-off civil servant, Lusaka, June 1993.

34. Interview with an unemployed graduate, Lusaka, June 1993.

CHAPTER FIVE

NEW POLITICS,
NEW CHALLENGES, AND NEW
CONTRADICTIONS IN ZAMBIA

The crisis, contradictions, and conflicts confronting the new MMD government have been enormous. It has required a combination of maturity and accommodation to identify pressing national issues and map out responses which would strengthen the hold of the movement on power. First, the defeated UNIP government was very bitter. Kaunda, the fallen UNIP leader, kept referring to the MMD and its government as irresponsible "small boys." Other leading members of UNIP initiated several campaigns to discredit the new government. It thus became necessary for the new government to devise mechanisms to contain this effort at building a counter-political bloc in Zambia. Second, many members of the MMD had served UNIP dutifully and loyally for decades. Adapting to a new government, new leaders, new symbols, new ideas, and a new philosophy of government and governance was not going to be easy. The MMD needed to map out an agenda for weaning these people away from the UNIP traditions and towards solidarity with the new party and government. Third, the party's emphasis on openness, democracy, participation, accountability, social justice, and human rights were in some respects new, as the UNIP government had gone against all these in the latter part of its reign. It was necessary to work out an agenda that would guarantee basic freedoms without encouraging anarchy. The new government had to learn to be fair, just, open—but very firm. Fourth, though the MMD had enjoyed tremendous diplomatic, financial, and other kinds of support from donors, lenders, and other international bodies, the new government now needed to cut an image of independence and control. It had to carefully retrace its steps from the seemingly total surrender to the IMF, the World Bank and the Western powers, especially the United States and the United Kingdom. This was a risky development because the Zambian economy was totally down and almost out and was going to rely heavily on those nations, organizations, and interest groups for aid, loans, concessions, credit, and support. Finally, fifth, the MMD had to find a way to retain the support of its teeming members who were expecting "miracles" to follow the defeat of the UNIP and the ascendance of the MMD. The people had all turned against KK and the UNIP out of frustration, alienation, unemployment, inflation, social decay, human rights abuses, corruption, abuse of office, the neglect of the rural areas, infrastructural dislocation, and general difficulties in their daily lives. The MMD had campaigned with the slogan "The Hour Has Come," and the people were all too eager to see what the "hour" brought with it and how it would be different and better than the past. Unfortunately for the MMD, the people were too impatient to listen to excuses, so that how the movement was going to contain and/or respond to the rising expectations was going to be critical.

Though President Chiluba and the movement have tried as much as possible to deal with the issues above, they have not succeeded on any front. The new challenges have continued to task the capability, resources, unity, vision, and organization of the MMD. The president has been accused of clannishness and indecision. He has been accused of bringing his personal religious interests and biases into government and of being no longer capable of distinguishing between the church and the state. Now that even the vice-president has become "born again," the issue of religion has taken a higher place in national decision-making and debates. The movement has not really succeeded in converting itself into a real political party. Frequently, it speaks with many voices, party discipline is lacking, and intense power struggles and conflicts continue unabated. Many ministers of state have been accused of indiscipline, corruption, and abuse of office.

Allegations of drug-pushing were levelled against several of the ministers, and Chiluba was accused by several prominent persons of shielding the accused ministers from justice. Because of deepening economic and social crisis, support for the party has started to wane as people fail to see any significant improvement in their conditions of living. The *Kwacha*, the national currency, continues to depreciate to unprecedented levels, inflation remains high, interests rates prevent business people from borrowing, food remains scarce, no new jobs are being created, and the top politicians and ministers continue to live in opulence in the midst of poverty.

Lack of discipline and effective control within the movement and the inability of the new MMD government to satisfy individual, regional, class, community, and group pressures and demands have encouraged splits within the movement leading to the emergence of other parties which have engaged in virulent attacks on the government. Such a situation obviously encouraged the greatest political challenge and test to the government's resolve in the "Zero Option" controversy when the UNIP was accused of plotting a coup to overthrow the Chiluba government (see below). Just as the Kaunda government was put to the political test by the Leshina and Watch Tower episodes, the MMD was tested early in its rule by the Zero Option controversy. Beyond the Zero Option issue, however, the MMD has had to deal with the drug issue, drought, religious fanaticism, discipline within the party, and generally increasing disaffection with its inability to immediately make a difference in the lives of the people. Without doubt, these are serious challenges for a new regime.

Reaching Out to Zambians: Adjusting to New Realities

As soon as the MMD was sworn into power to govern Zambia, it tried to reach out to the people. In speech after speech Chiluba made it clear that the MMD government had inherited an empty treasury, huge foreign and domestic debts, and a very difficult political terrain on which to mount its reform programs. It restated its faith in the market and in the policies and programs of the IMF and the World Bank to see Zambia through the very difficult times. Chiluba never tired of reeling out to listeners the millions of dollars that had come from lenders and donors and how such support was essential to the survival of the country and the new government. Beyond foreign support however, the Chiluba government believed that only a diversified economy and a self-reliant productive base would provide the answer to the numerous contradictions and crises plaguing the country. As the Finance Minister Ronald Penza noted, Zambia was "steaming ahead with reforms, including privatization to liberalise the economy." He noted however, that "high inflation and hefty foreign debt remain major headaches."[1] These problems, coupled with a near total collapse of infrastructures and an almost total erosion of investor confidence despite democratization efforts, made it difficult to achieve the goals of dismantling the state's 80-percent control of the economy and selling of 19 major enterprises as part of its privatization drive. The Zambia Privatisation Agency (PAZ), which had scheduled another 32 medium-to-large-scale industries for sale to private investors by September 1993, ran into difficulties because the rate of economic recovery had been very slow. Annual inflation was over 180 percent in mid-1993 and the removal of subsidies from agriculture and petroleum only worsened an already bad situation.[2] Of course, without adequate measures to redistribute the gains and pains of adjustment and educate the populace to accept the constraints of restructuring as a necessary step to recovery, the outcome of these programs only alienated the people from the state, its agents, and its agencies.

By mid 1993 the government had suspended duty on basic food commodities such as vegetable oil, maize, rice, and wheat.[3] Import duties were scrapped to encourage importers to bring in these items especially, as the drought of 1991–92 had devastated the agricultural sector and inflation was ravaging the economy. As discussed earlier, the government outlined a major program to generate employment in the private sector while carrying out a comprehensive privatization and commercialization program. It also embarked on a policy aimed at trimming the size of the bureaucracy so as to cut waste, mismanagement, and its huge wage bill. These efforts did not yield immediate results in spite of the good intentions of the MMD government. Small-scale industries continued to go bankrupt at an alarming rate. For instance, Liyali Enterprises, an indigenous battery-producing company, shifted its operations to "reconditioning batteries from scrap" because it lacked the foreign exchange to import sulfuric acid and other inputs.[4] The Copperbelt Bottling Company also shut its Tip-Top and Cobo producing plants and settled for imported concentrates from Swaziland. When it launched a new drink, "Iron-Brew," the concentrates were imported from South Africa. With such redirection of production patterns, local farmers who had relied on supplying these firms with fruits were bankrupted.[5] Dickson Kasminda reported in May 1993 that eighteen firms

173

in Southern and Copperbelt provinces closed down or drastically retrenched workers due to shortages of inputs and other raw materials and foreign exchange. These closures rendered over 5,000 workers jobless. In other instances, many local industries were priced out of the market by second-hand *salaula* dealers.[6] New businesses were not being established. Local business interests, especially the Asians, realizing that the Kwacha was being devalued regularly, kept their funds in foreign exchange and away from the banks. Corruption continued to ruin public policies, task the credibility of the government, and divert scarce resources to private pockets.[7] Frauds in banking institutions became so rampant as to prompt a public appeal from Ronald Penza, the finance minister.[8] Infrastructures continued to deteriorate, with far-reaching implications for other sectors of the economy. For instance, as potholes dotted all the major streets, traffic jams delayed movement, and the prices of goods and services increased as it started costing more to move goods and services from the rural to the urban centers. The era of rapidly rising population and urbanization had "not been matched with a similar expansion of social services. The number of schools, clinics, police stations and even markets had remained static for several years," and the MMD government lacked the resources to make a difference in these areas.[9]

More importantly, the MMD could no longer continue to count on using what was inherited from Kaunda as an excuse for its own poor performance. Melinda Ham is quite specific on the fact that a "reason for the MMD's rapidly decreasing popularity in every province is its failure to make any tangible improvements in peoples's standard of living. Instead, the electorate believe they are suffering more now than under Kaunda."[10] Moreover, as Jowie Mwiinga has noted, "the first two years of the Chiluba presidency were characterized by dashed expectations. Chiluba's government, which rode to power with the promise of transparency and accountability, quickly proved to be anything but transparent and accountable."[11] In a situation where "cases of high level corruption and financial abuse, of which there were not a few, went unpunished, as did other excesses of senior government officials,"[12] it would be impossible for Chiluba and the MMD to keep reform programs on track, maintain the momentum of the democratization program, and convince Zambians that it is important to make collective sacrifices for the national good and for the future. The Zambia Confederation of Chambers of Commerce and Industries is of the view that "the current industrial policy is a fantastic formula for poverty creation." As the *Zambia Daily Mail* has noted, though the adjustment program is supposed to increase opportunities and lead to recovery and expanded growth, "many businessmen now believe that government's doctrinaire adherence to total liberalisation will kill domestic industries."[13]

This is a major problem for the MMD. It is rather early in its life span, given the massive mandate it received in the 1991 elections, for major sectors like manufacturers and trade unions to be challenging the industrialization and reform programs of the MMD. At one level it would seem that the MMD had lost touch with these very important constituencies; at another level, it would appear that not only had communication broken down, but also that these constituencies had lost faith in the ability of the new government to make a difference in the area of economic recovery. Fackson Shamenda, who succeeded Chiluba as president of the ZCTU, has also argued that liberalization would lead to exploitation of the working classes and only industrialists would benefit from the privatization program of the MMD. To him, the MMD must avoid "over-privatisation" because if "everything is privatized, the private sector is likely to become so powerful with nothing left for the masses."[14] This position is completely contrary to that of the MMD, which advocates total privatization of the economy.

The government has been forced to take several unpopular measures in order to keep donor and lender support and to keep the structural adjustment program on track. These measures, according to Chiluba, have meant a "lot of hardship" to a people already brutalized by decades of mismanagement and repression.[15] So far, the MMD, at least until very recently, has been able to get away with most of its painful remedies because of the popular support which swept it into power. Without doubt, some of these policies are necessary in a rapidly changing world where the market is the moving force of production, exchange, and consumption. However, the MMD is certainly not doing enough to educate and mobilize the people. Many Zambians want to be patient and to bear the social costs of adjustment. Unfortunately this desire to be patient has been completely eroded by the opulence and waste in which the elites, particularly the ministers and top political figures, live. As a respondent noted:

> How can they ask us to tighten our belts when they expand their own. We are no fools. We voted in the MMD because they promised us a better life. So far, we are still awaiting this better life. I am yet to see any serious difference between Chiluba and Kaunda and we are tired of excuses upon excuses which do not affect the rich.[16]

Though Chiluba admits that "if our people don't see a better standard of living, they will think democracy isn't a better alternative,"[17] in mid-1993 the government was forced to remove subsidies from fuel. The price of petrol and diesel went up by 30 and 100 percent, respectively. This shot up the price for petrol in Lusaka from K226 to K293 per liter, and diesel increased from K130 to K268 per liter. Kerosene went up from K110 to K177. In cities such as Livingstone the cost of petrol was excessively higher, increasing from K266 to K373 per liter. The May 1993 fuel-price increase was the fourth fuel-price hike in 1993 alone. The increases were condemned by traders, school children, the trade unions, farmers, the Truckers Association of Zambia, and the United Transport and Taxis Association.[18]

The impact on the economy was immediate. Minibus operators increased their fares by between 50 and 150 percent. The Zambia National Farmers Union (ZNFU) announced that the price of maize would be adjusted from K5000 to K9000 per bag because of the fuel-price increase.[19] Electricity costs went up by 240 percent and the Consumer Protective Association (CPA) had to warn the government to be "mindful of social impacts in their pursuance of economic adjustment programmes."[20] Labor leaders made it clear that following the rising cost of living, they were going to demand higher wages. It will be dangerous for the MMD and the program it has set for itself to lose the support of the labor movement. It will be personally embarrassing for Chiluba who was president of the ZCTU for over a decade and a half. The opposition parties roundly condemned the government for making life tougher for the already poor, especially those in the rural areas. Tenthani Mwanza, the president of the National Party for Democracy (NPD), called for the immediate reintroduction of subsidies in order to avoid chaos in the country.[21] The MMD has so far done a poor job at continuing mobilization and education of the populace. Opposition to its programs continue to mount because people do not understand them and the impacts are not evenly distributed. With local industries unable to borrow due to very high interest rates of about 120 per cent, unemployment remains high and the state remains the main employer in the economy.[22]

Power Struggles at the Provincial Levels

As Zambians were beginning to feel that economic recovery could probably never occur under the MMD, the increasing factionalization and fractionalization within the party

177

created new distractions and contradictions, with implications for stability, party discipline, and credibility. These struggles were largely caused by and reflective of: (a) patronage claims within the MMD, as a continuation of the UNIP tradition; (b) the struggle for control and spheres of authority and accumulation; (c) the survival of strong UNIP tendencies, such as the privatization of public office along with its resources; and (d) the weak nature of MMD party structures and very low party discipline. As well, the deepening struggles for power within the party were a reflection of the diverse interests which comprised the MMD: the so-called "recycled politicians" or "recycled democrats" of Zambia.

A major front of power struggles within the provinces which reached a head in 1993 was in the Northern and Southern Provinces. In the Northern Province, Daniel Kapapa (the minister of the province) became embroiled in a controversy with the Ministry of Works when he refused to release ten official vehicles which had belonged to UNIP leaders but were in his custody.[23] There was also a dangerous power struggle between Kapapa and Emmanuel Kasonde, who was dismissed as finance minister in mid-1993. Kasonde had been provincial chair of the MMD and when he became minister, rather than ask his deputy to run the affairs of the party in the province, he put Kapapa in charge. On his return to the province following his dismissal, Kapapa refused to surrender the position to Kasonde. This divided the party into two warring camps and an ugly war of words raged between both party leaders.[24] The struggle for power practically stifled party activities and showed that the MMD still lacked party discipline and clear ways of running affairs at the local level. As well, there were practically no effective and consistent conflict resolution mechanisms in place to take care of such embarrassing and explosive political struggles among party stalwarts.

A more serious consequence of these power conflicts was the way in which they fractionalized civil society. Here was a new political party and a new government which had to contend with institutions, alignments, ideologies, and personalities that had been groomed by UNIP for 28 years. The last thing the MMD needed was a power rift within its own ranks. Thus, rather than focus on mobilization, education, constituency building, and leadership training, these regional power rifts served only to create enemies, warring camps, and deep divisions. The situation served only to weaken the party and create opportunities for opposition interests.

The situation in the Northwestern Province was not helped by the failure of the MMD government to deliver on most of its promises to the people of the area upon coming to power. The province "is large, poor, neglected and underdeveloped. The spiral of economic decline and political neglect is forcing many people in the province to question their support for the ruling party," the MMD.[25] The general feeling in the Northeastern province is that the MMD has abandoned them. It has failed to tar the road from Solwezi, the capital of the province, to Kabompo and Zambezi; it has failed to improve the condition of chiefs; and it has failed to alleviate the suffering of the people. Such conditions only add to the growing influence and campaigns of opposition parties.

In the Copperbelt, there was a major power struggle between MMD cadres and provincial minister Kangwea Nsuluka. The minister had suspended the Cadres for alleged antiparty activities. Following an impasse within the region, the cadres appealed to the National Executive Council (NEC) of the MMD, which granted an "amnesty" to the suspended party members. But Nsuluka refused to recognize or acknowledge the amnesty granted by the NEC and this deepened the crisis to include the NEC, the provincial minister, and the cadres.[26] When four leaders of the party attended a meeting addressed by Nsuluka at Chingola Civil Centre, the minister had the police throw them out of the

179

meeting, insisting that they were still on suspension.[27] Intervention by MMD Disciplinary Committee chairman Elias Chipimo, Legal Committee chairman Ludwig Sondashi, and elections chairman Sikota Wina failed to sway Nsuluka, and Chipimo was forced to refer the matter to the MMD National Executive Committee.[28] The important point in this case is the limited control which Chiluba and the MMD NEC had over provincial ministers like Nsukula. Even when Chiluba directly cautioned Nsuluka against destroying the party in the "sensitive" Copperbelt Province, the minister remained adamant.[29] This could in the future be very dangerous if such powerful and stubborn ministers were to switch their loyalties to the opposition. More importantly, such inability to discipline MMD members swiftly and decisively, demoralizes the rank and file of the party which begin to see the administrative—particularly disciplinary—structures of the party as weak and ineffective. This might just force them to seek protection from patrons outside the official structures of the party.

In the Southern Province, there was a general feeling of neglect and marginalization by the MMD. According to a former defense minister who is now MMD MP for Siavonga and chairman for the Southern Province, Frederick Hapunda, "it is amazing how we have been neglected. There is so much corruption in the government that it is capable of discrediting the party if not checked. In the Southern Province, we are the back bone of the party, we gave it our total support, but pro-UNIP regions are enjoying the benefits of our sacrifices."[30] In the 1991 general elections, the MMD won in all of the 19 constituencies of the Southern Province. The number of votes received by Chiluba in the province was the highest in Zambia. In the 1992 local government elections, the MMD won 97 percent of the local government seats. It was also a record performance compared to other provinces. In spite of these indicators of support, the MMD chairman for the province is of the view that:

> It is...disheartening that national leaders have waged
> a war of attrition against the party leadership in the
> province for the simple reason of trying to hide their
> evil actions elsewhere. For unknown reasons more
> regard is shown by the national leadership for people
> from areas where the MMD is generally doing badly.
> People from Southern Province have been sidelined
> in appointments to government, parastatal, civil ser-
> vice or diplomatic service in comparison to those
> from other provinces. It is unacceptable that a
> province with a history of loyalty continues to be
> ignored, insulted and marginalised in the Third
> Republic as was the case in the Second Republic.[31]

Hapunda supports his claims by pointing out that of the 30 opposition political parties that had emerged by mid-1993 to challenge the MMD in Zambia, none had taken a firm root in the Southern Province, where the "people are totally in support of Chiluba." Rather than be rewarded with ameni-ties and opportunities, Hapunda argues, "the people of the Southern Province are forgotten people, left without jobs, loans, security nor any definite means of a decent life. They are organizing the party (MMD) without vehicles, without bicycles, money, nor stationery—virtually nothing."[32] Constant attacks on the leadership in the Southern Province by prominent MMD leaders like Labour Minister Michael Sata and attacks against a Southern Province cultural orga-nization, *The Bantu Botatwe Ngoma Yamaanu Cultural Association*, is also seen as an attempt to undermine the need for cultural unity and social expression in the Province. To this extent, "the people of the Southern Province feel somewhat unprotected and unwanted by the party and this will force the province to defend itself and its rights in the most appropriate manner."[33]

As a follow-up to this promise to defend itself, leaders in the Southern Province started joining issue with MMD national leaders. They took out paid advertisements in the papers to articulate responses to what they perceived as attacks against the province and to inform other Zambians of conditions of neglect and marginalization. More importantly, they passed resolutions at the Monze Consultative Meeting of December 12, 1992 calling for an immediate MMD national convention. They drew attention to the fact that a mid-term national convention was actually provided for in the party's constitution "to allow members to assess themselves and the party." The leaders of the province were convinced that in spite of the good work of the MMD, issues of credibility were becoming rather more critical. They highlighted issues of abuse of power and office, corruption, drug trafficking, allegations against ministers which gives the impression that the government itself was involved in drug trafficking, hence "its tolerance of the scourge." The Southern Province MMD then went ahead to set up its own commission of inquiry to investigate the drug-trafficking allegations. Finally, the MMD leadership in the province expressed its opposition to "the current price of maize, withdrawal of subsidy on free dipping...the high cost of farm inputs" which were important since it is an agricultural province. It felt that it was necessary to review the performance of the Social Action Programme (SAP) which "had brought a lot of hardships on the people" and encouraged virulent attacks directed against the MMD. For the Southern Province MMD, these attacks could have "been softened had people been seeing some tangible results on potholes, grading of feeder roads, medicines in hospitals, improved schools, improved public transport and several other areas."[34] In order words, as far as the province was concerned the MMD government was a disaster for the people and for Zambia. It is precisely this sort of disaffection and opposition that the Zero Option Plan wanted to capitalize upon and deepen to the point of political unrest.[35]

It must be noted, though, that some MMD leaders believe that the problem with the Southern Province party leaders is "political ambition." The controversial Michael Sata further inflamed the Southern Province politicians when he stated that "the people of Southern Province had suffered because of political prostitution and Political rejects who had joined the bandwagon in forming the MMD."[36] He argued that many MMD members did not understand the democracy which the MMD had brought to the nation and that "at the rate events were going, the party would be destroyed." In a dispute over the removal of former provincial chairman Mwami Maunga for not submitting an audited report, Derrick Chitala, MMD National Deputy Secretary, argued that "they removed Maunga because he is close to Chiluba. The problem with Hapunda and his colleagues is that they feel they should be ministers the way they were in UNIP. They are calling for conventions because they want one of them to be president."[37]

These divisions have tended to encourage opposition parties to challenge the MMD. In fact, many believe that even if the MMD survives till the 1996 general elections, with all the alignment and realignment of political forces in the provinces, with the scandals and allegations of corruption, with political stalwarts unable to work together, a fairly viable opposition could eat deeply into the territory of the MMD. More importantly, the conflicts and struggles show that the MMD suffered very seriously from indiscipline. Many ministers have no respect for the party's constitution or the NEC. As the *Times of Zambia* put it in an editorial:

> The situation now is positively unsettling....In the Southern Province, there is clear animosity and irreverence directed at some members of the National Executive Council (NEC). On the Copperbelt, NEC has been effectively under challenge and now in the Northern Province there are equally some unsavory developments. It is an unhealthy picture that is emerging. It could herald the break up of the MMD as we have known it with

dire consequences for the country. Democracy should not be misconstrued to mean lack of authority. Under the guise of democracy some MMD cadres are doing things that should never be done in a well organized party. There is no basis for instance for challenging NEC on party matters unless the organization is to have no leadership hierarchy. There is equally no basis for singling out ranking members of the NEC and dragging their names through the mud using very intemperate language at that. These actions undermine authority in the party and they are not compatible with democracy.[38]

The *Daily Mail* also noted that the squabbles within the MMD are "unproductive to the nation," that the squabbles have a lot to do with leadership styles, "mistrust and suspicion between the provincial leadership and those from other provinces."[39] It is clear to political observers that unless Chiluba and the MMD NEC become more decisive and take charge of the affairs of the movement, it will become embroiled in so many conflicts that it would be unable to govern or maintain law and order. By mid-1995, these divisions, coalitions, and realignment of political interests along ethnic and regional lines provided the basis for the emergence of very powerful, well-organized, and well-financed opposition parties led by former MMD ministers, founding members, stalwarts, and those who could not be disciplined by the party's administrative machinery. How much damage these new parties would be able to do to the MMD would become evident in elections in the future.

Corruption and Accountability Under the MMD

Under the Kaunda dispensation, corruption was a household word. Patron-client relations were used to lubricate the edges of corruption, and cultural norms were even used to rationalize the privatization of power and public resources. In its last days in office, the UNIP "spent billions of Kwacha during the election campaign, much of which cannot be accounted for because the UNIP shredded vital documents before surrendering power."[40] The MMD had campaigned on the promise to run a corruption-free, transparent, and accountable government that would be very sensitive to the aspirations of the Zambian people. Unfortunately, this has not happened. The promise to operate a "new political culture of openness and accountability" also has not materialized. While it has tried very hard, mainly due to pressures from donors and lenders, to run a sound budgeting and record keeping system, the MMD has had great difficulties with controlling the behavior of ministers and influential party members. The corruption within the MMD government is adjudged by many to be more pervasive, more sophisticated, and more damaging than what had obtained under Kaunda. All those I interviewed, who were not leading members of the party, readily subscribed to the widespread view that corruption was the greatest headache of the MMD. Why has this been the case?

The first explanation has to do with the accumulative *base* of the Zambian bourgeoisie, which is still largely in the structures and institutions of the state—which remains the largest employer, contractor, importer, and source of contracts in spite of privatization and commercialization programs. A weak and largely unproductive dominant class will always rely on the state for accumulation through corruption. The second reason for the continuing corruption is that all the leaders of the MMD, including Chiluba, had been leading members of UNIP and had been effectively schooled in UNIP traditions. Many had been retired, dismissed, or demoted for various acts of corruption and mismanagement. Many had joined the MMD only because avenues for accumulation through corruption in UNIP had been closed and they could not bear the idea of living without looting. When the MMD came to power, they grabbed political positions and continued to misappropriate funds as usual. The third reason is that Chiluba has remained rather indecisive and unable to translate his words of commitment and honesty into action. One reason for this, among others, is that the very persons involved in corruption and other crimes were equally his sponsors and founders of the MMD. Combined with his religiosity and unwillingness to disgrace such prominent and longstanding political figures, he gave the impression of a willingness to tolerate and accommodate such corrupt politicians.

The power struggles within the MMD (see above) were not helped by the ways in which ministers abused their offices and continued plundering public funds. Admittedly, not all ministers have been corrupt. The general impression around the country, however, was that the ministers were so rich and comfortable that they lacked the capability or credibility to fight corruption, strengthen the party, and take care of the needs of the people. The Minister for Foreign Affairs, who had been very prominent in Zambian politics since his early twenties, was constantly being accused of one moral misdeed or fraudulent act or the other, including association with "dubious foreign investors."[41] In an editorial on the state of the nation and the MMD government, the *National Mirror* noted that in its first eighteen months in power the MMD, which had "pledged to give Zambians a corruption-free, responsible government with a human face and one accountable to the electorate to whom it owes its mandate," had failed woefully to deliver on all fronts.[42] According to the paper, "within this short period, (the) MMD (has been) marked by inconsistencies. None are so glaring and serious as the ones involving national leaders in corruption and drug trafficking."[43] Furthermore, the paper argued, ministers who had been offered tax-free pay packages and all other incentives to put them above board were a contradiction to the declaration of Zambia as a Christian nation and the declared goals of the MMD to stamp corruption out of the political scene for good.

The most glaring and popular case of drug trafficking was made against Princess Nakatindi Wina, Minister for Community Development and Social Services and wife of Arthur Wina a founding member of the MMD.[44] The drug scandal also tainted Deputy Speaker of the Assembly Sikota Wina, who had actually been arrested on drug-trafficking charges at the Bombay airport in 1984. He was alleged to have fled India dressed in a Northern Sudanese *djellaba* (long white gown) with a forged Sudanese passport. The most prominent of Zambia's drug traffickers is probably foreign affairs minister Vernon Mwaanga. He, too, had been arrested on drug-trafficking charges at the Frankfurt airport in 1984. He avoided a lengthy jail term by invoking his diplomatic immunity. In 1994, his son Maliko was arrested in Lusaka along with two former military officers for being in possession of high-grade cocaine worth over £70,000. Ministers and parliamentarians like Derrick Chitala, Ronald Penza, Mathews Ngulube, and the former vice-president Levi Mwanawasa have used their political positions to grab acres of land belonging to the University of Zambia. Though Chiluba ordered the ministers to return the land to the university, most of it had already been resold in direct contravention of the 1985 Land Use Act. Several ministers have also used their position to acquire land in a conservation area east of Lusaka after compelling the ministry of lands to deregister the area. This brazen act has begun to affect the Chalimbana river, which is gradually drying up. World Bank director for Southern Africa Stephen Dening was forced to warn Chiluba in mid-1993 of the grave consequences of not addressing the corruption-and-drug issue. In fact, donors withheld about $1.3 billion in aid money to force Chiluba to clean up his administration and get rid of corrupt ministers. In spite of pressures from donors, lenders and the opposition parties, President Chiluba refused to fire the ministers, arguing that an "irresponsible press" was responsible for blowing up the issue of corruption and that

187

in any case they (especially Princess Nakatindi) had not been found guilty of any offense beyond rumors and general allegations. When officials of the Drug Enforcement Commission sought permission from the President to "record a warn and caution statement" from Princess Nakatindi, Chiluba refused to grant them the permission to do so. In mid-June 1993, Chiluba altered the drug laws and gave himself powers to fire the head of the drug commission. This weakened the Commission and eroded its autonomy.[45] Such slowness to action has only discredited the movement and government and opened an avenue for donors, lenders, and Western governments to tie foreign aid to viable policies against corruption and drug trafficking.

In December 1993, donors withheld $96 million of a pledged $860 million until clear policies on corruption and drug trafficking were put in place. As well, the appearance of nonchalance to increasing corruption in government has exposed Chiluba and his government to virulent attacks from ordinary Zambians and opposition forces.[46] Donatella Lorch has noted that "Today Zambians say their government has become as corrupt as the authoritarian state it replaced. Graft is endemic in institutions ranging from the police department to the soccer association, Zambia's biggest source of pride....apathy and disillusionment seem to have replaced the exultation that swept Zambia when Mr. Kaunda peacefully yielded to Mr. Chiluba in November 1991."[47] As well, there is a widespread view in Zambia that "Chiluba may have been compromised by his more sophisticated and moneyed backers, who funded and executed his campaign....he has been unable to control them because he lacks the political refinement of the likes of Mwaanga and Wina, whose political history goes back at least 30 years. Most of Chiluba's ministers are successful businessmen, some of them tycoons by world standards. Chiluba, on the other hand, was a credit officer until 1991."[48] In some respects therefore, it was a case of making a government impotent by an unseen "shadow government" which dictated the policies of state. These powerful business interests which had funded Chiluba's campaign had no interest in altering the distinctively dependent and commercially-based Zambian economy, and they had no interest in using the new enthusiasm for democracy to sponsor a viable national project.

The opposition has capitalized on this development to expand its own credibility and weaken the MMD as a party and a government. In their campaigns against the MMD they have publicized scandals like the building of houses at Chilenje for government ministers and government businesses that benefitted from Japanese grants to upgrade their capital stock. There was also the K28 million maize deal which involved Gibson Nkausu and Gilbert Mululu, deputy ministers for agriculture, food and fisheries, and for communications and transport, respectively. As well, finance minister Ronald Penza had been accused of several financial irregularities involving the use of his office to benefit his private businesses. These and many more scandals encouraged the opposition to challenge the MMD directly and to argue that it no longer had the mandate or moral authority to rule the nation. For instance, Davis Mwaba, the leader of the United Patriotic Party (UPP), argued that "No one should remain in doubt anymore. The MMD government is not taking this loved country of ours anywhere. If not, then only backwards. The MMD government has drug barons holding some of the highest offices in the land and making every Zambian arriving at any outside airport a subject of suspicion...and Chiluba pretends not to know."[49] He went on to call on the Chiluba government to resign and seek a fresh mandate from Zambians. In January 1994, Vernon Mwaanga, a long standing top-notcher of UNIP, the country's foreign minister for decades (save for brief periods), resigned from the government in order to facilitate investigations of drug trafficking. As Lorch has noted,

Mwaanga may be regarded as a charismatic politician and diplomat, but "to diplomats and opposition leaders, he is one of Zambia's most powerful drug traffickers and a symbol of the corruption that threatens to thwart the country's transformation to a stable democracy."[50] With Mwaanga's resignation, the number of ministers who have resigned from office in the 27 months of the MMD government on charges of corruption and mismanagement nounted to seven. Seven others have been dismissed on similar charges. The minister for legal affairs, Roger Chongwe resigned in order to protest continuing corruption in government as well as over policy differences with Chiluba. The vice-president, Levi Mwanawasa and the new minister for legal affairs, Ludwig Sondashi, resigned in July 1994 for similar reasons. When such credible and very important politicians desert a government citing corruption, one cannot ignore the implications for the legitimacy of such a government. Though the MMD-dominated assembly succeeded in finally passing the Ethics Bill in August 1994, there is no doubt that the Chiluba administration will find it almost impossible to shake off the general perception in the country that it is as corrupt as the Kaunda government, if not more so!

A Crisis of Performance and Popular Challenges to MMD Power

Though the MMD had received substantial support from the working class, and Chiluba himself had emerged from their ranks, the trade unions were not patient with the MMD. Perhaps this was a result of poor education and mobilization programs or the result of the excessive personalization of the political campaigns which blamed Kaunda and UNIP for all the country's predicaments. Within a couple of years, salary matters had generated severe contradictions and conflicts between the state and the trade union movement. As Melinda Ham has noted,

...there is a growing sense of betrayal among the Zambian people that the MMD has failed to deliver on its promises. The new government has not improved the quality of voters' lives. Although liberalization of prices and imports has put more goods on the shelves, people have less money to buy them. Because of spiralling inflation, the majority are worse off now than under Kaunda. Workers have fought back, staging over 50 strikes in the last eight months (of 1992) to demand a living wage.[51]

A trade union leader interviewed in Lusaka told me that "if Chiluba thinks that he can joke with us because he was a former trade union leader, he should think twice. Note my words, he is a *former* trade union leader. Now he is a president, a part, in fact, head of the government. We are ready to fight him and the politicians to a standstill. So far, I cannot see any evidence that they have some respect for workers." Similar angry words were uttered by hundreds of workers—across gender and ethnic groups—whom I interviewed in Zambia. At the University of Zambia, all the students I interviewed were very bitter at the inability of the MMD to "show respect for workers," and to "cultivate a special relationship with the masses." It was the opinion of many students that the MMD has been hijacked by "imperialist agents" and "local capitalists." Most of the women were particularly bitter because the government "has not put our special circumstances into consideration. They treat us just like *things* just like the former government did. We have no rights and our children suffer a lot."[52]

In May 1993 public servants in Kitwe went on strike to "force the government to resume stalled negotiations for salary increases."[53] The Civil Servants Union of Zambia (CSUZ), the Zambia National Union of Teachers (ZNUT), the Zambia United Local Authorities Workers Union (ZULAWU), and the National Union of Public Service Workers (NUPSW) all took part in the strike against the government. In early June 1993, teachers in Kitwe embarked on a strike action to back up their demands for better wages. Within twenty-four hours, the strike had spread to "almost all government departments across the country, including Lusaka."[54] Appeals from union leaders like ZNUT chairman Mwembe Sichone and government officials, as well as promises to resolve the problems through negotiations, failed to convince the workers to return to work.[55] As a worker in Lusaka put it, "we were fed up with promises. We suffered for twenty eight years listening to speeches. Now the MMD has come again with speeches. What is going on here? Whom are they fooling?"[56] The strike was joined by workers in Kabwe, Mkushi, Namwala, Isoka, Solwezi, and Kasama. The CSUZ accused the government of being "evasive" on the demands made by the workers and complained of political interference from the Ministry of Labour and Social Security, which tried to manipulate the union leaders in order to end the strike.[57]

The anger of the workers, especially the women, with the MMD must be put in proper context in order to understand why the elasticity of hope and pain has become so weak— in fact, inelastic. For the peasants, many have simply withdrawn from the market or withdrawn into their rural traditions of self-help and self-sufficiency. Many smuggle their products across the borders to neighboring countries where prices are better and the foreign currency much stronger than the Kwacha. Like the workers, they have learned to rely more on very ingenuous coping mechanisms in the face of "abandonment" by the state and increasing hardships. The bureaucrats simply privatized their positions and were spending more time on private business deals than on government assignments. These constituencies all relied on the MMD to improve their lives "as soon as it became the government." The room for understanding, tolerance, and accommodation was therefore very slim.

The quality of life in Zambia before and since the election

has been nothing to write home about. In 1993 the United Nations Development Programme (UNDP) showed that Zambia experienced a major drop of about 30 points in its Human Development Index. Of the 173 countries listed in the Index, Zambia was ranked at number 130. This was due largely to increasing deterioration in the quality of life and the total failure to rehabilitate social infrastructure in the country.[58] A poorly implemented structural adjustment program had imposed unprecedented hardship on the people. The policies of commercialization and privatization in the context of a run-away inflation and massive retrenchment of workers meant an inability to meet the basic needs of the people. For a nation which had inherited $2 billion in reserves at political independence, the current conditions of decay, general deterioration, hunger, disease, poverty, violence, insecurity, uncertainty, and hopelessness among nonbourgeois forces is rather shocking. There is a consensus among Zambians and scholars that the UNIP government, in spite of suffocating propaganda, paid no serious "attention to poverty issues or to the equitable distribution of the burden of adjustment....By the end of its tenure, the UNIP regime was in such poor standing that no economic policy it implemented could inspire public confidence."[59] The MMD was therefore quite aware of this failing and of the challenge it posed to the task of democratic consolidation in post-UNIP Zambia.

Zambia has one of the highest case loads of Acquired Immune Deficiency Syndrome (AIDS) in the Southern Africa region.[60] Birgitta Rantakari, wife of the Finnish Ambassador to Zambia, referring to a survey by Zambian NGOs, revealed that "ninety per cent of prostitutes in Zambia are HIV positive."[61] The AIDS crisis is so severe that the government constantly takes out paid advertisements in local newspapers with President Chiluba's photograph warning the people that "We are heading Towards a Zambia with no people" and inviting the younger generation to join in the fight against the deadly disease.[62] The Chiluba government, in another advertisement carrying the president's picture, announced that it had increased funds for the fight against AIDS from K50 million in 1992 to K224.5 million in 1993. Prostitution increased with increasing poverty and increasing desperation within families. Violent crimes and armed robbery also experienced dramatic increases. Several members of parliament had their cars snatched in Lusaka and it became very unsafe to move around in what was once a very peaceful city.[63] The police were so ill-equipped that it became a point of sour jokes in the major cities. In fact, the situation with the police was so bad that it was only partially rescued from its terrible state when it received a donation of "very advanced BMW motorbikes, some bicycles, VW Golf cars and ...huge Man trucks."[64] Even these did not help the ability to fight crime and maintain law and order.[65] As well, people could no longer afford the high cost of health care, and self-medication and quack doctors came to dominate the health-delivery system. In Mwinilunga, for example, the Zambia Enrolled Nurses Association (ZENA) discovered that "47 per cent of all the children in the area were stunted, not growing, because of poor diet and unhygienic conditions...43 per cent of the children were underweight due to undernourishment and poor living conditions."[66] Most hospitals lacked doctors, while facilities for basic health-care delivery and nurses were in short supply. Part of the problem was poor funding from the government to hospitals which essentially catered to the poor, who could not be relied upon as a source of capital generation. According to Inonge Mbikusita-Lewanika, member of parliament for Senanga, by mid-1993 the government had "not released K40million for" the Senanga District Hospital and this had "greatly hampered" operations at the hospital.[67]

In most rural communities people still lived in filth without basic amenities. Yet, the MMD had received substantial support from the rural areas in the 1991 elections. Many rural dwellers complained that the parliamentarians have behaved just like UNIP politicians, abandoning the rural areas and taking refuge in the comforts of the city. Schools lack basic facilities and libraries are empty. Schools at Chitibuka, Mukumbo, and Lumpuma, for instance, were so lacking in facilities that children "squatted on the floor while the institutions did not have trained teachers. Trained teachers had deserted the area because of the dilapidated structures and poor facilities."[68] Unfortunately, in spite of the terrible state of infrastructures and services, the central government has consistently underfunded the provinces. For instance, by the middle of 1993, only 17 percent of funds requested by Southern Province for social sector rehabilitation had been released by the government. This made it impossible to rehabilitate deteriorating institutions and roads and to provide much needed services.[69] The conditions at the University of Zambia were no different. Professors were having a hard time surviving on the meager incomes they earned, and the prospect of attending conferences—even in South Africa or Botswana—was completely out of the question. The library was outdated and offices looked rather desolate with poor facilities. The urban centers were in an equally terrible state, as unemployment and inflation erased whatever minor gains Zambians had reaped from the democratization process. Bus shelters were converted into 'homes' by the homeless, genuine and "emergency" beggars could be seen all over the city of Lusaka, and able-bodied youths could be seen roaming the streets.[70] The Central Statistics Office (CSO) announced recently that "the number of children forced to work at least part-time has increased to 2.7 million and could reach three million by the end of the year (1995)." The government has also admitted that 72 percent of Zambians live in poverty, and while in 1994 $1.2 million was allocated to the government's Social Safety Net program to assist the vulnerable, this was reduced to a mere $600,000 in 1995. In a country which is the most urbanized in sub-Saharan Africa, where the 8.5

million population is projected to hit 13 million by 2010, inability to design and implement effective programs to contain the frustrations of the poor will have far-reaching implications for political stability and the overall quality of life.

For many in the villages and cities, their hopes are now reposed in the activities of the NGOs and Voluntary Development Organizations (VDOs). In Zambia there are 130 indigenous and international NGOs and about 1,093 registered cooperatives. There are also hundreds of community and self-help organizations that are not registered but are effectively organized around ethnic, clan, class, gender, religious, and other interests. Where the state seems to have failed, the NGOs seem to be working hard to reconstruct roads, build pit latrines, teach basic skills to women, help with agricultural systems, and give hope to the poor. Urban Self-Help Push, for instance, though with support from the government and foreign donors, has succeeded in funding programs which have provided employment for over 4,000 people, mostly women.[71] In spite of a heavy dependence on foreign funding which at times compels them to alter their priorities, and the usual problems of low administrative and technical capacities, local NGOs have been effective at the community levels and have developed a strong network with the poor. The net effect is the steady erosion of state hegemony and credibility and the strengthening of grassroots consciousness which would strengthen civil society and provide a basis for challenging the state. Of course, a widening of the gap between the state and the poor would easily provide room for the opposition to strengthen itself and directly erode possibilities for consolidating democracy in Zambia.

Religion and Economic Recovery in MMD Zambia: The Merger of Church and State

While Chiluba's commitment to market reforms and liberal democracy is not in doubt, and though the party has clearly stated these positions in its manifesto, the influence of Chiluba's "born again" Christian convictions seems to be affecting national morale and the government's ability to respond to practical issues. Not only is the nation's television dominated by local and imported religious programs, but the country seems to have been invaded by all sorts of televangelists and religious preachers all claiming to cure one ailment or the other and capitalizing on the president's avowed belief in Christ. When Zambia had a drought in 1991–92, it was attributed to God, who supposedly was punishing the people for turning away from him. When the drought ended and the rains came, President Chiluba organized a national thanksgiving service to thank God for the rains. He personally led the nation in offering prayers to God. At that gathering in the Holy Cross Cathedral in Lusaka, a priest had the boldness to declare in the hearing of the president and Zambians that Christians now had the power to determine the rise and fall of the Zambian nation. Chiluba even attributed "the peaceful transition to multi-party politics in 1991" to the commitment of Zambians to prayer. In his words, "the MMD was born out of prayer because the entire nation had prayed hard for peace when power was changing hands."[72] When American evangelist Reverend Ernest Angley visited Zambia on Chiluba's invitation in June of 1993, he was given a red carpet reception, met by Chiluba who personally attended his rally at the stadium. Though Angley had promised to cure the sick, poor, deaf, lame, and dumb, the Zambia Council for the Handicapped and several Catholic and Protestant priests dismissed his visit as "well orchestrated religious entertainment" which should be taken "with a grain of salt."[73] The Zambia Council for the Handicapped actually "warned members against attending sessions being organized by the visiting American evangelist...they would just be disgracing themselves and their disabilities."[74]

The reality is that in today's Zambia there is really no distinction between the secular and the religious, and many prominent politicians, party loyalists, and business persons have become "overnight Christians" and "born again" Christians in order to get close to the government. Perhaps the greatest challenge to the notion of Zambia as a Christian nation is in the deepening economic and social crises which continue to make day-to-day living a herculean task. As well, given the corruption within the government pointed out above, it has been very difficult to convince enlightened Zambians that the government and the MMD are serious about the new religious outlook imposed on the country.[75] As Pastor Nevers Mumba of Victory Ministries in Kitwe has noted,

> Zambia has failed to live up to the proclamation of being a Christian nation because of corruption among leaders and lack of an agenda by the church to fulfil the obligation...leaders in government lack a moral code. They are into prostitution and preoccupied with amassing wealth. They are an embarrassment to the nation."[76]

Without doubt, the vast majority of MMD members have no idea of the implications of declaring Zambia to be a Christian nation. In their views and politics, they wish to run the country as a secular state with religion being a private affair. This is not how President Chiluba sees it since he has elevated religion to the prime position on the national agenda. His open bias towards the Christian faith has given some overzealous members of the MMD and Christian community the courage to make disparaging remarks about other faiths and religions.[77] Students of the Theology Association of Zambia (TAZ) accused Christians of being responsible for "the rising tension with Moslems in the country." According to Brighton Hacitapika, TAZ chairman, ever since the declaration of Zambia as a Christian nation by President Chiluba in 1991, Christian fanaticism had crept in, in great quantity and could be blamed for the tension.[78] Some adherents of the less popular religions in Zambia have urged the government to learn from the predicaments of countries like Nigeria and the Sudan, where religious conflicts have claimed thousands of lives, wasted resources, taken the national question to unprecedented heights, and almost permanently divided the people.

Unfortunately, Chiluba's religiosity has not helped him one bit in increasing his credibility or that of his government, which continues to be plagued by infighting and unbridled corruption. As Jowie Mwiinga has noted,

> Chiluba, a self-styled "born again" christian, meanwhile, continued to gloss over the excesses of his ministers. He turned a blind eye to shocking social transgressions of senior government officials. Several ministers were implicated in messy adulterous affairs last year, while several others married second wives in spite of the law. "Judge not," the president said, when challenged to arrest immorality in his cabinet, "and thou shalt not be judged."[79]

Such slick biblical responses mean little or nothing to workers who have been laid off without compensation or to graduates and school dropouts who roam the streets and bars idling away their time, drinking countless bottles of *Mosi* to escape the realities of a very challenging and uncertain future. Many who thought that his religious piety would "serve to introduce a spirituality, morality and some righteousness into government" and make "our leaders realise that they owe their positions to the people"[80] have become disappointed, as they now feel that "Chiluba is a fake Christian or born again. All he is doing is hiding behind religion to do nothing. Will God cover the pot holes, bring inflation down, or take care of growing problems of crime and prostitution?"[81] Yet, the problems of Zambia, even as the MMD admits, were created, nurtured, and reproduced by the history of the country, the character of the economy and the global market, and twenty-seven years of misrule and corruption run by the UNIP government of Kaunda.

Chiluba's responses to these problems have included: calling for honesty, prayers, and belief in God; calling on donors to honor pledges made to the government in 1991 and 1992 following the victory of the MMD; calling on the World Bank and the IMF to take charge of specific projects, to provide additional foreign exchange, and to move rapidly on the commercialization and privatization agenda of the MMD government. Like Kenneth Kaunda, he has also relied on cabinet reshuffles and the sacking of ministers, at times without notice (see above). Stan Kristafor and Ephraim Chibwe were sacked as ministers for their alleged racism and irregular financial activities, though no comprehensive and clear explanations were provided for these "irregular" dealings. Four other ministers including Arthur Wina, holder of MMD Membership card No. 0001, were sacked in April 1993 with no clear explanations, though Wina and Humphrey Mulemba had become very disillusioned with the party and were known to have been nursing ideas about forming an opposition party at that time. In fact, Wina believes that "all the democratic principles" for which the MMD stood had evaporated with the capture of state power, that Chiluba was very interested in perpetuating his political life and careers, and some of the sackings were attempts to weed out from the party potential challengers to his power. Accusing Chiluba of being one of the major causes of the MMD's loss of direction and for derailing the party with "selfish motives," Wina contended that "there are a lot of rotten eggs in our government, and those are the ones who should go. There have been reports relating to government contracts being awarded to friends by ministers, of ministers trafficking in drugs...of rescuing bankrupt banks through influence...."[82]

In mid-1993, finance minister Emmanuel Kasonde was

sacked (at a press conference held by Chiluba) for flouting "financial regulations and for alleged dubious maize imports."[83] Following the resignation of Vernon Mwaanga, Nakatindi Wina, and deputy speaker of the assembly Sikatu Wina, who all were alleged to be deeply involved in drug trafficking in early 1994 (see above), pressures were mounted on Chiluba by donors and the private media to resign or, at the very least, to sack his entire cabinet. Chiluba, who had traditionally defended all his ministers, claiming that they were all clean, refused to sack the entire cabinet and firmly ruled out possibilities of resignation. Though minister for development cooperation Dean Mungomba and minister for health Boniface Kawimbe publicly confirmed that members of the government were involved in drug trafficking, and finance minister Ronald Penza had promised the donor Consultative Group on Zambia that the MMD government was going to take drastic measures to cure the smear of drug trafficking, Chiluba's responses were cosmetic. First, he sacked the two ministers who had the courage to speak out about corruption and drug trafficking in the government. Next he censored (and later sacked) the finance minister for admitting to the donors that such a problem existed within the government. Police inspector-general Dariuis Kalebo was sacked for not curbing the increasing crime wave in the country even when it was clear that the police were badly trained and poorly equipped and that morale was low in the force. More importantly, the rising crime wave was directly related to joblessness, retrenchment of workers without benefits or safety nets to tide them over the hard times, and the deteriorating conditions of living. Sacking the police chief was therefore merely diversionary and a superficial response to the crime problem. Chiluba then moved some of his ministers around, e.g. moving Newstead Zimba to Home Affairs. Zambians and donors were shocked that "none of the ministers linked to corruption by the investigating wings of the government were sacked...."[84] Such changes in government without any explanations sent mixed signals to donors and lenders as well as investors that something was seriously wrong within the government. This is the more so when the reshuffling does not remove the ministers who are known to be inefficient, corrupt, and simply incompetent. Reshuffling "becomes a mechanism for diverting attention from the real issue, protecting favorites in power, and consolidating the position of the president. In the final analysis it weakens the party and Zambians suffer."[85] His recent action seems to have convinced more Zambians that Chiluba is "too weak of character and too limited in exposure to effectively run a country,"[86] and has encouraged opposition elements, trade unions, students, donors, the Church, and pressure groups to argue that Chiluba was firmly on the side of crime and corruption: "I could not believe what the president did. It is now clear to me that I have wasted my time supporting Chiluba and the MMD. Our country is going down the drains. The president is scared of the drug dealers. He has lost control. He punishes those who do not steal and actually rewards those who steal. I will not be surprised if somewhere down the road, we find that his election money came from these criminals and barons. God save Zambia."[87] Such feelings, which are widespread, do not augur well for Chiluba, the MMD, and democracy in Zambia. Though some younger MMD politicians like Samuel Miyanda would argue that "it takes time to set things right" and that "Chiluba is doing his very best, Zambia is a tough country to govern," Jowie Mwiinga has noted that "[i]ncreasingly, Zambians are beginning to feel they have been short-changed by the Chiluba establishment. Most are now beginning to regard the Kaunda years with nostalgia."[88]

Dealing with Donors in a Condition of Weakness

One challenge which the MMD faced even before it came to power was how to deal with the West, with international institutions like the IMF and World Bank, with South Africa, and with creditors. The South African issue was quickly resolved. The decision was to reopen relations at a formal level even before the democratic elections which saw the ascendancy of Mandela and the African National Congress (ANC). Zambia was heavily dependent on South Africa anyway and most shop shelves in Lusaka are filled with goods imported from South Africa even in the days of apartheid. The decision then to formalize relations with South Africa was made easier by the ongoing negotiations between the apartheid state and the ANC, the formal termination of apartheid, and the release of Mandela. But it has not been quite as easy and straightforward dealing with the West, particularly the World Bank. For a country that owes so much money and had come to rely on foreign aid and other forms of support to survive, it lacked the autonomy or capacity to chart an autonomous path.

Zambia is so poor that the extent of its dependence on the West is astonishing. Several government vehicles show that they were donated by one Scandinavian country or some international agency or the other. The government is unable to rehabilitate its roads. Because of the poor state of roads, there is the joke that if you saw anyone driving straight on Zambian roads, that person was probably (or certainly) drunk. The construction of the Kapiri-Chingola road was funded by the Danish Development Agency at a cost of 190 million Kroners. The Kabwe-Lusaka road is being funded by the European Community at a cost of $15 million. The USAID is spending $18 million to construct the Kajima road. The roads from Munali hills to Mazabuka are being funded by the Norwegian Agency for Development at a cost of K136 million.[89] Issues of electricity supply, water purification, pest control and the like are all dependent on foreign funding. This is why UNIP members continued to contend that the MMD was a creation of the West, supported by the West, to do the bidding of the West. Western diplomats are given extensive coverage on national television and there are practically no boundaries on issues they can comment on. They speak with such authority that any observer would mistake them for ministers in the Chiluba cabinet. For instance, while teachers were on strike over wage increases, the IMF representative Mr. John Hill at a lecture at the University of Zambia announced that "government will not increase teachers salaries by the percentage they are demanding or retrench them because of limited funding, most of which was donor supplied."[90] He announced that the government of Zambia could not "afford to increase teachers salary by more than 30 per cent," as against the 144 percent the teachers were asking for. Noting that Zambia was heavily dependent on foreign funding which the donor countries raised from taxes in the West, he then threatened that "Zambia risked being cut-off should the donors suspect that the money was being misapplied." Mr. Hill then informed Zambians that the country's "civil service was too large, inefficient and its production capacity too low."[91] Of course no Western government would tolerate such a discussion of its public policies by a representative of a foreign agency who was not even a national. But with Zambia's near total dependence on the IMF and World Bank, and with leaders who do not believe in "rocking the boat," there was little or nothing it could do.

Another example which elicited a response from a minister was when the World Bank representative Isaac Moreithi, at a seminar presentation, stated that Zambia's defense expenditures "had been higher than in most sub-Saharan African countries except those countries involved in internal or external military conflicts for the period between 1985–90...the government on average spent at least 100 per cent more on the military than on education and 2900 per cent more than on transport, power and energy."[92] These and other statements so enraged minister for defence Ben Mwila that he threatened to deport the World Bank representative because the statements "were not only alarmist but suspicious in its origin because it bordered on infringing the nation's sovereignty and defence and security."[93] While the statements were valid and did demonstrate the continuation of misplaced priorities, even under the MMD, it is debatable that it was the duty of the World Bank to make such pronouncements. After all, though the Cold War has ended, the United States' defence budget is still at an all time high at $280 billion. Add to this figure another $30 billion for the CIA and FBI, and we get a figure just as high as the Cold War era. Yet, no African ambassador or diplomat is commenting on this at press conferences in Washington, D.C. And the U.S, of course, is the world's largest debtor, owing some $4.5 trillion! Without doubt, in the coming decades, Zambia and the MMD government, if it remains in power, will have to find ways of winning back its independence from such external bodies as the IMF and World Bank. This will be no easy task unless the economy improves sufficiently to make Zambia less dependent on foreign aid, creditors, advisers, and other forms of support.

Expanding the Political Terrain: The Emergence of Opposition Forces

The existence of a credible opposition is one of the hallmarks of a working democracy. In fact, a good opposition can not only keep the government on its toes but also ensure that accountability, respect for the constitution, and other possible vices are checked. Unfortunately, African politics has tended to see the role of an opposition as that of an unrepentant enemy of the incumbent government. This is why whenever the control of state power changes, the former government also becomes the enemy to the new government. As we have indicated earlier, the bitterness in which politicians give up power is directly related to the role which power plays in private accumulation and the survival of those who are not in power, or linked to those in power. Very few African politicians leave office without becoming rich, and most of the wealthy persons in the continent made their "seed" monies through direct and/or indirect linkages to the state and its resources. The MMD came to power as the only credible challenge to UNIP. It won a landslide victory and expectations were high. Promises were legion. It promised everything and almost all Zambians believed that, as the MMD's campaign slogan puts it, "the Hour Has Come."

However, since 1991, over 34 opposition parties have emerged in Zambia. More than half of these parties can be dismissed as nuisance organizations, designed to advance the interests of a handful of disgruntled politicians, regional patrons, and clan/ethnic lords, and those who have been marginalized from current power and accumulation processes. Then there are a few that are quite serious in their challenge to the MMD. In the context of factionalization and fractionalization within the MMD, it is possible to see how they can do a lot of damage to the ruling party. Many Zambians, frustrated at the inability of the MMD to demonstrate how really different it is from Kaunda's UNIP, have flocked to the opposition. Of course, the existence of the opposition and their ability to operate openly is evidence of a major change in the politics of Zambia. Under Kaunda, that was not possible. The open operations of the numerous parties certainly attests to a growing and vibrant civil society. Yet, it could just as well be evidence of continuing fragmentation of civil society, with possibilities for degenerating into anarchy if not adequately managed.

Rumors about the formation of a stronger, better-organized, and more democratic party which would involve all the political heavyweights in Zambia and which would shatter the future of the MMD started making the rounds immediately after the October 1991 elections. The first breakaway faction from the MMD was the Caucus for National Unity (CNU), which was led by Muyoba Macwani and which first emerged on the political landscape in February 1992. Though initially a dissident group within the MMD, it officially broke with the ruling party on July 25, 1995, a few days after one of its founders, Akashanbakwa Mbikusita Lewanika, quit the government in protest against the failure of the parliament to investigate growing corruption in the system. The CNU could not get a single cabinet minister to join it in its effort to split the MMD. The CNU also failed to recruit any prominent political figure or member of parliament. Though it accused the MMD of corruption, of nepotism, and of being undemocratic, it failed to attract any serious attention from Zambians. The CNU actually believed that it could defeat the MMD in the 1996 election, as it declared that it would form the government following such an exercise. One of its cofounders, Baldwin Munakumabu Nkumbula, had actually sued the government for what he described as a poor handling of a cholera outbreak in late 1992. It was Nkumbula's view that Chiluba was "too weak" to implement radical change in the country. Within a short time the CNU broke into two factions. The other faction was led by Patrick Katyoka, and it called itself the Congress for National Unity (CNU). To be sure, these former MMD members must have felt dissatisfied with the party for failing to meet their personal expectations or they genuinely believed that the MMD was not what they had anticipated. It did show that there were cracks within the MMD. This early challenge to the MMD did not augur well, as the rank-and-file of the party could not comprehend the basis of the quarrels and factionalization within the new party and government. While it did allow for disgruntled politicians to quit the MMD, it also took away very powerful leaders who had the capacity to give the MMD not only a solid foundation, but also a national image.

Next came the Democratic National Congress (DNC), led by former UNIP stalwart Enos Haimbe, which tried to present itself as the replica of Harry Nkumbula's African National Congress. When the Minister for Labour and Social Welfare Michael Sata announced that some core leaders of the MMD, including some NEC members, were forming a political party of their own, fears were once again awakened as to the future of the MMD. The DNC quickly distanced itself from MMD members of parliament and ministers. This declaration raised debates as to the existence of a so-called *Third Force* within the MMD. The *Third Force* was supposed to be a major movement within the MMD which drew its support from Southern, Western, Northwestern, and Central Provinces. Its goal was to recruit major and influential MPs and ministers. Initially, the party was to be announced on May 1, 1993, but the tragedy of the Zambian soccer squad allegedly put the plan on hold. It was then rescheduled to announce its break away from the MMD at the national convention. Michael Sata, who continued to hammer on this issue, went as far as pointing an accusing finger at the *Banti Botatwe* as an organization designed to provide the platform for the new party. With such statements Sata was accusing the MMD leadership in the Southern Province of being behind the move (Baldwin Nkumbula is from the Southern province). The *Third Force,* it was believed, advocated a federal structure governed by regions rather than the current unitary arrangement. This would guarantee some autonomy for the provinces and give the provinces more control over their resources.

Though over 34 opposition parties have emerged in Zambia thus far, one of the most credible of these is perhaps the National Party (NP)—could this be the long-awaited, so-called *Third Force*? The NP was launched on August 16, 1993 and formally registered on September 10, 1993 with Inonge Mbikusita-Lewanika as its interim chairperson. As Melinda Ham rightly notes, "Its formation marks the most serious division in the ruling Movement for Multiparty Democracy (MMD) government since it was elected in October 1991."[94] The NP leader had been MMD member of parliament for Senanga in the Western Province. Eight other MPs, which included three former cabinet ministers and a deputy minister, joined Lewanika in deserting the MMD and pitching their camp against it. It is clear that the NP had overcome some of the limitations and disappointments which the CNU suffered from. It was not really surprising that some of the top MMD notchers who resigned to join the NP included Emmanuel Kasonde, who had been dismissed as finance minister and was embroiled in a battle with Kapapa over the provincial chairmanship of the party. Former minister for youth, sports and child development Baldwin Nkumbula and former minister for technical education and vocational training Akashambwata Mbikusita-Lewanika, both of whom had resigned as ministers in 1992 but remained within the MMD, also joined the NP. Humphrey Mulemba and Arthur Wina, former minsters for mines and for education, respectively, are also in the forefront of the NP. Former UNIP secretary-general, Kennedy Shepande also pitched camp with the NP.

The new NP leaders accused the MMD of lack of direction, subservience to foreign interests, nepotism, authoritarianism, and unbridled corruption. Akashambwata Lewanika argued that there was "a critical national crisis of leadership and governance in Zambia....The promises of our multiparty democracy have been grievously undermined by underhanded, dishonest, and alarmist politics."[95] The party was particularly angry at the MMD for not taking allegations of corruption and drug trafficking within the cabinet seriously. The NP has tried to present itself as a national party in response to criticisms from MMD officials describing it as an ethnic or regional party. It describes itself as a "receptive and listening" party, giving the impression that the MMD had become arrogant, aloof, and totally out of touch with the problems and people of Zambia. The leaders have a lot of past records to draw on: some of them had been founding members and officers of the MMD, and some had opposed the imposition of the state of emergency on the grounds that it violated the principles of democracy for which the MMD had fought. Two of the leaders had been the very first to resign from the MMD government in protest against the way the party was being run. Nkumbula and Kapwepwe also come from families with longstanding records of political activity in Zambia and the Southern Africa region. Many of the NP leaders are quite popular in the country and have a record of speaking their minds on burning national issues. Breaking new ground, and showing that it had vision and courage to challenge traditional political styles in Zambia, its chairperson was the first female party leader in the country.

Without doubt, the MMD would have to look inward and reconstitute its politics in such a way as not to be crushed by the opposition. Performance, sensitivity, and credibility are the key issues. Poor, hungry, disillusioned, alienated, and desperate people have no patience with long speeches, oratory, or promises. The situation becomes worse when they can see their "leaders" living in luxury while they feed the people with words. Though at the moment it would appear that "most of the opposition parties are disorganized and lack resources necessary for a viable role in national politics"[96] and that the MMD still has full control of the mainstream media (comprising two daily newspapers, a radio and television station), these would be insufficient to counter an organized opposition, especially in an environment in which the vast majority are becoming extremely disillusioned. A coalition of opposition political parties will do some damage to the MMD in any election. The creation of the Zambia Opposition Front (Zofro) on June 11, 1994, is evidence of this possibility. Zofro is an opposition coalition made up of the Labour Party (LP) led by Chipeza Mufune, the Independent Democratic Front (IDF) led by Mike Kaira (who also leads Zofro), the National Democratic Alliance (NDA) led by Yonam Phiri, the National Party for Democracy (NPD), and the Zambia Progressive Party (ZPP). There is no doubting the fact that the activities of these parties and the coalition will erode the influence and membership of the MMD unless it puts it house in order. There are other parties like the Democratic Party (DP) led by Emmanuel Mwamba (a wealthy businessman), the United Democratic Congress Party (UDCP) led by former prime minister Daniel Lisulo, and the National People's Salvation Party (NPSP) led by Lubwe Lambanya. As well, there are previously existing parties like the Movement for Democratic Process (MDP) led by Chama Chakomboka, and the Multi Racial Party (MRP) led by Aaron Mulenga. It would be interesting to see how the political realignments in the country work out in the 1990s and beyond.

Notes

1. "Zambia Still on Reform Course," *Times of Zambia* (June 2, 1993).
2. Ibid.
3. Evans Milimo, "State Waives Duty on Staple Food," *Financial Mail* (Lusaka) (May 11-17, 1993).
4. ———, "Battery Firm Cries for Loan," *Financial Mail* (Lusaka) (May 11-17, 1993).
5. "Firm 'Shocks' Minister," *Times of Zambia* (June 2, 1993).
6. See Dickson Kaminda, "18 Firms Shut," *Zambia Daily Mail* (May 15, 1993). According to Chrispin Mwenya, Secretary of the National Union of Commercial and Industrial Workers (NUCIW), textile and cloth workers were the hardest hit because "most people now prefer to buy from Salaula traders where quality clothes are affordable. Some of the companies affected in this closure are Zambia Fashions, Star Clothing, Town Country, Zenith Zambia Limited, Manhatta Factory, Partex Industries, Sparrow Garments, Rabin Garments, Anstal Industries, Texprint, Dolly Day Fashions and Factory and Zambia Textiles Limited.
7. See Joe Chilaizya, "Fraud Cover Up? Zimco Investigator Claims Powerful Figures Wanted to Silence Him," *Weekly Post* (Lusaka) (May 14-20, 1993.
8. Pauline Banda, "Bank Frauds Worry State, Says Penza," *Zambia Daily Mail* (June 2, 1993).

9. *Zambia Daily Mail*, "Editorial Comment" (June 2, 1993).
10. Melinda Ham, "Zambia: An Outspoken Opposition," *Africa Report* (November-December, 1993), p.33.
11. Jowie Mwiinga, "Chill for Chiluba," *Africa Report* (March-April, 1994).
12. Ibid.
13. "Economic Suicide?" *Zambia Daily Mail* (May 24, 1993).
14. Fackson Shamenda, President ZCTU Interview with *Search* (Ndola, Zambia) (December 1992).
15. Rob Wright, "Chiluba Sets Zambia on New Course," *Africa Recovery* (April 1992), p.4.
16. Interview Lusaka, Zambia, June 1993.
17. Frederick Chiluba, quoted in Rob Wright, "Chiluba Sets Zambia on New Course" (op. cit.), p.4.
18. See: "Fuel Price Up," *Times of Zambia* (May 23, 1993), Nigel Mulenga, "Fuel Pricing: Just What Went Wrong?" *Zambia Daily Mail* (May 24, 1993), and "Kitwe Commuters Prefer to Walk," *Zambia Daily Mail* (May 26, 1993).
19. Mutale Mwamba, "Maize Output Threatened," *Zambia Daily Mail* (May 26, 1993).
20. "CPA Warns Ova Price Hikes," *Times of Zambia* (May 26, 1993).
21. "Opposition Calls for Vital Subsidies," *Weekly Standard* (May 31-June 6, 1993). See also "Structural Adjustment: A Prescription for Poverty?" *The Weekly Post* (October 1-7, 1993). In this report the *Weekly Post* revealed that more than 15,000 Zambians had written to the IMF, the World Bank and the Minister for Finance on how the structural adjustment program was negatively affecting their lives. This was part of an international campaign mounted by Oxfam. The newspaper published some of the pathetic letters.
22. See Melinda Ham, "Luring Investment," *Africa Resort* (September-October 1992); Philemon Nyirenda, "High Interest Rates Kill Growth," *Times of Zambia* (May 22, 1993); and "How People are Killed By Economic Reforms," *The Weekly Post* (October 1-7, 1993). For a pro-government perspective on Zambia's reform program see Derrick Chitala, "How MMD is Now Curing Zambia's Economic Disease," *The Weekly Post* (October 1-7, 1993). Chitala is Deputy Minister Special Duties at State House

and National Deputy Secretary of the MMD.

23. Mutale Mwamba, "'Fighting' Kapapa in Row Over Vehicles," *Zambia Daily Mail* (June 2, 1993)

24. See Hastings Nyasulu and Pelekelo Liswaniso, "Miyanda Clarifies Leadership Rows: Kasonde's Still MMD Boss," *Zambia Daily Mail* (May 27, 1993) and "North MMD Splits into 2 Camps: Kapapa Vs Kasonde," *Times of Zambia* (May 25, 1993).

25. "Focus on North-Western Province," *The Weekly Post* (September 10-1, 1993).

26. See "Banned MMD Cadres Now Appeal," *Times of Zambia* (june 3, 1993).

27. See "Four MMD Officials Tossed Out of Meeting," *Times of Zambia* (May 15, 1993). The affected officials were Dr. Ladislus Kamata, Chairman, Mr. Imasiku Sasa, the Vice-Chairman, Mr. Emmanuel Simuwi the Secretary and Baron Kaunda, the Youth Representative. This incident took place in the presence of the Deputy Minister for Defence, Mr. Chitalu Sampa and the Mayor for Chingola, Mr. Johannes Steyn.

28. See "NEC to Discuss Copperbelt Suspension," *Times of Zambia* (May 21, 1993).

29. See "Chiluba Cautions Nsuluka," *Times of Zambia* (May 29, 1993).

30. Interview with Frederick Hapunda, Lusaka, June 1993.

31. Frederick Hapunda, "Southerners Feel 'Insulted'" *The Weekly Post* (July 9-15, 1993).

32. Ibid.

33. Ibid.

34. Ibid. See also: Doris Kasote, "Southerners Call for Corruption Inquiry," *The Weekly Post* (July 9-15, 1993), and Teddy Chisanga, "Subsidies Earn Bad Name as Free Market Economy Takes Over" (Ibid.).

35. Between June 26 and 27, the MMD Provincial Committee in the Southern Province met at Choma and passed very strongly worded resolutions calling on the Chiluba government to immediately institute commissions of inquiry to look into the allegations on drug trafficking and corruption in government. See Doris Kasote, "Southerners Call for Corruption Inquiry" (op. cit.).

36. "Sata, Chipimo Tell Off Critics," *Times of Zambia* (May 24, 1993).

37. Elias Chitenje, "Wrangle Brews over Maunga's Re-Instatement," *The Weekly Post* (December 24-30, 1992). In fact Chitala dismissed the resolutions passed at the Provincial Conference arguing that the MMD NEC was not notified of the meeting and there was no way of determining if they had a quorum. The December 5, 1992 meeting at Nawaggali where Hapunda was elected to replace Maunga was according to Chitala not monitored by an electoral commissioner.

38. Editorial Opinion, *Times of Zambia* (May 25, 1993).

39. Editorial Comment *Zambia Daily Mail* (May 27, 1993).

40. Carol Graham, *Safety Nets, Politics, and the Poor: Transition to Market Economies* (Washington, D.C.: The Brookings Institution, 1994), p. 158.

41. Masauto Phiri, "Mwaanga's Dubious Foreign 'Investors'" *The Weekly Post* (September 10-16, 1993) and Jowie Mwiinga and Tendal Banda, "Government Corruption Tops Paris Club Agenda," (Ibid.).

42. "Reflection," Editorial in *National Mirror* (May 31-June 6,1993).

43. Ibid.

44. See "Nakatindi Wina Linked to Drugs," *The Weekly Post* (May 28- June 3, 1993).

45. Shortly after this alteration, Chiluba sacked Kamoyo Mwale the Head of the Drug Enforcement Commission who had actually been appointed by Kaunda. Within the MMD many leading members believed that a single proven case of drug trafficking against any minister would destroy the government and party hence Chiluba was reluctant to act in spite of abundant evidence provided be security agencies.

46. See "Drug Dealers Deserve Harsh Punishment," *The Weekly Post* (April 30-May 6, 1993).

47. Donatella Lorch, "In Zambia, a Legacy of Graft and a Drug Scandal Taint Democratic Reforms," *The New York Times* (International) (January 30, 1994).

48. Jowie Mwiinga, "Chill for Chiluba," *Africa Report* (March-April, 1994). Chiluba had dropped out of high school after only two years, worked in Tanzania at a sisal plantation as a clerk and became a leading trade unionist in Zambia. His trade union activities gave him national prominence. A very articulate speaker, he is regarded as an effective

trade union leader. His skills as a unionist have been over-whelmed by the complexity and difficulties of politics where he now has to deal with more powerful; richer and more experienced politicians.

49. Davis Mwaba, "Why the MMD Government Should Seek a Fresh Mandate," *The Weekly Post* (Lusaka) (April 30-May 6, 1993). In several respects Mr. Mwaba's call is a politically opportunistic one to open the way for his party to contest the elections if it were called.

50. Donatella Lorch, "In Zambia, a Legacy of Graft and a Drug Scandal Taint Democratic Reforms," (op. cit.)

51. Melinda Ham, "Zambia: Luring Investment," *Africa Report* (September-October 1992), p.41.

52. Interview with a female public servant, Department of Agriculture, June, 1993, Lusaka, Zambia.

53. "Public Workers go on Strike," *Times of Zambia* (May 28, 1993).

54. Hastings Nyasulu, "Pay Talks Start," *Zambia Daily Mail* (June 2, 1993).

55. See "Strikers Defy Union Leaders," *Times of Zambia* (June 2, 1993).

56. Interview, Lusaka, June 1993.

57. "Teachers Strike Spreads: Unions Blamed," *Times of Zambia* (June 3, 1993).

58. "Zambia's Rating in Sharp Drop," *Times of Zambia* (May 28, 1993).

59. Carol Graham, *Safety Nets. Politics and the Poor* (op. cit.), p. 156.

60. See Guy Scott, "Getting to Grips with the Politics of Life and Death," *The Weekly Post* (September 10-1, 1993).

61. Mutale Mwamba, "90% 'Good Time Girls' HIV- Survey," *Zambia Daily Mail* (May 14, 1993). Mrs Rantakari is also Chairperson of the Tasintha Home for Prostitutes, a home created by Zambian NGOs to help prostitutes start a new life.

62. See one of such adverts in *The Weekly Post* (April 30-May 6, 1993). See also Martin Wamunyima, "Mission Eases Agony of AIDS Patients," *Times of Zambia* (May 29, 1993).

63. See for instance "Gunmen Rob Ndola Woman," *Times of Zambia* (June 2, 1993), and "Kitwe Gunmen Snatch Car," *Times of Zambia* (May 21, 1993).

64. See Editorial Opinion, *Times of Zambia* (June 3, 1993), p. 1, and "Police Scout for Cars," in Ibid.

65. See Martin Wamunyima, "Transport Crisis Bedevils Police," *Times of Zambia* (May 15, 1993), and Anthony Kunda, "Half-baked Police on Edge of Ruin," *The Weekly Post* (September 10-16, 1993).

66. "Measles Hit Mwinilunga," *Zambia Daily Mail* (June 2, 1993).

67. "Hospital Cash Not Released," *Times of Zambia* (May 21, 1993).

68. "Chief Sends SOS," *Times of Zambia* (May 21, 1993).

69. "State Releases South Funds," *Times of Zambia* (May 21, 1993).

70. See Tendal Banda, "Poverty Transforms Bus-Stop Shelter," *The Weekly Post* (September 10-16, 1993), and "Even Beggars Face Growing Competition," *The Weekly Post* (May 28-June 3, 1993).

71. Carol Graham, *Safety Nets. Politics and the Poor* (op. cit.), pp. 172-183.

72. "Chiluba Hails Zambians," *Times of Zambia* (May 26, 1993);

73. "Catholics Tick-Off Angley's Sessions," *Times of Zambia* (May 29, 1993). See also "Victory Crusade Leaves Much to be Desired," *The Weekly Post* (July 9-15, 1993).

74. "Council Dismisses Healing Crusades," *Times of Zambia* (May 28, 1993). The Council was of the view that evangelists like Rev. Angley were false and had never cured anyone. An official of the Council actually said "people like that are thieves in the name of the lord. How many people has he cured in his own country. Chiluba is the one encouraging these clowns and actors to come here and waste our time." Interview, Lusaka, May 1993.

75. Within the Zambian government the level of corruption is simply mind-boggling. This is the more so given the limited resources available in the entire country, at least, when compared with Ghana or Nigeria. For instance, corruption, and illegal connections cost the Posts and Telecommunications Corporation (PTC) K100 million every week. Interference in the PTC's operations by government and political figures cost K3 billion every week. See "Shady Deals Rock PTC," *Times of Zambia* (May 29, 1993).

76. "Christian Nation Idea a Flop," *Times of Zambia* (May 15, 1993).

77. For a critique of this development see Gilbert Mudenda, "Chauvinism, it is said, is the Last Refuge of the Scoundrel," *The Weekly Post* (May 28-June 3, 1993). President Chiluba has been featured several times giving his personal testimony on South African Christian Television and on other international television broadcasts.

78. "Christians Responsible for Uproar," *The Weekly Post* (July 9-15, 1993).

79. Jowie Mwiinga, "Chill for Chiluba," *Africa Report* (March-April, 1994).

80. Interview with a former minister, Lusaka, Zambia, June, 1993.

81. Interview Lusaka, Zambia, June, 1993.

82. Dingi Chirwa, Tendal Banda and Masautso Phiri, "Chiluba's Reshuffle Undermines Confidence," *The Weekly Post* (April 23-29, 1993); Masautso Phiri, "Chiluba's Reshuffle Reflects His Political Power Game," in Ibid; and "Collective Irresponsibility?" Editorial Opinion (Ibid.)

83. "Why Kasonde was Sacked," *Times of Zambia* (May 29, 1993).

84. Jowie Mwiinga, "Chill for Chiluba" (op. cit.)

85. Interview with Dr, Jotham Moomba, University of Zambia, Political Science Department, June 1993.

86. Jowie Mwiinga, "Chill for Chiluba" (op. cit.)

87. Personal communication with an MMD activist, Lusaka, Zambia. March, 1994.

88. Jowie Mwiinga, "Chill for Chiluba" (op. cit.)

89. See Remmy Kabali, "MMD Goes Into Action," *Search* (Ndola, Zambia) (December 1992).

90. Peter Chilambwe, "IMF Official says Government Will not Increase Teachers' Pay," *The Weekly Post* (July 9-15, 1993).

91. Though Hill insisted that his lecture was private and did not wish to be quoted in the press, a private lecture is usually not delivered on the premises of the country's main university campus with the public and media in attendance.

92. Elias Chitenge, "Mwila Threatens to Deport World Bank

Man," *The Weekly Post* (January 22-28, 1993).

93. Ibid.
94. Melinda Ham, "Zambia: An Outspoken Opposition (op. cit.), p. 31.
95. Melinda Ham, ibid, p. 32. The MMD, drawing a lesson from how it built up its own membership through resignations from UNIP, held an emergency crisis meeting in April 1993 and expelled some "suspects" from the MMD including Guy Scott former Agriculture Minister and the youngest MP for Mkushi North, Rolf Shenton.
96. Jowie Mwiinga, "Chill for Chiluba" (op. cit.)

CHAPTER SIX

UNIP MAKES ANOTHER BID
FOR POWER: THE CRISIS OF
DEMOCRATIC CONSOLIDATION
IN ZAMBIA

New democratic regimes in Africa face monumental problems. The previous chapter considered some of the critical socioeconomic challenges which have confronted the MMD since its ascendancy to power in 1991. For new democracies like the MMD, the sources of pressure can be varied: internal, external, cultural, social, ideological, donor, and/or lender sources. In the first place, new democracies are largely the precipitates of a general disillusionment with authoritarian, military, or other undemocratic forms of government which became unacceptable to the people and failed to receive support from the West in the aftermath of the Cold War. Secondly, they rode to power posing as clear and drastic alternatives to existing corrupt, repressive, and violent regimes. They made promises to the people and received overwhelming mandates to improve the general conditions of life by checking inflation, corruption, crime, waste, mismanagement, unemployment, homelessness, rural-urban drift, and drug trafficking. The new democratic movements and governments have also promised to respect human rights, put an end to personal rule and the privatization of public office, and generate processes to empower the people, their organizations, and their communities. Finally, third, they rode to power with widespread support from international organizations, lenders, donors, international observer teams, and the good will of a democratizing world.

The inability of such new "popular" governments to take full control of the state, set up structures to mediate and contain opposition and contradictions, or, at the very least, to meet some of the immediate expectations of the electorate can set in motion a process of rapid delegitimization. In fact, the electorate in Africa seems to be fed up with promises of one sort or the other. They have become rather skeptical of politicians who seem not to differ much from those of the early days of political independence. As one respondent angrily retorted in an interview: "What you are seeing in this country is the near total failure of democracy to make any significant change in the lives of the people. Such conditions encourage all sorts of negative responses. It is a pity that the MMD has not done much to distance itself from the terrible experiences of the past three decades."[1]

This skepticism, deepened by continuing economic crisis and the numerous constraints on the new regime, is beginning to dampen the enthusiasm for democracy and to pose serious challenges for the new wave of democratic governments in Africa. As Richard Sandbrook has noted, the "pendulum, now swinging so strongly toward liberal-democratic, free-market solutions, may later swing back as many of their fulsome promises remain unfulfilled."[2] Conditions of uncertainty, weakness, instability, corruption, and poor performance have encouraged opposition elements to challenge incumbent governments through legal and extra-legal means: "Africa's hostile conditions encumber not so much *transitions* to democracy as the *consolidation* of enduring democracies. Without a civil society willing and able to resist authoritarianism, democratic transitions may only be cosmetic, designed mainly for foreign consumption, or cyclical (as in Latin America), with democratic tendencies reversed by *coups d'etat*."[3] The preconditions for democracy discussed above (see Chapter One) equally point to the problems of consolidating democracy in underdeveloped formations. Yet, as we have demonstrated in earlier chapters, the Zambian case throws up so many negative coalitions, contradictions, crises, and conflicts, that the chances for consolidating and reproducing a viable democratic tradition and culture can be described as very slim. Not only did the MMD inherit a terribly mismanaged economy, plagued by debt, inflation, unemployment, urban dislocation, rural decay, hunger, disease, and capital flight; it also has been unable to prove itself a more credible alternative to the UNIP government in spite of the massive good will it enjoyed from Zambians, donors, lenders, and Western governments. In fact, it has been unable to retain the support of its main constituency, labor. The Chiluba government has had to implement very painful structural adjustment programs in order to satisfy investors and donors without adequate policies to protect vulnerable groups. This has eroded its initial support and created a large constituency for opposition interests.

The new democracy in Zambia has faced challenges from a variety of sources. Provincial, ethnic, religious, and social cleavages and distrust have continued to "complicate or even undermine the give-and-take of democratic competition."[4] The "weakness of classes that have elsewhere championed democracy" has constituted itself into an obstacle to "democratic consolidation"; democracy has not succeeded in eliminating "the clientlist basis of unproductive resource allocations and poor public management"; and it has failed to "introduce much equity, rendering utopian the widely proclaimed goal of 'equitable growth'."[5] Thus according to Sandbrook, while the new democracy has "contributed to a new political climate in sub-Saharan Africa," the political environment it had engendered "embodies several unresolved contradictions and unduly sanguine expectations."[6] These "unresolved contradictions" are generating not only disillusionment and frustration with the MMD in Zambia but with democracy as supported by the donors and lenders in general. As Robert Pinkney has noted, "Choosing between competing parties is hardly a worthwhile exercise unless the successful parties can then use the machinery of state to repay their debts to their constituents, whether in material terms or in a modest reshaping of society to reflect current values and priorities."[7] Unfortunately for the MMD and the Chiluba government, it has not been able to either repay debts to constituents or reshape society in a way which address the pressing needs of nonbourgeois forces in Zambia. As Pinkney notes, at a general level:

> A democratically elected government moving into the presidential palace following the departure of the authoritarians might feel like Napoleon entering Moscow. A famous victory has been won, but where are the spoils? And once people have discovered that little has changed, or can be changed, as a result of their votes, why should they be anxious to defend democracy?[8]

Barry Gills and Joel Rocamora have noted that new democracies "remain extremely fragile and threatened by political upheaval.[9] Samuel Huntington has also argued that "Democratic governments succeeding authoritarian governments faced a much more serious, emotion charged, and politically sensitive" environment.[10] Such challenges included, according to Huntington, what to do "with the symbols, doctrines, organizations, laws, civil servants, and leaders of the authoritarian system. Beneath these issues often lay fundamental questions of national identity and political legitimacy."[11] Where a new democracy is confronted with problems of legitimacy, the intransigence of the defeated authoritarian regime, deepening economic crisis, insurgencies, ethnic and communal conflicts, regional challenges to central authority, severe socioeconomic inequality, extreme poverty, a huge foreign debt profile, and inexperience in containing the forces of disintegration and manipulation in the political process, it becomes even more difficult to consolidate democracy and to move to the stage of democratization (assuming that this was on the agenda in the first place).[12] Finally, Pinkney has noted that the capacity of the state in Africa to transform society and reproduce a viable democratic tradition is very weak.[13] Most of the transitions in Africa, ironically, have been packaged and led by the very same elements or at the very best, their direct protegees, who bankrupted the state, ruined the economy, accentuated ethnic, regional, and religious suspicions and conflicts, and failed to improve on the relations and patterns of production and exchange since political independence in the 1960s.[14]

What follows in this situation is that the old contradictions, coalitions, conflicts, and crises survive. New regimes are thus prone to containing legal and extralegal challenges. Such challenges distract them from whatever agenda brought them into power, and scarce resources are diverted to security and survival strategies. The credibility of the new government erodes rapidly and there is a new "authoritarian nostalgia" which replaces the initial enthusiasm for democracy.[15] It is in this context that we can fully appreciate the crisis of the MMD in Zambia as well as increasing disillusionment with Chiluba and the government. Though the MMD is a conservative rightist party which rode to power with popular support, even its pro-market agenda has run into problems because the domestic base of support is lacking. Zambia is still an underdeveloped, debt-ridden, foreign-dominated, technologically backward, and unstable society dominated by a very corrupt and largely unproductive elite presiding over a non-hegemonic state. These issues have not been addressed and multiparty election can only do so much without resources and a viable political playing field.

The rest of this chapter deals with the 1993 "Zero Option" episode in Zambia in which the Frederick Chiluba MMD Government accused the opposition United National Independence Party (UNIP) of planning to overthrow it through a coup d'etat. This crisis forced the new democratic government to impose a state of emergency, to the great displeasure of donors and international human rights organizations and Western governments. It also generated heated debates as to the viability of Zambian democracy and demonstrated some of the very serious internal pressures which new "democratic" regimes face in developing social formations. As well, the response to the state of emergency from international human rights organizations like Africa Watch tended to give the impression that the "drive for democracy" means that governments are no longer entitled to take national security measures to protect themselves and their citizens.

The "Zero Option" Episode: Stretching the Limits of Zambian Democracy

Every African government has reason to watch its back, as opposition elements will often take advantage of its vulnerability, ineffectiveness, and problems to discredit or unseat it. Challenges to the government are nothing new to Zambia. From working-class and peasant riots through religiously motivated challenges to military coup attempts, the country has managed to survive such uprisings and developments since 1964. As well, it has, since political independence, had to contend with the hostile minority regimes in Southern Rhodesia (now Zimbabwe) and apartheid South Africa. When the UNIP and Kenneth Kaunda lost the 1991 elections by a landslide to the MMD, most of its leaders including Kaunda were stunned beyond belief. The constitution had no clear rules on transitioning from one government to another. Because the UNIP had actually assumed it would win the election, even if by a narrow margin, it had made little or no preparations for a transition. The transition was therefore characterized by all sorts of mudslinging, accusations, and counter accusation. Till this very day, some die-hard supporters of the UNIP still believe that what happened was a mistake, that Kaunda was "merely on vacation," and that the MMD would not last a year in power. This time frame has had to be revised after each year of continuing control of state power by the MMD.

Kaunda has constantly described the MMD as a "mad government," run by corrupt and inexperienced young people. He constantly referred to the MMD leaders as "frightened little men" and after he lost the election and in spite of the international interest in the elections, Kaunda had actually prescribed civil disobedience in September 1992 at Namayani.[16] In a demonstration of anger and frustration Kaunda declared that "the MMD government was like a foreign one which should be fought in the same way UNIP had fought the colonial government."[17] Within the UNIP, younger members felt that what was required was "young blood" and leaders who will match the MMD's populist strategy and expose it as a "conservative, opportunistic, and reactionary political outfit" which has already "sold out to lenders, donors and Western governments."[18]

After twenty eight years of UNIP domination of the social, political, cultural, economic, philosophical and spiritual life of the country, one major task which the MMD faced was how to deal with UNIP supporters within its ranks, the security forces, the presidency, the armed forces, and the bureaucracy. Without doubt, this was a very difficult challenge as many were not too willing to openly declare for the MMD just in case it could not hold on to power and UNIP were to regain control. The campaign had been very bitter and rough, and the MMD on coming to power did not treat Kaunda with the dignity of a former president. He was relieved of several "perks" he had enjoyed in power, the UNIP Headquarters was seized, and hundreds of UNIP stalwarts in the bureaucracy, intelligence services, and diplomatic and other critical positions were sacked and replaced with MMD supporters. This created a lot of bad blood and encouraged those who had been displaced to identify with designs to unseat the MMD from power. Of course the treatment meted out to Kaunda was simply a taste of his own medicine and largely a precipitate of his bitter and unguarded statements about the MMD at home and abroad which served to increase tensions and hostility to the government. Thus, from all sides of the political divide, anger, humiliation, arrogance, intolerance, and a lack of a accommodation created conditions for extralegal responses to the contestation for power.

It is in this context that we can appreciate the origins of the "Radical Programme of Action for UNIP"(RPAU), alias the "Zero Option Plan."[19] The document acknowledges that the MMD took power following a peaceful transition process and the defeat of UNIP. It attributes the defeat however, to "hatred by the Americans of President Kaunda. The hatred of President Kaunda surfaced during the American adventures in Iraq. The open support of Iraq demonstrated by President Kaunda irated [sic!] the Americans." The authors of the program felt that Kaunda was very influential in the sub-region and in the continent at that time, especially in the Organization of African Unity (OAU), the Southern Africa Development Community (SADC), the Preferential Free Trade Area (PT), and the Economic Community of West African States (ECOWAS) and the Americans had felt that he could mobilize support for Iraq in the African continent. The RPAU also contended that Kaunda was capable of influencing Zaire and Malawi, that South Africa was embroiled in its internal crisis and was therefore an unreliable ally in the Gulf crisis, and that with the decline of communism and the disintegration of the Soviet Empire, America had to move fast to "destabilize the satellite communist/socialist central African countries. The most stable of these countries with an influential leader was Zambia."

This position of course assumed that Zambia was, by some stretch of the imagination, a socialist—even a communist—nation and obviously oversimplifies the issues involved in the Gulf crisis while outlandishly exaggerating Kaunda's influence in Africa at the beginning of the 1990s. While Kaunda was certainly influential in Southern Africa, to claim any substantial degree of influence in the ECOWAS would certainly be an exaggeration. Given the depth of Zambia's economic crisis and the extent of socioeconomic dislocation in Zambia by the end of the 1980s, it is doubtful that Zambia could be conveniently described as a "very stable nation." Before Kaunda left office he was confronted with not just massive desertion of UNIP by top politicians but also massive and persistent strike actions by students, peasants, and workers, as well as an attempted military coup.

The RPAU claimed that South African and Malawian intelligence agencies were used by the West to ensure the fall of Kaunda and UNIP: this assistance was in "the form of providing a base for information gathering...and other logistics," dissemination of massive disinformation and misinformation directed against UNIP within Zambia, and general support for the Angolan rebel group UNITA and for pro-Western dissidents in Zaire who were encouraged to mobilize public opinion against Kaunda. RPAU also claimed that the Mozambican rebel group RENAMO was used on the operational side, such as "insurgent attacks to create low morale among the Zambian Armed Forces. All in all the West (America) resolved: KAUNDA MUST GO." Again this would look like an effort to blame practically every individual or organization not in the mainstream in the Southern Africa

227

subregion for the fall of Kaunda. The document provides no evidence but makes these claims to lay the foundation for its prescriptions. On the domestic front, the Zero Option Plan claims that popular forces were also used by the West to unseat Kaunda:

> The trade unions through the ZCTU were then being prepared for action—CIVIL DISOBEDIENCE. The students were incited to lead the breakdown in law and order. This was done through their various organizations. Obviously preparations for this started immediately there were signs that President Gorbachev was reforming communism. The west also used arm twisting tactics by attaching their aid to the human rights record of Zambia, scaling down the Civil Service and the discontinuation of subsidies, privatisation of parastatal companies including ZCCM etc.

The Plan went on to complain about the resurgence of ethnic loyalties which it claimed had been "silenced by the introduction of the One Party State in 1973," accused the Bembas of wanting "to rule the country and their aim is to rule it by any means—Hook or Crook," and noted that the MMD was formed as "a lose alliance and still is. The name was connoted [sic] by the Americans (Mr David) was the initiator as he had done in other African countries—notably Kenya." The document contended that there was a major ethnic rift within the MMD which made it vulnerable, so that several staunch supporters of the MMD had been co-opted into the intelligence service or rewarded with diplomatic appointment, but the vast majority who had not been rewarded with jobs following the movement's victory were disgruntled. Those who were appointed as ministers "have turned to corruption to enrich themselves through their businesses under the pretext of liberalisation and market economy." Furthermore,

As a result of inexperience in managing national issues, corruption, etc, the nation has experienced Cholera outbreaks, inability to control the epidemic, inflation, deaths in police cells, inability to properly manage the famine disaster, failure to maintain the country's social infrastructure like schools and hospitals.

Generally, the population is now disgruntled with the present government. This has been displayed by a low turn out at by-elections and the local government elections.

This sounded more like a vivid description of Zambia in the last decade of Kenneth Kaunda's rule. The Zero Option Plan did not mention that the MMD was still grappling with the legacies of the UNIP which for 27 years succeeded in virtually destroying the socioeconomic base of Zambia, ran up an unprecedented foreign debt, and ran down all infrastructures. It is true that the MMD had not really done much to improve on the situation, but with skeptical donors and creditors, a decaying infrastructure, stagnating industry and agriculture, drought, urban restlessness, and uncertain political loyalties, there was not much the MMD could really achieve. The MMD had been in power for less than two years and was already being blamed for problems it inherited from Kaunda! The Plan directly accused the MMD of being a creation of the West and erroneously asserted that the one party state foisted on the nation by Kaunda took care of ethnic conflicts in Zambia. On these grounds, it was convenient to attribute to the politics of the MMD the deepening ethnic and provincial conflicts that were unleashed with the end of the one-party state.

These accusations and allegations make sense when we consider the declared aims and methods of the Zero Option Plan. The document was very definitive in its aims: "to wrestle power from the MMD government in order to form a government responsive to the people's needs. This must be done before the 1996 general elections." The goal, therefore, was not to give the MMD another chance at renewing the mandate given to it in the October 1991 election. To ensure that this was achieved, the Zero Option Plan noted that UNIP could capture power in either of three ways: *(a)* ballot box (elections), *(b)* civil disobedience, and/or *(c)* armed insurrection. For the purposes of its immediate goal the Zero Option document opted for the second method: civil disobedience. This would aim at "making the country ungovernable and creating a sense of insecurity thereby offering the authorities no opportunity of proper governance." Specifically, there was a need to organize a strong opposition to the MMD government by organizing trade unions, students' organizations, retrenched intelligence officers and army/police officers, retrenched parastatal executives, unemployed youths (*mishanga boys*), propaganda through the media, alliances with opposition parties and interest groups, and discouragement of investors and donor funding.

In the trade unions, alliances were to be forged with conservative anti-MMD union leaders, supporters of the MMD in union positions were to be challenged and replaced, and the trade union movement as a whole was to be penetrated. Rather than focus exclusively on the leadership, it was deemed essential to first identify influential individuals and unions in the labor movement and to begin the process of penetration at the "shop steward level or branch level etc. Once the bottom leadership can be changed or influenced then it would be easier to usurp the top." To win the allegiance of union leaders, "a token extra financial funding would be necessary once the bottom echelon (was) under control."

The supportive unions were to be encouraged to call strike actions, create confusion in industry and the bureaucracy, organize riots and sit-ins, "rough up executives in companies," and make demands for salary increases in order to fuel inflation. This way, the UNIP can gradually but decisively wean the labor movement away from the MMD. The UNIP was counting on the fact that policies of retrenchment, privatization, and desubsidization were already weakening the support which the MMD initially enjoyed from the working classes.

The students' movement was also to receive special attention. The focus was to be mostly on primary and secondary school levels. As well, the colleges and the University of Zambia would be reorganized to support UNIP. To do this effectively, militant students, organizations and the UNZA students' union must be co-opted, money must be set aside, even a monthly allowance to win the support of the leaders, and a "sense of revolution should be dinned into school boy/students, for example with the escalation of school fees, high cost of uniforms, etc, students in Secondary Schools should be encouraged to defy authorities by going to school without uniforms." With such conditions of control and manipulation, the UNIP can precipitate a major crisis in the school system which would "spread like bush fire to other schools," especially in Lusaka, and thus pose a challenge to the patience and credibility of the government.

The Zero Option Plan also called for the mobilization into the opposition of all military and police officers as well as business executives who had been laid off. Since they were most likely to be disgruntled with the MMD, and since they have a "bone to pick" with the present government, they "were bound to be reliable allies" in the struggle to unseat the MMD from power. These retired or dismissed officers would be sources of information about the activities and problems of the government. Since some of them had received training in such arts as "creation of alarming rumors which should send frightening waves into the general public," they could be relied upon to help destabilize the system. Some of the officers would also be used to "physically incite the general public against the government. The public is unhappy about the general state of the economy, the archaic transport system, cholera, corruption, etc. These officers could be used to organize demonstrations along the lines of Tienamen Square, Romania, etc. The rural population could also be incited so that *chaos would reign throughout Zambia*" (emphasis added). The unemployed youths or *mishanga* boys are defined by the document as the "most important and effective sector of the community," and UNIP "must identify and create leadership among these people." The leadership must be paid monthly allowances and be encouraged to:

a) spread "propaganda against the government. They can be sponsored to ride in minibuses to various locations while criticizing the government";

b) perpetrate "thefts in and around town centres";

c) perpetrate "petty crime in and around the town centres. The Police must be made to fail to contain the situation. This would be the nucleus of all the chaos in the country and therefore needs to be better remunerated. This group should be encouraged to commit crimes against Western foreigners, crimes like pick-pocketing tourists (white)."

These were certainly frightening plans. Obviously the Zero Option authors were not thinking of life in Zambia after the MMD. Many of the *mishanga* boys are thugs, thieves, and persons with very low self-esteem. To recruit such persons for serious political action, fund them, and rely on their anti-social activities to win the seat of power was tantamount to opening up the party and the government it hopes to form to all sorts of blackmail and disorder. The Document also laid out clear plans for frightening away foreign investors from Zambia. Top UNIP leaders were to be required to issue strongly worded statements that it was "not safe to invest in Zambia at the moment," that the UNIP government will "nationalise companies which have been privatised during the reign of the MMD government," and everything was to be done to "discourage funding from the West" as this has been the basis of MMD power and popularity. While this would have the immediate effect of keeping away investors who would not want their businesses nationalized, how did the UNIP hope that it could convince them to return once it was in power?

To make its propaganda against the incumbent MMD effective, the Zero Option Plan recommended that the UNIP must set up its own newspaper and that it was "desirable to also set up our own covert radio station" in order to reach the rural population and counter the government's propaganda. It recommended that a special Cell must be created to implement the Plan because the present Central Committee of UNIP was full of informers. Because adequate funding was necessary and the party lacked sufficient funds, the Plan recommended that "Efforts must be made to obtain assistance from friendly parties and governments like our Arab or Islamic governments of the Middle East e.g. Iran or Iraq, or the PLO or Libya." The Plan prescribed a policy of constant harassment and attacks on the MMD, its officers, and its programs:

> It is important that the party takes advantage of certain situations which occur day to day. Whenever we notice a crack in the MMD our aim should be to widen that crack e.g. the Southern Province Wrangle and many others. The party should make full use of its only MPs. Efforts should be made to encourage MPs to talk to dissident MPs in the MMD for a possible breakaway. The party should be thinking about a merger of MPs with other MPs in MMD in order to create a crisis.

The Plan was definitive on the fact that UNIP would not come to power in Zambia again "unless it creates chaos in the government....Leaders must be prepared for self-sacrifice. The party must transform itself into a revolutionary one." This would enable UNIP to put "sufficient pressure on the government so as to sufficiently weaken it and eventually bring it to a halt and thus pave the way for new Presidential and General Elections which will probably lead to the ushering in of the Fourth Republic by the end of this year (1993)." Finally, the Zero Option Plan noted that by losing two by-elections in October 1991, UNIP cadres were seriously demoralized and this made it urgent to mount a "Revamp UNIP campaign." The details of how to implement the Plan were to be made known only to a small subcommittee and the actions would be "covert."

The State Responds to the Opposition: Nipping the Zero Option Plan in the Bud

This document, which eventually came to the knowledge of the security forces only because UNIP members discussed it in public, was clearly a dangerous document. If implemented, it had every potential of destabilizing the nation and leading to instability, violence, political impasse and possibly a military coup. The task of consolidating democracy which the World Bank, donors, lenders, and Western governments, as well as international non-governmental organizations have harped on very recently would have experienced a major setback. It was clear that for some of its members, UNIP had become a desperate party and was willing to come to power through extralegal means. However, it needs to be pointed out that not all UNIP members supported the Zero Option Plan. The Plan was a clear reflection of a serious power struggle within UNIP itself—between "radical" supporters of the Plan led by Wezi Kaunda (the son of Kenneth Kaunda), Rupiah Banda (UNIP Secretary for International Relations), and Bwendo Mulengela (UNIP Publicity Secretary) on the one hand and more conservative and "reformist" factions led by UNIP president Kebby Musokotwane on the other. In a country that had been so terribly mismanaged and where the new

234

government was not making much headway in terms of structural reforms, it would have been quite easy to cause chaos and achieve the aim of destabilizing the country.

When the Zero Option Plan became known to the public, especially after the *Times of Zambia* published excerpts from the document on February 24, 1993, President Chiluba moved quickly to nip the plan in the bud. He declared a state of emergency on March 4, 1993. In declaring the state of emergency on national television, Chiluba announced that: "Zambia is threatened. Our young democracy is at stake. The danger is real and the consequences if not attended to are grave. The political climate is being systematically poisoned by a few of our citizens who are bent on plunging this nation into chaos." The president described the Plan as a "carefully crafted agenda for destruction." Reassuring the people that their rights would not be unduly trampled upon, Chiluba promised that his government "will uphold the conditions in which our people will enjoy to the fullest extent possible their democratic rights. Therefore, only those who break the law and wish to bring anarchy will face the wrath of this state of emergency." By March 5, fourteen top UNIP officials (including seven members of the central committee) and members including the three sons of the former president, Wezi Kaunda, Tilyenji Kaunda and Panji Kaunda had been arrested and detained. Several other members of the party were to be arrested later, with a few being released after security screening. Wezi Kaunda, Cuthbert Ng'uni, and Bonnie Tembo were charged with "treason felony." Wezi Kaunda was charged with one count of preparing the document with other unknown persons between January 1 and February 19 of 1993 and of possessing the *Zero Option Plan*, which was classified as a seditious document. He was also charged with another count of distributing the Plan at Freedom House (UNIP Headquarters) on February 10th to members of the UNIP Central Committee "to entice them to join his scheme to usurp power from the government."[20]

Cuthbert Ng'uni was charged with "treason felony" and accused of authoring the Plan and of distributing it to UNIP Central Committee members. Tembo was charged with treason felony and of being in possession of an intelligence document. Steven Moyo, the former head of the Zambia National Broadcasting Corporation (ZNBC), was also arrested, as was Henry Kamima, the former director general of the Zambian Intelligence Service. The latter was accused of retaining an intelligence document titled *Brief on the Security Situation in the Country*, which he had prepared for Chiluba before he (Kamima) was sacked from his position in early 1992.[21] Christopher Mukoya, a former intelligence officer who was in charge of UNIP security in the Copperbelt, was detained and accused of possessing an official document entitled *Security Brief for F. X. Chungu, Director General of Zambia Intelligence and Security Service on the Occasion of His Visit to North Western Province Between 27th and 28th April 1982*. Lemmy Siwisha, a provincial intelligence officer based in Solwezi, was accused of giving the intelligence document to Muyoka and was therefore charged with communicating classified official information, and of failure to secure a classified official document. The Chiluba government also severed relations with Iraq and Iran, accusing them of interfering in Zambia's internal affairs. The two countries, together with the PLO and Libya, had been specifically mentioned in the Zero Option Plan. The former president was a personal friend of Saddam Hussein and had overtly supported him during the Gulf War.

The one point which the MMD government wanted to demonstrate was that it was fully in control of national security and could deal decisively with the forces of instability irrespective of who was involved. Chiluba also saw the episode as an ample opportunity to restructure the security system and take measures to consolidate the hold of the MMD over the bureaucracy and intelligence services, which were "still filled with pro-UNIP stalwarts."[22] However, the response of the Chiluba government generated intensive debates in and outside the country. To some, it was a betrayal of the country's democratic ideals. It showed that the attacks against the state of emergency when Kaunda was in power were opportunistic. It showed that Chiluba was a ruthless politician who would not hesitate to deny Zambians their liberties. Many who held this position were of course, UNIP members. To others, the response was adequate. Desperate conditions required desperate and strong responses. It was Chiluba's "softness" that made it possible for Wezi Kaunda and his UNIP compatriots to even contemplate the Plan. If Chiluba missed this opportunity to rally Zambians against UNIP and to strengthen the party and the democratic enterprise, he might never get another opportunity. The UNIP needed to be taught a lesson and made to realize that the MMD was in charge. Yet, to foreign interests, the state of emergency was unfortunate. It showed that Zambian democracy was still weak and uncertain. There was no way in which a democratic government could justify a state of emergency. Below, we look at these issues in some detail.

The State of Emergency Debate:
Western Double Standards?

It is natural that democratic forces should show concern over any policy which constrains personal and collective liberties. Since the neocolonial state in Africa has historically capitalized on any form of popular challenge to trample on the freedoms and liberties of the people, organizations in civil society have traditionally distrusted the restrictions of liberties, even if done in the "national interest." After all, ruthless dictators in Nigeria, Kenya, Equatorial Guinea, Zaire, and Uganda at one time or the other justified their actions in the interest of the nation. The

Zambian situation was somewhat different since it would be futile to adopt an absolutist position on issues of national security. The MMD government had two options: first, to regard the threat as minor and because it was trying to consolidate democracy and please donors, treat it with levity. Second, it could demonstrate that it was a legitimate government with a very popular mandate, and establish a tradition of opposition to all efforts to seize state power through extralegal, and clearly illegal and corrupt means. The real issues under such circumstances would be: whether the state of emergency had been imposed legally; whether the liberties of those who were not involved were trampled upon; whether the liberties of those accused were respected; and whether the imposition of emergency measures was an excuse to satisfy other sinister ends.

During the state of emergency, UNIP was allowed to hold protest marches and rallies; public and privately-owned media wrote angry and harsh editorials against the government; and prominent politicians—even UNIP leaders—were allowed to speak out against the state of emergency. Of course, the UNIP and other opposition parties capitalized on the action to discredit Chiluba and the MMD and to show that the ruling party was not as strong as is generally believed. As the Zero Option Plan itself had recommended, UNIP leaders were to capitalize on all cracks in the government to embarrass and pressure the government. However, the declaration of a state of emergency caused a great uproar and much debate within the government, the country, and the international community, and among Western nations, donors, and lenders who had touted Zambia as a model for peaceful transition, commitment to market reforms, popular government, and working democracy in Africa. Naturally these interest groups felt shocked and disappointed to see such a harsh measure as the state of emergency—which Kaunda had imposed on Zambia permanently almost throughout his stay in power—reimposed on the country.

They also felt embarrassed that their "model of democracy" was seemingly moving in a different direction. Many Zambians felt it was a bad omen, the terrible beginning of a chain of repression and human rights abuses. The nightmare of the Kaunda days, when the state of emergency was used as a tool to repress the opposition and silence critics of the government, quickly came to mind.

Within the MMD there were those who felt that the state of emergency violated all the democratic principles for which the movement stood and therefore opposed it. Within the Chiluba cabinet, powerful ministers—such as Roger Chongwe, Godfrey Miyanda, and Ludwig Sondashi—opposed the state of emergency[23]; the majority of the ministers, however,supported its imposition.[24] Of course, it was easy for the Chiluba government to get the bill empowering itself to impose the state of emergency through a parliament in which it controlled an absolute majority.

UNIP president Kebby Musokotwane admitted that the Zero Option Plan was a UNIP document, written by some members whom he refused to identify. The document, he admitted, had been in circulation for more than three months among members of the Central Committee of UNIP but was not adopted as a party policy paper. In spite of this admission, and in spite of the clearly subversive contents of the Zero Option Plan, international agencies and Western nations actually condemned the state of emergency or expressed serious reservations. Amnesty International declared that the detainees were all "prisoners of conscience." Amnesty never told the world to whose "conscience" it was referring to—Zambians', the nation's, donors', UNIP's, or the lenders'? Amnesty International is based in a country which puts people to death almost daily and has over a million of its citizens in jail for various offenses against the state and other citizens. Are these million-and-more persons all prisoners of conscience? UNIP leaders who were not detained showed a strong degree of support for the party by calling several press conferences and publicizing the conditions of the detainees as much as possible. That this was possible during the state of emergency showed the vibrancy of civil society and the degree of tolerance which political pluralism had introduced. This would not have been possible in pre-1991 Zambia. Lusaka-based diplomats met with Chiluba and expressed the reservations of their governments. Some thought the state of emergency was an "overreaction," while others thought that existing laws could have taken care of the problem. But in America (to use one example), existing laws alone were not enough to respond to the insane bombing of the Federal Building in Oklahoma City. The president and Congress have passed legislation and are discussing more, as well as unprecedented powers to enable the state better protect itself and its citizens against attacks. This has included the hiring of more secret service agents, the monitoring of international and cellular telephone calls, and the provision of more resources to security agencies. African diplomats did not meet with president Bill Clinton to express any reservations about these decisions and actions: it was an internal American affair! Within Zambia, the ZCTU condemned the state of emergency and described it as intimidatory. The Law Association of Zambia (LAZ) argued that there was no way that personal freedoms would not be abused and that the state of emergency was a direct challenge to popular democracy. While these and other criticisms show that there is extensive domestic and foreign interest in Zambia's democracy and democratization programs, they also show that critics and foreign governments and organizations either apply double standards or have very limited appreciation of the pressures new regimes face. In any event, a concrete understanding of the dangers posed to the MMD by UNIP and the Zero Option Plan is definitely lacking.

Without necessarily supporting the curtailment of the liberties of communities, constituencies, and individuals, we ought to recognize the truth that every government has a right to independently interpret its security situation, evaluate the power of and dangers posed by the opposition, and take appropriate measures to protect itself and its citizens. The very first and most important task of any serious government is its survival, the guarantee of national peace and stability, and the creation of an environment in which citizens can attain the highest levels of their productive and creative abilities. To be sure, this must not be "at all costs" or at the cost of personal and collective rights of the citizenry. The developed countries have never taken the issue of their own security lightly. They spend billions of dollars every year on building, expanding, and maintaining their internal and external intelligence operations. They employ thousands of undercover security agents in virtually every sector of society at great cost to taxpayers. Any challenge or real or perceived threat to the state is confronted with despatch. Even during the riots in Los Angeles, the United States government did not hesitate to send soldiers into the area to maintain law and order. Phones are bugged and the secret services have never been short of funds. The FBI and CIA alone spend about $30 billion each year on their operations. The response to the militant politics of the anti-Vietnam activists, the Black Panthers, and even David Koresh and the Branch Davidians in Waco, Texas, by U.S security forces shows that the developed, stable, and resource-endowed states of the West do not play around when it comes to security matters. Already, militia movements in the United States are being put under surveillance, and conservative radio announcers and talk-show hosts are being directly accused of posing a security threat to America. When some members of parliament challenged Boris Yeltsin's authority in Russia, he moved against them with heavy military artillery and received the full endorsement of the United States and other Western nations. The fact that a government is pursuing a democratic agenda does not mean that it should tolerate or accommodate threats to

its security and survival or pay more attention to the feelings and positions of foreign governments and donors. In
fact, if the Zero Option Plan had succeeded, the very same
lenders, donors, and Western governments would have recognized the new government; after all, it is not individuals
but countries that are accorded diplomatic recognition. The
very same Western interests worked with apartheid South
Africa for decades in spite of the sanctions from the
Organization of African Unity (OAU) and the United Nations
because their national interests were often uppermost in
their geostrategic and economic calculations. In any case,
Western governments certainly do not consult African leaders on matters of their own internal and external security.

It is therefore very difficult to find much reason in the
world's reaction to the imposition of a state of emergency by
a popularly elected and independent government. I was in
Zambia at that time and there was practically no evidence
that there even was a state of emergency. The situation only
allowed Chiluba to arrest and detain those who were directly
involved in drawing up and circulating the plan which outlined clear programs for creating anarchy, violence, disorder, tensions, and, in the final analysis, the fall of the
government. Any government worth its salt and interested
in its own survival must react to the presence of such a document, especially if it has been designed by people with a
score to settle, or by people with the resources, connections,
and determination to unseat the government. The fact that
a particular government is pursuing a democratic enterprise
does not mean that it sacrifices its capability for autonomous
action or that it must accommodate all sorts of challenges,
even those likely to see it out of power, just to satisfy the
interests of outside financial donors and lenders.

Generally, the Western world was unhappy at the imposition of the state of emergency. Even liberal international
organizations like Africa Watch condemned the state of
emergency. In a report on the state of emergency, issued

after it was lifted, Africa Watch noted that "it is extremely concerning that a state of emergency was declared at all by a government so recently elected on a platform of respect for civil and political rights."[25] Describing Zambia as a "model for democracy," it was the contention of Africa Watch that because Chiluba received 76% "of the presidential vote," and the MMD controls 125 of the 150 seats in parliament, and Chiluba had been "a prominent trade union leader who had himself been detained by Kaunda," it had no business in declaring a state of emergency no matter how much it was threatened by the opposition. As well, because the MMD had campaigned on a platform which "stressed the need for change, promising liberalisation of the economy, which was largely under state control, and democratization of the political system," and because the party "denounced the semi state of emergency under which Zambia had been ruled," it had no business declaring a state of emergency, as this negated its declared commitment to "the protection of civil rights, democratic pluralism and political accountability."[26] Even when referring to the Zero Option Plan and all the treasonable contents of the document, Africa Watch still contended that Chiluba "offered no further evidence that the Zero Option Plan represented a threat to national security nor any other justification for declaration."[27]

Such positions do not help the cause of democratization and political stability in Africa. What further evidence does a new government which is still confronted with a struggle for legitimacy and survival in a terribly decaying and tension-ridden society *need* to present before the international community to convince them that it is necessary to contain challenges to its survival? In fact, Chiluba does *not* need to convince Africa Watch or any other body before deciding, in the first instance, that the security and stability of Zambia are threatened by a group sitting down to write on paper how to overthrow a legitimately elected government. Unfortunately for Zambia and several—in fact, most—

African states, they will continue to face such evaluations of their independent efforts at political and economic restructuring for a long time to come, largely because of their continuing near-total dependence on, and vulnerability to, external forces.[28]

On May 25th, the Chiluba government revoked the state of emergency during ceremonies marking Africa Freedom Day and released all those who had been detained. In so doing, Chiluba left no one in doubt that in spite of its commitment to democracy, the government would clamp down on "trouble makers."[29] The president made it clear that the state of emergency had achieved its aims and that "Those who threaten the security of our people and the enterprise in democracy in which our people have invested will be dealt with fairly but firmly." Chiluba pointed out that his government was fully "determined to preserve" Zambia's "young democracy...it is our future." It had been very difficult for the state to prove the charges against the detainees, especially in the context of extreme domestic and international pressure.[30] It was also prudent to revoke the emergency in order to satisfy donors and lenders who were beginning to argue loudly that "Zambian democracy was on a life support machine" and who were actually beginning to link further aid and credits to the "restoration of full democracy."[31] To be sure, the lifting of the state of emergency was welcomed by all, including Chiluba himself.

In his address to the nation, Chiluba pointed out that "The decision to impose the state of emergency was painful but necessary." The Canadian High Commissioner Ambrey Morantz and the American Ambassador Gordon Streeb publicly expressed their delight at the revocation of the state of emergency. Bishop John Mambo of the Forum for Democratic Process (FODEP) contended that "The state of emergency had brought embarrassment outside Zambia because our democracy was being questioned." However, there were also those who felt that the state of emergency

had been necessary to show to the opposition that Chiluba
was capable of tough actions:

> Whatever people say, they cannot deny the fact that
> Chiluba shattered the invisibility of UNIP and its
> leaders with the state of emergency. The president
> showed that he had the guts to go the whole way,
> western support or no western support. The arrests
> of the three children of Kaunda especially Wezi
> Kaunda who sees himself as the next Kaunda to rule
> Zambia, showed that there were no sacred cows in
> the country. To have kept them in jail for 70 days,
> got the state of emergency through parliament and
> stood his ground, showed that the MMD was in power
> and in control of Zambia.[32]

Conclusion

Perhaps the real problem is that many Zambians have been
encouraged to overexaggerate the importance of their efforts
at democracy. After all, it was not like a transition from military rule to popular democracy. Whatever its faults, the
UNIP had established democratic institutions, and scheduled elections were held regularly under the one-party "participatory democratic" system. Zambia is not the only
democratizing country in Africa. More importantly, the transition was possible largely because Kaunda lost credibility,
copper prices fell, he was caught in the contradiction of his
own ideology, he lost touch with the people, UNIP had
become stagnant and bereft of new ideas, and leading members of UNIP—including Chiluba and the vast majority of
the MMD leadership—opted out of the party to form the
opposition. Above all these was the massive financial, logistical, and material support which the MMD enjoyed probably much more than any other prodemocracy movement in
Africa in the post-Cold War era. The Western world and the
Scandinavian countries have convinced most Zambian political leaders that they are probably the only genuine democratic country in Africa. In fact, in 1992, the Swedish Labour

Movement awarded the Peace and Freedom Prize to the ZCTU for "being instrumental in the reintroduction of a multiparty system in Zambia."[33] What will they award to Zambians who resisted one-party rule, fought against repression, and without whose support the MMD could not have won the elections? This sort of patronizing attitude by Western institutions has often tended to divide Africans and generate false expectations. Hence, such positions as: "It is all too clear that Zambian democracy is being watched. As far as the international community is concerned, it is Africa's model," and "Zambia shoulders heavy responsibility in the region to ensure that democracy works. It has been a leading light already and it is important that it continues to be or else democracy is doomed," are clear exaggerations of the significance and implications of democratic transition in Zambia.[34]

The state of emergency was definitely a major test for the Chiluba government and for Zambian democracy. Since the government did not proscribe UNIP, did not constrain the activities of the media, and had allowed the democratic process to continue uninhibited, the government only did what it had to do to control and prevent such divisive and dangerous political positions and options. As the Algerian government did when it acted against the fundamentalists in the interest of the nation, the Chiluba government was faced with its own fundamental challenges; the imposition of the state of emergency in Zambia must be seen in that light. Democracy is not the ultimate stage of societal development and should not be an excuse for anarchy or retrogression. Opposition movements in Africa must learn to work hard, mobilize people, alter national discourses through dialogue and organization, and use legal and political means to challenge incumbent regimes rather than seek shortcuts to power at the expense of national peace and stability. Yet, it is important not to focus exclusively on *democracy* but rather to realize that, ultimately, what determines what is possible—even the character of the opposition, and the ability of the state and elites to manage contradictions and so on—is *the nature of civil society*. The Zero Option episode certainly jolted the MMD government into realizing that it had to perform and take full charge of the affairs of state, if it is not to be unseated by opposition forces. Melinda Ham was also correct in noting that "the emergency has also demonstrated how fragile Zambia's democracy is, that the division of powers between the executive and legislative wings of government are blurred, and Parliament has little power to challenge the cabinet. UNIP, the only existing viable opposition, is weakened and faced with a split, which raises the worrying specter of another de facto one party state."[35] If these critical issues are not addressed, there is no reason not to expect a better articulated agenda for promoting social unrest and regime turnover in Zambia in the future.

Notes

1. Interview with an MMD member of parliament, Lusaka, June 1993.
2. Richard Sandbrook, *The Politics of Africa's Economic Recovery* (Cambridge: Cambridge University Press, 1991), p. 121.
3. Ibid., p. 91.
4. Ibid., p. 96.
5. Ibid., pp. 117-118.
6. Ibid., p. 120.
7. Robert Pinkney, *Democracy in the Third World* (Boulder: Lynne Rienner, 1994), p. 159.
8. Ibid.
9. Barry Gills and Joel Rocamora, "Low Intensity Democracy," *Third World Quarterly* Vol. 13, (3) (1992), p. 507.
10. Samuel Huntington, *The Third Wave- Democratization in the Late Twentieth Century*, (Norman and London: University of Oklahoma Press, 1991), p. 211.
11. Ibid.
12. See ibid., pp. 252-255.

13. See Robert Pinkney, *Democracy in the Third World*, op. cit.
14. Claude Ake, "Is Africa Democratizing?" Text of the 1993 Guardian Lecture, reproduced in *The Guardian* (Lagos) (December 12, 1993).
15. Samuel Huntington, *The Third Wave*, op. cit., p. 255.
16. "Zero Option: What the Zero Option Saga Means," *The Weekly Post* (May 21-27, 1993).
17. Ibid.
18. Interview, Lusaka, July 1993.
19. This document was reproduced in full in *The National Mirror* (March 15-21, 1993).
20. Masauto Phiri, "What Charges Have Come Out?" *The Weekly Post* (May 21-27, 1993).
21. The Chiluba government was very aware of the divisions within UNIP between the radical and reformist factions. Kebby Musokotwane, the president of UNIP and leader of the reformists was not arrested or detained as it was clear that the document could not have come from that faction. Chibembe Nyaluge, UNIP Secretary for Youth Affairs and Lucy Sichone, UNIP Political Secretary who belong to the reformist camp were detained briefly and released.
22. Interview with an MMD official, Lusaka, June 1993.
23. Roger Chongwe is Minister for Legal Affairs, Geoffrey Miyanda is Minister without Portfolio and Ludwig Sondashi is Minister for Labor.
24. In its rush to announce the state of emergency, Chiluba had wrongly invoked Article 31 of the Constitution which actually prevents the government from restricting individual rights and freedoms. This error was corrected when he invoked Article 30 of the Constitution which allows for the imposition of a full state of emergency. This error was a major sign of weakness and confusion within the MMD government especially as the government had some of the more seasoned and experienced legal minds on its side. These include the Vice-President Levi Mwanawasa, Legal Affairs Minister Ludwig Sondashi, Attorney-General Ali Hamir, Local Government Minister Roger Chongwe, and Presidential Legal Advisor Vincent Malambo.
25. Africa Watch, "Zambia: Model For Democracy Declares State of Emergency," Vol. V, (8) (June 10, 1993), p. l.
26. Ibid., p. 2.

27. Ibid., p. 3.
28. Africa Watch took the position that "Unless more con-
    crete evidence of criminal action is offered by the govern-
    ment, the charges look dangerously like a simple effort to
    restrict political opposition to the MMD." One might ask:
    To whom is this evidence to be presented? This sounds
    more like imposing American political and legal values on
    other societies: The "Be Like Mike Syndrome." What
    might threaten the American state might not threaten the
    Zambian state and vice versa. One can look at the
    American political system and see hundreds of unusual
    political arrangements and activities which might never
    be contemplated in other societies. Yet, these have not
    become the focus of any international debate because
    they take place in the polity of a hegemonic power!
29. "Emergency Scrapped," *Times of Zambia* (May 26, 1993).
30. See Margaret Nyimba, "8 Detainees Freed, Rearrested,
    Charged," *Times of Zambia* (May 22, 1993), and Andrew
    Sakala, "Released Suspects Greeted with Pomp" (ibid.)
31. See Samuel Ngoma, "Emergency Lifting Cheers all,"
    Times of Zambia (May 29, 1993).
32. Interview with an MMD Member of Parliament, Lusaka,
    June 1993.
33. "ZCTU Wins Prize," *The Weekly Post* (December 24-30,
    1992). Yet, the ZCTU remains an undemocratic body
    compulsorily affiliated to the MMD the way it was affili-
    ated to UNIP. Many of ZCTU's leaders do not agree with
    the policies of the MMD. See interview with Fackson
    Shamenda, President of the ZCTU in *Search* (December
    1992) and Mutete Kashimani, "ZCTU Still Undemocratic,"
    Search (December 1992).
34. Samuel Ngoma, "Emergency Lifting Cheers all, " op. cit.
    The transition program in Kenya and Malawi where the
    leaders initially opposed any form of mobilization for
    democracy, and the violent conflicts in Mali and Nigeria
    tasked the efforts of pro-democracy groups much more
    than in Zambia. See Githu Muigai, "Kenya's Opposition
    and the Crisis of Governance," *Issue* XXI, 1-2 (1993);
    Jacques Mariel Nzouankeu, "The Role of the National
    Conference in the Transition to Democracy in Africa: The
    Cases of Benin and Mali," *Issue* XXI, 1-2, (1993); and
    Julius O. Ihonvbere, "Dead End to Nigerian Democracy?:

Explaining the 1993 General Abacha Coup in Nigeria," Marcia Jones, (ed.), *Proceedings of the Association of Third World Studies*, (Statesboro: Georgia Southern University, 1995).

35.   Melinda Ham, "Zambia: History Repeats Itself," *Africa Report* (May-June 1993).

CHAPTER SEVEN

THE FUTURE OF DEMOCRACY
AND CIVIL SOCIETY IN AFRICA

Given the socio-economic conditions of Africa and
the fact that up to 80 per cent of Africa's working
people are peasants, multi-partysm is more likely
than not, in the first instance, to lead to conservative victories, and a multi-coloured cloak of legitimacy. Thus the multi-party state is unlikely to be
any more responsive to either the needs or
expressed wishes of the majority of Africa's population than the one party and military states have
been.[1]

Nations cannot be built without the popular support
and full participation of the people, nor can the economic crisis be resolved and the human and economic conditions improved without the full and
effective contribution, creativity and popular enthusiasm of the vast majority of the people.[2]

This work has examined the democratization processes
underway in Zambia with particular emphasis on the role
of social forces and popular organizations in the recomposition of political spaces and the strengthening of civil society. To be sure, the evidence is clear that Africa still has a

long way to go before it can become truly *democratic*, and before it can set up the necessary political, social, and economic institutions required to maintain the democratic process. It is only now being widely appreciated that "Liberalization of politics may mean pluralization of interest articulation, but not democratic government. Instead, it may yield demands for sub-national micro-states, extremist ideological clashes and opportunities for cross border interventions."[3] Yet, a beginning has been made. As we demonstrated in the first chapter, the ongoing struggle for democracy *and democratization* is the product of a combination of internal and external forces. The fall of the Soviet Union as a nation and a superpower, the triumph of market forces under the supervision of the IMF and the World Bank, and the emergence of the United States as the sole hegemonic force in the world have far reaching implications for the democratization processes in Africa.[4]

These changes in the global system, as well as those within Africa, have led to the interpretation of democracy solely as a *procedural* matter, emphasizing multiplicity of parties, periodic elections, multiplicity of candidates during elections, the existence of a constitution and parliament, the guarantee of basic freedoms, and the independence of the judiciary. These are processes which can easily be *imposed* on society from above by urban-based elites with very limited political objectives. As has been demonstrated in Zaire, Togo, Nigeria, Kenya, Zambia, and Ghana, *procedural* democracy is not all that difficult to set up, especially when donors make further aid conditional on some sort of political pluralism. Of course, because the process lacks the necessary foundation and support in civil society, it can break down just as easily if the elites have too narrow a vision or lack cohesion or political consensus. As Harvey Glickman has noted,

> Governments are still unable to arrest economic decline, but it is clear that politics in Africa is "open-

ing up." Ironically, as the world has discovered in Eastern Europe and Central Asia, more freedom can mean more strife. And, liberty and consent in politics do not equal economic progress and prosperity. Nevertheless, it is also clear that authoritarian rule has lost whatever legitimacy it may have had, although a number of states persist in shaky military or one-party governments despite pressures for change of varying intensity.... As well, lingering or rekindled civil wars still daunt efforts to create governments or country wide acceptance....[5]

Trends in Reform Politics and the Democratization Process

It is true that the "post–Cold War, aspiring new world order makes democratic government the modular political envelope for a variety of political social trends."[6] Yet, these "trends" are not value-free. They in large measure reflect the dominant political, economic, and ideological interests of the forces which condition and determine relations in the increasingly unequal global division of labor. The Cold War might have ended, but the poverty war goes on and the divide between the rich and poor nations remains as wide as ever. True, a process of globalization is occurring as states lose their sovereignty to supranational or transterritorial structures. But, Africa, already marginalized in the global capitalist order, remains unimportant in the economic and geostrategic calculations of the developed nations. In terms of foreign aid, economic concessions, immigration policies, investments, and other indicators of a so-called new global order, Africa is hardly considered.

The political and economic agenda of international finance capital and of the Western nations at the moment tend to give preference to political arrangements which merge economic and political interests and structures to reflect the overall goals of global capitalism. Such arrangements, at least in Africa, give a veneer of democracy but hardly restructure the political landscape, the power balances, the relations of power and production, or the ability of the social formation to maintain some autonomy from powerful external forces and interests. Thus predatory rule continues, the nation is held hostage by a handful of corrupt elites (for, even though multiple parties exist on the political terrain, they are more the "properties" of certain individuals who often are the presidential candidates), and masses of people remain mere objects of manipulation and exploitation.

A second dimension of the current processes in Africa is the overblown expectations on the part of the Western nations and donors from Africans and African political elites. True, the record of the African bourgeoisie on all fronts is disastrous and, in fact, shameful. They have squandered resources, intimidated vulnerable constituencies, suffocated civil society, mortgaged their economies, and pushed resource-rich Africa to the bottom of global relations. Following decades of massive repression, the elimination/containment of real and imaginary opposition, the neglect of the rural areas, urban dislocation, foreign domination and exploitation, social unrest, and marginalization in a highly exploitative global order, African leaders were forced to adopt very painful structural adjustment programs. Because, by and large, these programs could be implemented only through repression, African regimes subverted the courts, repressed popular forces, promulgated draconian laws and decrees, dismantled all the economic and political institutions set up since the 1960s, and opened up their economies to foreign capital in the name of commercialization, privatization, and liberalization. Invariably, these policies have changed little. They increased alienation, violence, distrust, unrest, instability, poverty, coups and counter-coups, and vulnerability to foreign control. As Martin Klein has rightly noted, adjustment policies which overlook the specificities and dynamics of African social formations have "often made a bad economic situation worse and have condemned a whole generation of young people to unemployment, to helplessness and to poverty. Often bitter and alienated, the Mishanga boys of Lusaka and the students of Bamako are the contemporary counterparts of Nkrumah's veranda boys and the key groups in most urban demonstrations. And behind them stands an even larger mass of people for whom independence has meant absolutely nothing, people who have neither love for nor commitment to leaders they did not choose and do not like."[7] It is this clearly weak and highly fractionalized and factionalized elite that the western nations and lenders are depending on to promote even *liberal* democracy, not to mention a genuine empowerment of the people and the democratization of society.

In the midst of the confusion, uncertainty, and desperation generated by externally imposed programs, the donors and lenders added new conditionalities of multipartyism, democracy, and respect for human rights. While this should have been part of the package at the beginning, it was introduced as an afterthought, a convenient way of pressurizing African leaders to open up political spaces, but also a convenient way of rationalizing decreased aid and investment in the region. The important issue, however, is the way in which donors have gone about the "no democracy, no foreign aid" campaign completely oblivious to the realities on the ground in Africa. After decades of Western—and, of course, Eastern bloc—support for African leaders in their irresponsibility, waste, terrorization of civil society, and misplaced priorities, to now assume that such desperate leaders, who are scared of giving up power for a variety of reasons, would simply turn to democracy seems somewhat naive. To assume that the same institutions and structures of society employed in repressing the people while trying to force monetarist IMF and World Bank prescriptions down the throats of the people can now be employed in mobilizing, educating, and empowering the people seems somewhat misplaced. As well, to assume that the very same elites that were responsible for decades of terror and tyranny, corruption, waste, and mismanagement, can simply turn around and pursue democratic programs seems to overlook very serious contradictions, coalitions, and conflicts which characterize social and political relations in Africa.

Of course, the Western media, observers, and scholars have jumped on the bandwagon of praising every simplistic political move in Africa as evidence of democracy and popular will. Even when Babangida of Nigeria gave all indications that he had no plans to leave office, he was seen as this great "democratic dictator," the soldier who was a "champion of human rights." This was even after he threw hundreds of Nigerians into detention without trial, waged a war against the media, and presided over one of the most decadent and corrupt regimes in human history. The Western media and observers, as well as their "experts," have started to treat African leaders as they treat East Europeans—like inexperienced politicians who know very little about democracy, governance, administration, the market, capitalism, state–society relations, and so on. This is very simplistic, patronizing, and in fact a very shallow appreciation of the capability of these peoples to do a lot of damage on their own or with the support of their Western allies. Many politicians in Zambia have often wondered why the West did not insist on these reforms since 1960 when they knew that it was the only way to capitalist development, and why they allowed the situation to deteriorate to present levels before rushing in their economic and political conditionalities. The net result is that even simple political moves are hailed as monumental manifestations of commitment to the market and to liberal democracy. The whole process of political and economic restructuring loses its originality, creativity, and the endogenous touch while

alien and foreign models, tastes, values, methods, and relations are grafted onto contradictions and conflicts that have
been generated from the dynamics of domestic alignment
and realignment of forces. This will only move Africa back
to the situation of the 1960s, and the policies introduced
will fail to restructure existing relations in any fundamental manner, thus generating frustration with liberal democracy and, consequently, opposition to it.

At the moment, it is important to critically evaluate the
processes of democratization. This in no way implies a lack
of support for the democratization projects in the region.
Rather, this is the only way to avoid the mistakes of the past,
and to comprehend the possibilities for a viable democratization project for the twenty-first century.[8] As we pointed
out in Chapter One, it is important that scholars and
activists draw a distinction between *democracy* and *democratization*. This way, we can distinguish between movements sponsored, led, and manipulated by the elites (which
also address elitist issues), from those which address grassroots-based programs and issues. The struggles by African
elites to manipulate political participation and discourses,
and to repackage primordial politics in the new language of
"democracy," "empowerment," "gender," and "peace,"
which pleases the ears of donors and lenders, is leading
Africa practically nowhere in its efforts at change in the
1990s. Without exception, the introduction of liberal
democracy has not resolved ethnic, religious, regional, and
gender inequalities and inequities. If anything, these have
become deepened to dangerous proportions threatening to
tear the state apart, pitting community against community,
and rapidly eroding the relevance of the state and its custodians.

These developments hold very far-reaching implications
for growth, development, peace, stability, and democracy
in Africa. There is no doubting the fact that in the context
of ongoing recomposition of political, strategic, and eco-

nomic relations in the emerging global order, Africa will be making a monumental mistake if it fails to restructure polit-ical and economic spaces with an agenda which acknowl-edges its historical experiences, specificities, balance of forces, and location and role in the international division of labor.[9] This is largely because the current efforts, as the opening statement clearly articulates, will run into several problems and contradictions arising from internal and exter-nal sources. As Martin Klein has noted:

> the new democratic regimes are going to have dif-ficulty. But let us recognize something about democ-racy. Democracy is not an abstract ideal. People do not choose democracy because they read about it. Democracy has invariably risen out of a struggle against autocracy. Sometimes revolutions begin for what seem trivial reasons. The American revolution was begun over some taxes and the quite reason-able expectation that the American colonies should pay for their own defense. Americans already had a tradition of political participation for large parts of the white male population, but the creation of a true democracy involved almost two centuries of struggle.[10]

Klein notes that "many of the new leaders will disappoint both us and their followers. They will disappoint us just as many of the guerilla leaders disappointed us when they moved into the cities to take power. Some proved to be cor-rupt. Even more proved to be incompetent at jobs for which guerilla warfare provided no training."[11] Poverty, ethnic vio-lence, intolerance, anger, hunger, disillusionment, years of alienation, and frustration with the slow pace of reform are going to remain challenges for decades to come. While I agree with Klein, a new political culture must be generated in Africa, a political culture which refuses to accept such behavior from the elites. Africans have suffered too much to tolerate more corruption, long and useless speeches, failures, the criminal looting of the treasury, misplaced priorities, and the continuing mortgaging of the economy.

New institutions must be created and civil society must be strengthened and leaders must be held accountable for their actions right from the first day in office. Of course, their failures must be measured in the context of African realities and the successes duly acknowledged. In fact, it would be a mistake to use political and economic indicators from the developed countries as a measure of how well African countries are doing. The situations and experiences are markedly different.

The African situation today is not only pathetic, it also encourages a high degree of pessimmism.[12] The region's deepening crisis has eroded possibilities for creativity and innovation and has devastated communities. As well, the crisis has weakened the state as well as the dominant classes and institutions, and has made Africa more vulnerable to outside manipulation than ever before. Hence "democracy" today means political and economic restructuring in line with the dictates of credit clubs, the IMF, and the World Bank via the imposition of orthodox structural adjustment packages. The crisis, which has greatly eroded the sovereignty of African states, has also shifted attention from the struggles of nonbourgeois forces at the grassroots, towards the often opportunistic and incoherent politics of the urban-based elites in the cities. It is with these elites that the donors and lenders negotiate the terms of their political and economic conditionalities.

We have also come to witness strange arguments to the effect that since the poor are "far from markets," the "most likely result, due to their economic and geographic condition, is that the poor will not be affected significantly by any adjustment program in the short run."[13] As Wamba-dia-Wamba has rightly noted, adjustment programs have been unable to guarantee growth, liberation, self-reliance, or democracy.[14] All over the continent, adjustment has hardly liberated the forces and factors of production to levels where an appreciable degree of growth and development can be visible. While in a few instances, fiscal and other macroeconomic indicators have undergone some changes, the sociocultural costs of adjustment have been devastating, and it will take decades for Africans to recover from ongoing dislocations and frustrations.[15] What is even more interesting is that, while the unequal distribution of the pains and costs of adjustment has pushed the masses away from the state towards support for opposition movements (as was the case in Zambia), the new democratic governments have seen their support and legitimacy evaporate as a result of the very same monetarist policies!

It is important therefore, to transcend the usually interesting and astonishing media reports, and to focus on activities at the grassroots which challenge the manipulative tactics of the elites, and the often inaccurate prescriptions of external interests. This will enable us to demonstrate the continuing trend of elite decadence, corruption, waste, repression of the people, asphyxiation of civil society, mismanagement, and general inhibition of the democratic process which have culminated in the current conditions of decay, subservience, and poverty. Democracy is not only failing to resolve primordial contradictions and conflicts, it is not in any way enhancing self-reliance, autonomy, and development in Africa because support from the West is halfhearted, and the ideological foundations of political prescriptions simply consolidate dependency. This is not to deny the formidable efforts of genuine popular and grassroots organizations all over the continent. Yet, democracy in Africa will make very limited progress until it directly addresses the structural roots of the region's predicament, and revolves around the experiences and aspirations of the majority of the people. There is a need for a new political platform capable of transcending the legacies and politics of the likes of Eyadema in Togo, Bongo in Gabon, and

Babangida and Abacha of Nigeria. The defeat of Banda in Malawi, for instance, is only the beginning of a very long and bitter struggle to, first of all, recover from the disaster he visited on the country.

In their efforts to placate the West, to keep foreign aid flowing in, and to reassure investors as to their degree of "new openness," African leaders have tried to ape Western political forms in the most pedestrian ways possible. For instance, after the Babangida junta refused to register any of the independently formed political parties, it simply created its own two parties—the Social *Democratic* Party (SDP) and the National *Republican* Convention (NRC)—in an effort to, even in name, reflect the American reality as much as possible. Thus African states lose the economic and political autonomy necessary to determine the content and context of the political and economic restructuring processes in their respective nations. The long discredited "spirit of modernization" ideologues of the 1960s seem to have been revived, with efforts to define democracy in Africa as an instrumental process which can be made to accommodate Western models in spite of different historical experiences, different contradictions and conflicts, and different locations in a highly exploitative and unequal global capitalist order. What we have in place today are corrupt and desperate regimes and elites, presiding over foreign-dictated economic and political programs, and participating in an international division of labor which is structured to marginalize the continent. The subservient and weak position of African states has not only created a new colonialism, but has reduced African elites to the status of "ignorant school boys" who must be constantly educated by Western and Japanese bureaucrats and politicians on the meanings and virtues of democracy and adjustment.[16] One example will suffice.

At the review of the United Nations Programme of Action on African Economic Recovery and Development (UNPAAERD) in New York in September 1991, the OAU took

261

the position that:

> During the life-span of UNPAAERD, African
> economies did not witness any significant change
> for the better...from all economic indicators, the con-
> tinent of Africa appeared to have been by-passed by
> (the) positive developments in the world system.
> African economies were required to make ... adjust-
> ments and achieve economic growth in the face of
> severely compressed incomes and rising debt over-
> hang. This is an impossible dilemma.[17]

The donors and lenders, particularly the European
Community, Japan, the IMF, and the World Bank, took a
completely different position on the African predicament.
The United States contended that most African states had
not put in place "serious and sustained" economic reform,
that there must be a "shift from a government dominated
approach to development to a private sector-led approach"
and that "democratization... will lead to better governance
and fiscal accountability."[18] Even the United States—the
world's largest debtor nation with a trade deficit of well over
$4 trillion and on practically all counts, an economy in seri-
ous crisis in spite of its democracy—has not shown any consistency in its prescriptions for the African predicament.
George Bush lost his job as President of the United States
on account of his inability to revive the economy, control
inflation, generate employment, stop bankruptcies, and
reduce foreign competition. The massive defeat of
Democrats by Republican candidates in the 1994 mid-term
elections was due largely to the sluggish nature of the economy and the poor public perception of performance on the
economic level. The point therefore is that even the United
States has not put in place a "serious and sustained" economic reform program for the world to emulate. The Savings
and Loans scandal, which is costing the nation over $500
billion, reflects the fact that "fiscal accountability" cannot
always be guaranteed even with Western-style democracy.

More importantly, it is wrong to pressure African states to "roll back the state" when in the West the state is still a major actor in economic matters—bailing out businesses, conducting research and development for businesses, seeking foreign markets for private business, subsidizing health care, education, public transportation, and guaranteeing and subsidizing local businesses that invest in certain parts of the world. The West continues to subsidize farmers and also to control prices. It provides social insurance and all sorts of assistance to the poor, such as Food Stamps and other entitlements. By May 1995, the Clinton administration was planning to impose sanctions on Japan for not purchasing more American cars: to the best of my knowledge the White House does not manufacture cars. This is the state engaging another state to open up markets for private capitalist accumulation. Thus to give the impression that Western capitalism has developed only because the state does not participate in the economic sphere, is simply wrong. It is equally a very dangerous prescription in an underdeveloped economy, where the dominant elites are weak and nonhegemonic, and where the economy is under foreign domination. The state has always been part of the process of change, accumulation, growth, development, and democratization. The real challenge in Africa is how to *reconstitute* the state to make it more efficient, accountable, stable, and effective in mediating class contradictions and promoting growth and development.

It would appear that the unmediated prescription of "rolling back the state" and total privatization and commercialization of the economy is more of a strategy to promote the interests of the dominant actors in African economies—foreign capital. In any case, it is a historical fact that none of the present developed nations—not even the successful Newly Industrializing Countries (NICs)—developed *democratically* and without a strong and highly interventionist state. The rights of people, especially women, children, and minorities, were guaranteed only after the market was consolidated and after the institutions to sustain the market and democracy were established and consolidated and legitimized. It is also incorrect therefore, to give the impression that the West was *always* democratic, that its current state of development is the precipitate of its democratic history, and that it has resolved the problems of democracy. Only an acknowledgement of this historical fact will promote an honest appreciation of the constraints and contradictions of democratic consolidation in Africa without unduly pampering the state or popular constituencies. Of course, this is not to prescribe authoritarianism in place of democracy. Rather, our point is that the West and its institutions need to be more careful in their sermonising on democracy, and *we* must not forget that the West and the East built up the undemocratic and terribly repressive structures and political actors in contemporary Africa. According to Martin Klein,

> Nowhere in the world was there a tradition of democracy in the 18th century. France had no democratic traditions when it began its revolution. It created a revolutionary democratic tradition in 5 years and fought about it for the next 160. It took Britain two centuries to create the parliamentary democracy it later tried to bequeath to its former colonies. As late as 1832, Great Britain was ruled by several thousand wealthy property owners. Democratic traditions are created by people resisting autocracy or attacking privilege. We are seeing democracy created in the former Soviet Union, in Eastern Europe and in Africa—but it is the beginning of the struggle, not the end. Those who have power rarely yield willingly.[19]

The issues articulated by Klein above are often overlooked by donors and advocates of Western liberal democracy who assume that the progress towards democracy in Africa is too slow. When democratic efforts are mediated by political, social, and cultural realities on the ground, they turn their backs on the democratizing nations and blame the elites and the governments for being unable to operate a democratic system! It was a poor appreciation of the above-cited historical facts that led donors and Western NGOs to react so unsympathetically to the declaration of a state of emergency in Zambia in 1993 during the "Zero Option" episode. In reality, the march towards *democracy* will only *fuel* the real struggle for *democratization* in Africa. Development cannot occur without surplus extraction, the development of the factors and forces of production, the strengthening of the institutions and structures of production, and actual exchange. In social formations that are already underdeveloped, dominated, and marginalized, it is doubtful that these tasks can be done by following the prescriptions of the very same forces that underdeveloped the societies, that presently dominate them, and that have a very visible interest in their continuing underdevelopment and marginalization in the global system.

The Limits of the Prodemocracy Movements in Africa

Failed economic and political policies have thus increased repression, political desperation, and intolerance and violence in Africa. Regimes have now devised ingenuous ways of circumventing the growing pressures for accountability, democracy, and social justice. In other instances, elites are engaging in a struggle to penetrate political institutions in order to domesticate ongoing struggles for democracy. There is a need to be cautious in how we embrace the new political parties. Just because they are new and just because they carry the label "democratic" does not mean that "the Hour Has Come" and we must critically evaluate their politics in the context of African realities. There is obviously a yawning gap between pronouncements and documents on the one hand, and practices and praxis on the other. In Nigeria, for instance, the methods, goals, and instruments of politics are in no way better than those of the defunct first and second republics. In most instances, the new parties of the aborted third republic were much more disorganized, more corrupt, and more violent.[20] They were led by opportunists and people that Michael Sata of Zambia would refer to as "political prostitutes." They had no national project, no vision beyond the Central Bank and contract meetings, and no interest in generating new arguments, building new constituencies, and restructuring Nigeria's place in the global division of labor. Nigeria's "new breed" politicians lived for the day, tomorrow could take care of itself! In Zambia, the MMD was created and is still run by former UNIP stalwarts. Practically every minister who has resigned or has been dismissed by Chiluba has formed his/her own political party in Zambia. One begins to wonder as to what the real interests and objectives of these old political buzzards are. There is no difference between the leadership in "democratic" Ghana and those who ran the military dictatorship of Jerry Rawlings for almost a decade. The political parties refused to reach accommodation with each other, and Rawlings simply out-foxed them. Moi did the same thing to the prodemocracy movements in Kenya. Even the Forum for the Restoration of Democracy (FORD) splintered into two groups and, along with other parties, they were unable to concentrate opposition votes. It becomes necessary to be cautious when we seek to interpret the emergence of new political parties, prodemocracy movements, and other ostensibly pro-people organizations as the arrival of the democratic epoch. Many of the parties are new versions of the old ethnic and regional-based parties which failed woefully in the 1950s and 1960s. Others remain the properties of prominent politicians and "emergency millionaires," while several represent dubious interests masquerading as grassroots-based political parties.

Many of the prodemocracy movements—especially in the

francophone nations, but also in anglophone countries like Nigeria—have made loud demands for a "national conference" to set the agenda for the new politics. Such national conferences have already been called in several African countries (Benin, Congo, Gabon, Mali, Niger, Togo, Zaire) and have served as a viable and important avenue to open up new opportunities for confronting the power of the dominant classes. They have served as avenues for mobilizing opposition, forging a united front against incumbent regimes, and for redirecting the content of national politics in countries such as Niger, Cameroon, Central African Republic, Cote d'Ivoire, Guinea, and Madagascar. As well, the national conference has created opportunities for a broad discussion of national issues, identifying and selecting new leaders, and directly unseating and challenging current custodians of state power. Yet, we need to be very cautious in determining the forces behind these conferences, the goals that are established, and the methods for pursuing them. If such conferences are meant merely to attack the incumbent president, elect another potential "president-for-life," deal with political and not economic issues, its relevance will be tenuous. As well, if the conference is merely a tool in the hands of political opportunists and those marginalized from the center of current politics, it will eventually be hijacked and controlled by elements who are only marginally different from the current custodians of power. Finally, if the national conference is merely designed to create another political party dominated by political elites, intellectuals, and second-level politicians, then it will be unable to mobilize the people on a long-term basis or to provide an opportunity for strengthening civil society and thus ensuring the survival of democracy. In Zaire, Togo, and Cameroon, many leading advocates of the national conference have melted into the cabinet of the incumbent regimes, with no apologies for abandoning their constituencies. At one time in Gabon and Zaire, over a hundred political parties existed with direct interests in the presidency! In Nigeria, many leading members of the prodemocracy groups, including the Campaign for Democracy (CD), joined General Sani Abacha in November 1993 to dismantle the democratic institutions and effectively terminate the march to a third republic.

The only way in which the national conference can be relevant is if it is summoned by popular and grassroots organizations, visibly dominated by these organizations, focused on issues beyond the dictator and the elites, and organized around popular issues. Such a conference must also empower the people and their organizations; address environmental, gender, political, social, and economic issues; and work for short- and longer-term structural changes in the political economy. In short, it must not allow the "new breed" democrats to use democracy to kill or suffocate democracy. It must sufficiently open up the political system to prevent the new elite from using democracy to build authoritarianism. This is because the new authoritarianism is more subtle and more complex but quite unlikely to survive the onslaught of non-bourgeois forces.

Yet popular constituencies remain very vulnerable to manipulation and pressures from the elites. In Ghana, the prodemocracy forces were so opportunistic and divided that it was easy to marginalize and ridicule them in the political processes. A similar situation weakened the prodemocracy forces in Kenya, though they managed to win several seats in parliament. As soon as Section 2A of the Constitution was repealed by Moi in early 1992, five new political parties immediately sought registration: Forum for the Restoration of Democracy (FORD); The Democratic Party of Kenya (DP); The Social Democratic Party (SDP); The Labour Party Democracy (LPD); Kenya National Congress (KNC); Kenya National Democratic Alliance (KENDA); and Party of Independent Candidates of Kenya (PICK). As Githu Muigai has noted on this development, "No sooner had the parties been registered than it became clear that the problems of making multiparty politics viable were more difficult than had been envisaged. Ultimately there were two categories of problems: problems created by the government and KANU to derail the democratic process and problems inherent in the nature of the opposition itself and Kenyan politics generally."[21] The factionalization and fractionalization of the opposition, the failure to work for a consensus and to present the electorate with a clear alternative agenda for empowerment and democratization, significantly eroded its influence and chances in the elections. In Zimbabwe, though all the opposition parties are for the free market, against the one-party state, and against Marxism-Leninism, they are poorly organized, dominated by personalities of the early decades of independence, lack a sense of direction, and have not demonstrated a capacity to replace Mugabe's ruling Zimbabwe African National Union-Patriotic Front (ZANU [PF]). In fact, the leading opposition party, the Zimbabwe Unity Party (ZUM) led by Edgar Tekere, has "no campaign headquarters, not in the capital city, not in the provinces, not in the districts. Up to now ZUM operates from wherever its leaders happen to be. Candidates in the 1990 elections had to fend for themselves. There was no committee to plan strategy. Things were run on an *ad hoc* basis....After the elections, ZUM members and supporters expected an accounting and a party congress. There were none even to this day."[22] Masipula Sithole's view is that the "opposition parties are so weak that unity would not make a difference. There is a certain threshold of support a party must have in order to have local or national viability. None of the present opposition parties have this threshold of support."[23] It is possible to move from one African situation to the other and reach similar conclusions on the opposition, by whatever name or description they go.

This is rather unfortunate as one would have expected that the desperate socioeconomic and political conditions of Africa would have created a new political tendency among the elites. With the ongoing changes in the world, the scientific and technological revolution, and the revolution in information generation and dissemination, the new political parties in Africa are still mainly concerned with issues of raw power: power to dominate, power to loot, power to intimidate vulnerable groups, and power to relate directly with foreign capital to facilitate private accumulation. Political programs and alignments must begin to seriously examine the dangers which the African elite pose to the continent's peace and progress. The bourgeoisie which many Africanist scholars claimed to have seen in Africa (Kenya, Nigeria, Cote d'Ivoire, Ghana, Tanzania in particular) in the 1970s and early 1980s seem to have disappeared while socioeconomic and political conditions in the entire continent have hardly moved forward on any front.

Strengthening Civil Society in Africa: Constraints and Possibilities

In the past decade or so, hundreds of civil liberty organizations and popular movements as well as NGOs have been created in all African states in spite of opposition and harassment from the state and its security networks.[24] As Yoweri Museveni, president of Uganda, noted recently, "(t)oday an authentic grass roots movement for fundamental democratic change is unfolding in Africa. The people are winning in their demands for the removal of dictatorial and fascist regimes across the continent. These democratic struggles are older than the changes that have swept Eastern Europe since 1989."[25] It was the absence of this tradition of grassroots empowerment that has made it impossible for political parties to become mass-based and to survive; that has made democratic rights and liberties tenuous; and that has made it possible for military adventurists and political opportunists to hijack political power, repress the people, loot the national treasuries, and reproduce conditions of backwardness and subservience to external forces. It is important to note, however, that the process of building a viable civil society takes time, it evolves from the direct struggles of the people. Civil society cannot be legislated or created by donors and lenders. The current tendency to force a civil society on Africa is a wrong step in the wrong direction. A viable civil society would have to emerge from the contestations for power, the alignment and realignment of political and social forces, and the commitment of communities and organizations to networking, creating common grounds for political work, and to checking the excesses of the elites.

Several popular organizations and prodemocracy movements in Africa have clear-cut programs for empowerment and democratization of their respective societies. Without doubt, as the processes of networking and collective action increase in the years to come, holistic *national* programs, reflecting the interests and aspirations of the various national constituencies, will emerge in most African states. As Fantu Cheru notes, "Democratization of political and economic institutions both at national and international levels is a prerequisite for development."[26] While the "reform of the African state is a prerequisite of reform of the African economy" as Boutros Boutros-Ghali has rightly noted,[27] it is also true that an increasingly hostile international economy will not ease the pressure on the African economy to facilitate the necessary restructuring for development. As Boutros-Ghali has correctly noted, "economic liberalism and market forces all too often serve as a hypocritical rule that caters to special interests, those of the powerful who from their position of strength make the rules and even create the dogma, which everyone comes to regard as sacred."[28] The ability to create this "dogma" gives the creditors the power to appropriate the voices of the powerless and to interpret their own reality. In fact, the economic fundamentalism of the World Bank and IMF comes from this

271

tradition of exploiting economic and social weaknesses, and from desperation to impose ideas and programs, often untested, as universal and universally correct programs to which there are no alternatives. The truth is that the challenge of growth, development, stability, peace, and survival rests in the first instance with Africans themselves. There is an urgent need for a *new national economic, social, and political order* informed by the experiences, aspirations, and struggles of the people. Africa has not been short of responses to its deepening economic and political crisis, but only very few have been serious, pro-people, pro-democratic, and pro-liberation in content and context. There can be no hope for economic and political recovery and stability in Africa without a comprehensive transformation and recomposition of the political economy. As one African dictator once noted:

> Economic development nurtures democracy. On the other hand, under-development is a threat and obstacle to democracy. We commend the peoples of Eastern Europe and the Soviet Union for their decision to build democratic societies. We also note the significant financial and economic assistance which the Western industrialized countries and Japan have decided to offer them. This is in direct contrast to the virtual neglect of African affairs. If this neglect and this indifference continue, disillusionment may arise with democracy in the face of persistent and extreme economic hardship.[29]

African Non-Governmental Organizations (NGOs), through a steering committee which met in Nairobi, Kenya in April 1986, prepared a position paper for the Preparatory Committee for the General Assembly on the Special Session on Africa. In this document, they outlined a ten point strategy for change and progress in Africa:[30]

1) The African People must continue to expose the inequities of the present international economic, political

and social order, and demand full democratic participation in those organizations which make decisions relating to the ordering of international society, and the allocation of resources.

2) The African people must demand a fair and just return for the production of their labor in the international market, and reject international pricing and marketing arrangements which undervalue the products of African labor.

3) The African people must reject development projects imposed on our people either by international agencies or by our own leaders when they serve external interests rather than the interests of the ordinary people of Africa. Sometimes, these projects are suggested by foreign private and governmental interests to solve their own problems rather than those of Africa.

4) The people of Africa, especially those in the lower levels of society, must categorically decide their own development priorities. In precolonial Africa, people always placed food as the highest priority, whilst today the priorities are externally determined and people in Africa die for lack of food. These priorities must be put right.

5) In the context of rural development, we must emphasize the parallel and interconnected development of agriculture and industry so that, while agriculture provides food and raw materials for industry, the latter provides the necessary means of production to service agriculture. The initiatives to plan this kind of strategy must rest with the people themselves, and not be imposed by any outside agency or government.

6) When it comes to food production, due regard must be paid to the fact that the bulk of the food producers in Africa are women. Therefore, their legal rights to land, as well as their right to participate fully in all aspects of decision-making and allocation of resources must be respected and recognized.

7) Development projects in African countries must first and foremost service the needs of the national and local markets. Hence, the provision of inputs, credit facilities, water for irrigation, road network and storage facilities, electric power and telecommunications and extension services must first and foremost service the demands of products produced for local markets rather than for export markets.

8) We must reject the type of industrialization which is externally oriented, and which only serves to provide a market for imported machinery, and jobs for foreign technical and managerial experts. Our industrial strategy must be internal and African-oriented, not only to service the direct needs of our people, but also to employ our own material and human resources.

9) People must be represented directly in all democratic institutions from the village level to the national level. *Without a thoroughgoing democratic method of work, decisions will always be made in the name of the people rather than by them. Hence, we must demand consistent and thorough democratization of all institutions of decision-making* (my emphasis).

10) The African people can enjoy full democratic rights of participation only if their human rights and liberties are recognized. People must have full freedom to express themselves politically, to form associations and trade unions, to participate in all political activities without fear of repression, and to choose their own leaders. *Only by a full and thoroughgoing practice of democracy and people participation at all forums can there be any hope of getting Africa out of its present crisis.* All other efforts so far tried at international or local level are mere palliatives and attempts to tackle the symptoms of the crisis rather than its cause (my emphasis).

While the points outlined above reflect the yearnings of popular organizations in Africa, it does not outline an agenda for empowering popular organizations and challenging the statusquo and its custodians to capture political power. It is clear—and history has shown—that privileged elements who benefit from existing arrangements do not give up such privileges without serious and consistent challenges to their positions and power. The behavior of African elites since political independence, and the ways in which they have run down their respective economies and treated their peoples without respect, show that NGOs must develop critical and popular political programs for education, mobilization, and action.

Giving further political amplification to the 1986 effort, African NGOs met again in Arusha, Tanzania in February 1990 and adopted the *African Charter for Popular Participation in Development and Transformation*.[31] Adebayo Adedeji, the ECA's executive secretary, in his closing remarks following the adoption of the *Charter*, hoped that the document would launch Africa into a new era, "an Africa in which democracy, accountability, and development for transformation become internalized in every country and deep-rooted at every level in our society; an Africa where the enabling environment that promotes initiative and enterprise and guarantees the dignity of each human being becomes pervasive, and an Africa where the empowerment of the people and the democratization of the development process is the order of the day."[32] It was his hope that the implementation of the Charter through cooperation between the state, elites, private sector, donors, and NGOs would lead to "the new Africa of our vision where there is development and economic justice, not just growth; where there is democracy and accountability not despotism, authoritarianism and kleptocracy; and where the governed and their governments are moving hand-in-hand in the promotion of the common good, and where it is the will of the people rather than the wishes of one person or a group of persons, however powerful, that prevails."[33]

In spite of its limitations, the *Charter* has provided a

framework for *democratization* and empowerment on which African states and popular organizations can build. It not only transcends the Western prescription of multiparty elections, but begins by acknowledging the "unprecedented and unacceptable proportions" of the African crisis; recognizes that the crisis is not just an economic one, but also a "human, legal, political and social crisis," and takes the position that the only way out of the present crisis is to "establish independent people's organizations at various levels that are genuinely grassroots, voluntary, democratically administered and self-reliant and that are rooted in the tradition and culture of the society so as to ensure community empowerment and selfdevelopment."[34] The document notes that "unless the structures, pattern and political context of the process of socioeconomic development are appropriately altered" Africa's crisis cannot be overcome. Warning that "Africa is becoming further marginalized in world affairs, both geo politically and economically," the *Charter* strongly condemned "orthodox structural adjustment programmes, which undermine the human condition and disregard the potential and role of popular participation in self sustaining development."[35]

In its concrete prescription for popular participation in Africa, the *Charter* makes specific prescriptions for government, the media, youths, women, NGOs and VDOs, the international community, and organized labor. For governments, the *Charter* enjoins them to "adopt development strategies, approaches and programmes, the content and parameters of which are in line with the interest and aspirations of the people, and which incorporate, rather than alienate, African values and economic, social, cultural, political and environmental realities." African governments are urged to promote development in the context of a "popular participatory process," which "aim at the transformation of the African economies to achieve self-reliant and self-sustaining people-centered development based on popular participation and democratic consensus. To implement "endogenous and people centered development strategies," African governments are reminded in the *Charter* that "an enabling environment must be created to facilitate broad-based participation, on a decentralized basis," and that this is "an essential pre-requisite for the stimulation of initiatives and creativity and for enhancing output and productivity." For this to take place, governments need to extend "more economic power to the people through the equitable distribution of income;" enhancement of the "central role played by women in the economy;" promote "mass literacy and skills training," ensure "greater participation and consensus-building in the formulation and implementation of economic and social policies at all levels;" eliminate "laws and bureaucratic procedures that pose obstacles to people's participation;" increase employment opportunities for rural people and the urban poor; support small-scale indigenous entrepreneurship; strengthen communication capacities; and support efforts to achieve sub regional and regional integration in Africa.[36]

At the level of the people and their organizations, the *Charter* enjoins them to establish "autonomous grassroots organizations to promote participatory self-reliant development and increase the output and productivity of the masses." They are called upon to develop their "capacity to participate effectively in debates on economic policy and development issues"; promote education and literacy-skill learning to enhance popular participation; "shake off lethargy and traditional beliefs that are impediments to development" especially those that denigrate or undermine the status of women; change public attitudes to the disabled and integrate them into the main stream of development; create networks and collaborative relationships among their organizations; and their organizations should "support strongly and participate in the efforts to promote effective sub-regional and regional economic co-operation" in Africa.[37]

The international community is called upon in the *Charter* to support "African countries in their drive to internalize the development and transformation process"; the World Bank and IMF should learn to "accept and support African initiatives to conceptualize, formulate and implement endogenously designed development and transformation programmes"; technical assistance should be directed at "strengthening...national capabilities for policy analysis"; and the democratization of development in African countries should be furthered by "supporting the decentralization of development processes," and the active participation of the people and their organizations in the "formulation of development strategies and economic reform programmes and open debate and consensus-building processes on development and reform issues." Donors, lenders, and powerful interests in the global community are called upon to release resources for development "on a participatory basis which will require the reversal of the net outflow of financial resources from Africa;" reduce drastically the stock of Africa's debt and debt servicing obligations, and ensure that the "human dimension is central to adjustment programmes which must be compatible with the objectives and aspirations of the African people and with African realities. "[38]

The *Charter* recommends that the activities of NGOs and VDOs and their partners "should be fully participatory, democratic and accountable;" the media at national and regional levels are enjoined to "fight for and defend their freedom at all cost, and make special effort to champion the cause of popular participation and publicize activities and programmes thereof;" and women's organizations are called upon to "strengthen their capacity as builders of confidence among women," and to run their organizations as "democratic, autonomous and accountable organizations." Organized labor is enjoined to be voluntary, accountable and democratic, to promote mass literacy programs, organize rural workers, defend trade union rights, assist in the

formation of cooperatives, organize the unemployed for productive activities, pay special attention to effective and
democratic participation of women members, and "promote
work place democracy through the call for the protection
of workers' rights to freedom of association, collective bargaining and participatory management." Youths, students,
and their organizations are called upon to prepare and adopt
"an African Charter on Youth and Students Rights to include
the right to organize, education, employment, and free and
public expression," and African governments are called
upon to ensure the "full democratic participation of youth
and students" in national affairs, while the youth and students organizations are enjoined to be "democratic, voluntary, accountable and autonomous and should coordinate
their activities with workers', women's and peasant organizations."

In sum, the *Charter* is categorical in its endorsement of
the fact that Africa's predicament can only be addressed
through "an opening up of the political process to accommodate freedom of opinions, tolerate differences, accept
consensus on issues as well as ensure the effective participation of the people and their organizations and association."[39] The *Charter*, therefore, attempts to redirect the
attention and activities of Africans and the international
community to the urgent need to address the *political* and
human aspects of the African crisis. The underlying argument is that the most massive amounts of foreign aid and
international sympathy will do little or nothing for Africa if
the masses remain hungry, oppressed, alienated, and intimidated and the environment is not conducive to creativity,
innovation, and productivity.

Perhaps the most important part of the document is the
recommendation for the establishment of national and
regional monitoring bodies, and the identification of ten
major indicators of empowerment, participation, and
democratization:

1. The literacy rate as an index of the capacity for mass participation in public debate, decision-making and general development processes;

2. Freedom of association, especially political association, and presence of democratic institutions, such as political parties, trade unions, people's grassroots organizations and professional associations, and the guarantee of constitutional rights;

3. Representation of the people and their organizations in national deliberative and legislative bodies;

4. The rule of law and social and economic justice, including equitable distribution of income and the creation of full employment opportunities;

5. Protection of the ecological, human, and legal environment;

6. Press and media freedom to facilitate public debate on major issues;

7. Number and scope of grassroots organizations with effective participation in development activities, producers and consumers co-operatives, and community projects;

8. Extent of implementation of the Abuja Declaration on Women (1989) in each country;

9. Political accountability of leadership at all levels measured by the use of checks and balances; and

10. Decentralization of decision-making processes and institutions.[40]

The above indicators go beyond the prescriptions from the West—multiple parties, elections, parliaments, constitutions, and the adoption of monetarist economic programs—which are comparatively easier for the elites to implement and manipulate. Implementing the indicators recommended by the ECA and which have been accepted and adopted by the OAU will enthrone the power and struggles of the people and overthrow the waste, corruption, decadence, and subservience which has characterized elite dominance of the political landscape since the 1960s. This is not to say that the *Charter* has no limitations or weaknesses. It assumes a lot and even its monitoring program can and will do very little to contain the custodians of state power who have maintained themselves in power for decades through ruthlessness, corruption, and intolerance of new or opposing ideas. The *Charter* does not spell out sanctions that will be imposed on African leaders and countries which fail to implement the new indicators of democratization and popular participation, and it does not spell out clearly the protection and degree of autonomy which the regional and sub-regional monitoring bodies will enjoy.

The future of Africa lies ultimately with the process of empowerment. The pains and cost of structural adjustment have pushed nonbourgeois forces to the wall. These pains have forced normally docile people, communities, and groups to become highly politicized and active.[41] They are posing new questions, rejecting old ideologies and propaganda, joining in popular protests, and demanding the right to participate in the selection of their own leaders. This, certainly, is a major departure from the usual tradition in Africa. As Mohamed Halfani has rightly noted, "[m]ore organizations have severed their ties with the state and are seeking greater autonomy. Contemporary movements are shrugging off state patronage in order to reconstruct the substance and direction of local development. In some cases, their independence has put them on a collision course with governments."[42] While many of the grassroots organizations are mere service organizations without political programs, the services they render contribute to strengthening civil society in a general sense but do not play an integral part in the direct challenge to the neocolonial state and imperialism until they become politicized.

This reinvigoration of civil society is bound to encourage a struggle for *democratization* representing a steady process of mobilization, education, and empowerment of the people, their organizations, and their communities in such a way as to increase popular participation, accountability, civil liberties, and an enabling environment for growth and development. Democratization promotes the process of empowerment and the empowerment of the people puts them in charge of their lives and deepens the process of democratization. As Richard Sandbrook notes, empowerment "involves transforming the economic, social, psychological, political and legal circumstances of the currently powerless."[43] As well, empowerment "entails access to educational facilities and to the minimum resources needed to sustain households. Illiterate people who must devote all their energies to bare survival cannot empower themselves. This process further requires that people and their organizations have access to contending opinions and accurate information on the performance of power-holders...empowerment involves the difficult and hazardous task of constructing political institutions capable of mediating the conflicting interest[s] of classes, regions, sexes, and communal groups, and of safeguarding the voice and rights of hitherto oppressed groups and strata."[44] This is significantly different from the current processes of procedural democracy, which has been reduced to mere elections and the registration of multiple political parties. It is this level of democratization that the World Bank must support if it is serious about its new rhetoric. It is this process that the donors, lenders, and the United States must support if they are serious about a new global order and the restructuring of power relations in Africa. For, irrespective of ideological positions, the fact of the matter is that:

the process of reconstituting civil society is under way. Many old and new associations are striving to enhance their capacity to direct their own affairs. They are also rejecting their traditional roles as assigned by the state and are addressing issues of empowerment and social transformation. Today, many associations attribute as much importance to the participatory mode of their activities as to the concrete outcomes they achieve. The teaching of basic and functional literacy, the performance of theatrical plays, the assistance offered in litigation, the generation of new knowledge and information through research have acquired an importance beyond the immediate material benefits to the marginalized; their emancipatory and transformational impact is equally valued. African civil associations have thus become increasingly political.[45]

Even some of the prodemocracy organizations mentioned earlier are deepening their politics as they face isolation from the more politicized associations. In Ghana, younger politicans in the opposition are challenging the leadership of "old guard" politicians like Adu-Boahen and Hilla Limman in the effort to move politics away from the tired ideas and tactics of the 50s and 60s.[46] Disagreement on issues of ideology and strategies of struggle forced some individuals out of the Campaign for Democracy (CD) in Nigeria, culminating in the formation of the Democratic Alternative (DEAL), a more ideologically orthodox organization.

If Africa is to get out of its present quagmire, therefore, it must proceed along the path of empowering the people, their organizations, and communities. As Halfani has noted, "empowerment is the very essence of human development, not just a means to an end."[47] At present, the "democratization of Africa has focused on the power elite, who are the natural enemies of democracy. Although the elite has provided the vast majority of the leaders of the democracy movement, their involvement in democracy movements is mainly a tactical manoeuver."[48] Even the World Bank admits that political and economic reforms in Africa must seek to "empower ordinary people to take charge of their lives, to make communities more responsible for their development, and to make governments listen to their people.

Fostering a more pluralistic institutional structure—including nongovernmental organizations and stronger local government—is a means to these ends."[49] We must be careful how we use and prescribe "empowerment" though. The World Bank assumes that "empowerment" is compatible with free enterprise and a liberal democratic tradition. Yet "empowerment" is much more than just making it possible for the poor to participate in elections, or to choose between exploiters who will only pay lip service to their problems. The process of empowerment "involves transforming the economic, social, psychological, political and legal circumstances of the currently powerless"; it involves "the emergence of group identities (or community), the development of autonomous and coherent popular organizations, and the defence of, and education about, the legal rights of the popular sectors."[50] Finally, empowerment also involves a form of socioeconomic and political restructuring which will remove the locus of power from the current custodians of state power, and enable the currently disadvantaged to meet their basic needs, fully participate in decision-making, and provide opportunities to challenge internal and external exploiters. Thus, for people who have been brutalized, terrorized, exploited, manipulated, dehumanized, marginalized, intimidated, and repressed for so long, their empowerment is a signal for *liberation;* an opportunity to take charge, and a once-and-for-all opportunity to reorganize how they govern themselves and live their lives. It is doubtful if such a new agenda can be found in the current programs which support the power of the elites of Africa. People do not empower themselves to accept domination, poor leadership, and exploitation.

It is only through this process of empowerment, which "involves the difficult and hazardous task of constructing political institutions capable of mediating the conflicting interests of classes, regions, sexes, and communal groups, and of safeguarding the voice and rights of hitherto oppressed groups and strata,"[51] that the future of a democratic Africa lies. The construction of such accountable and democratic institutions and process will see the dismantling of the neocolonial state and its replacement with a national popular state. The national popular state will not only be democratic but it will also reflect the interests and aspirations of the working majority in the first place. It will respect human rights, promote growth and development, and create an environment which will enable Africans to attain the heights of their creative abilities. It is precisely this new level of creativity, commitment, patriotism, and participation that will make it possible for science and technology to be taken seriously, attract investors, encourage investment in production, define limits for state participation in the economy, check corruption and political excesses, and make interdependence the basis of economic relations with other regions and countries of the world. A strengthened civil society which will inevitably arise from the process of democratization and empowerment will check military adventurism, political and ethnic violence, and negate most of the inherited contradictions, coalitions, conflicts, and crises which have plagued Africa since the 1960s and which have consolidated the region's marginalization in the international division of labor. Claude Ake, writing on the character of the Nigerian political class, notes that "The ruling class in power has not changed at all. The same class, the same social forces have maintained power throughout, with irrelevant changes of sartorial image, ideological rhetoric, political style, and nuances of public policy. Although it has been steadily undermining its hegemony, it does not see that it is seriously threatened as of now."[52] While it is true that a few have "seen the handwriting on the wall" and restructured their politics accordingly, the vast majority remain steeped in corruption, opportunism, and manipulation and continue to demonstrate an unrepentant commitment to conservative political ideas. Any serious agenda for transformation and democratization must include a program for responding to the politics of this dominant class.

The attainment of the conditions described above will require two major conditions. First, there is an urgent need for "a transformation within a community and its members' consciousness, skills, resources, and institutions" as well as "rectifying the deformed economic and political structures" that currently breed atavistic behaviors.[53] Second, international organizations, donors, and lenders, as well as popular organizations around the world, will need to come to the direct support of prodemocracy activists in Africa. To be sure, there are countless opportunistic and mediocre organizations in the region parading themselves as prodemocracy movements. Many of the more serious organizations, however, lack the basic facilities to be effective and to expand. It is therefore essential to understand the origins, quality of leadership, size of membership, programs, nature of existing alliances with other popular groups, and field experience of any given African prodemocracy group before support is provided. Under these conditions, Africa and the new democracies must not be abandoned. The Zambian example clearly demonstrates a case where a new government with overwhelming nationwide support still needs external support to strengthen its ability to consolidate and reproduce democracy. This, rather than in merely replicating Western political institutions when the foundation/environment for the survival of the transferred structures and institutions are weak or very tenuous, is where the real struggle for Africa in the 1990s is located.

Notes

1. Adotey Bing, "Salim A. Salim on the OAU and the African Agenda," *Review of African Political Economy* (50) (March 1991), p. 61.
2. Economic Commission for Africa, *African Charter for*

Popular Participation in Development, (Addis Ababa: ECA, 1990), p. 17.

3. Harvey Glickman, "Editor's Introduction," *Issue: A Journal of Opinion* XXI, 1-2 (1993):3-4.

4. See Julius O. Ihonvbere, "Is Democracy Possible in Africa?: The Elites, The People and Civil Society," *QUEST: Philosophical Discussions* VI, 2 (December 1992) and "The State, Human Rights and Democratization in Africa," *Current World Leaders* 37, 4 (August 1994).

5. Harvey Glickman, "Editor's Introduction" (op. cit.), p.3.

6. Ibid., p.4.

7. Martin Klein, "Back to Democracy." Presidential Address to the Annual Meeting of the African Studies Association, 1991.

8. See Julius O. Ihonvbere, "Africa's Second Independence: A Political and Economic Overview," *Library of African Cinema* (San Francisco, CA: California Newsreel, 1993/ 1994).

9. Ernest Wamba-dia-Wamba, "Beyond Elite Politics of Democracy in Africa," *QUEST* VI, 1 (June 1991):29-42.

10. Martin Klein, "Back to Democracy" (op. cit.).

11. Ibid.

12. Lance Morrow, "Africa: The Scramble for Existence," *TIME* (September 7, 1992).

14. Ernest Wamba-dia-Wamba (op. cit.), p.29.

13. Jeffrey Herbst, *U.S. Economic Policy Toward Africa*, (New York: Council on Foreign Relations, 1992), p. 50. This line of argument overlooks the strong linkages between rural and urban dwellers, and demonstrates a poor understanding of the dynamics of production and accumulation as well as the ways in which rural producers have been incorporated into the domestic and global capitalist relations of power, production, and exchange.

14. Ernest Wamba-dia-Wamba (op.cit.), p.29.

15. See Julius O. Ihonvbere, "Economic Crisis, Structural Adjustment, and Social Crisis in Nigeria," *World Development* 21, 1 (January 1993):141-153; Baffour Ankomah, "Ghana's Reform Programme: How Long Will it be Before the Patient is Cured?" *African Business*, (March 1990):11-13.

16. See Julius O. Ihonvbere, "Political Conditionality and

Prospects for Recovery in Sub-Saharan Africa," *International Third World Studies Journal and Review* 3, 1-2 (1991):17-26.

17. Chu Okongwu, Minister of Budget and Planning of Nigeria, speaking on behalf of the OAU at the 1991 Review of UNPAAERD reproduced in "UNPAAERD speeches debate issues of debt, governance, and aid flows," *Africa Recovery* 5, 4 (December 1991):24.

18. Scott Spangler, ibid., p. 25.

19. Martin Klein, "Back to Democracy" (op. cit.).

20. See Julius O. Ihonvbere, "The Military and Political Engineering Under Structural Adjustment: The Nigerian Experience Since 1985," *Journal of Political and Military Sociology* 29 (Summer 1991):107-131, and Julius O. Ihonvbere, "Adjustment, Political Transition and the Organization of Military Power in Nigeria," UFAHAMU XIX, 1 (Winter 1991):22-42.

21. Githu Muigai, "Kenya's Opposition and the Crisis of Governance," *Issue: A Journal of Opinion* XXI, 1-2 (1993):p. 29.

22. Masipula Sithole, "Is Zimbabwe Poised on a Liberal Path? The State and Prospects of the Parties," *Issue: A Journal of Opinion* XXI, 1-2 (1993):39.

23. Ibid, p. 40.

24. See Timothy M. Shaw, "Popular Participation in Non-Governmental Structures in Africa: Implications for Democratic Development in Africa," *Africa Today* 37, 3) (1990):522.

25. Yoweri Museveni, Statement at the Kampala Forum reproduced in Olusegun Obasanjo and Felix G. N. Mosha (eds.), *Africa: Rise to Challenge*, (New York: Africa Leadership Forum, 1993).

26. Fantu Cheru, *The Silent Revolution in Africa: Debt. Development and Democracy*, (London and Harare: Zed Books and Anvil, 1989), p. 143.

27. Boutros Boutros-Ghali, *United Nations Focus on the New Agenda for Africa: New Concepts for Development Action in Africa*, (New York: UN Department of Information, 1992), p. 3.

28. Ibid., p. 5.

29. Ibrahim Babangida, (Chairman of the OAU), Address to the 46th Session of the UN General Assembly, New York,

October 1991

30. This section is drawn from Fantu Cheru, *The Silent Revolution in Africa* (op. cit.), pp. 155-156.

31. Economic Commission for Africa, *African Charter for Popular Participation in Development and Transformation* (op. cit.).

32. Adebayo Adedeji, Closing Remarks following the adoption of the *African Charter for Popular Participation in Development and Transformation* in ibid., p. 37.

33. Ibid.

34. Economic Commission for Africa, *African Charter for Popular Participation in Development* (op. cit.), p.20.

35. Ibid., pp. 18-19.

36. Ibid., pp. 23-24.

37. Ibid., pp. 24-25.

38. Ibid., pp. 25-26.

39. Ibid., p.19.

40. This paragraph is drawn from Ibid., pp.31-32. For a critical evaluation of this document see Julius O. Ihonvbere, "The African Crisis, the Popular Charter, and Prospects for Recovery in the 1990s," *Zeitschrift fur Afrikastudien(ZAST)* 11-12 (1991):25-41.

41. *The Economist* (February 22, 1992).

42. Mohammed Halfani, "The Challenges Ahead," in Richard Sandbrook and Mohammed Halfani, (eds.), *Empowering People: Building Community, Civil Associations, and Legality in Africa*, (Toronto: Center for Urban and Community Studies, University of Toronto, 1993), p. 201.

43. Richard Sandbrook, "Introduction" in Sandbrook and Halfani, (eds.), *Empowering People* (op cit.), p. 2.

44. Ibid., p. 3.

45. Mohammed Halfani, "The Challenges Ahead" (op. cit.), p. 201.

46. Prosper Bani, "The Changing Character of Politics in Ghana," mimeo, Department of Government, The University of Texas at Austin, August, 1994.

47. Mohammed Halfani, "Constraints on Empowerment," in Sandbrook and Halfani, (eds.), *Empowering People* (op. cit.), p. 33.

48. Claude Ake, "Is Africa Democratizing?" *The Guardian* (Lagos) (December 12, 1993).

49. World Bank, *Sub-Saharan Africa: From Crisis to*

Sustainable Growth-A Long-Term Perspective Study, (Washington, D.C.: World Bank, 1989), p. 55.

50. Richard Sandbrook, "Introduction," in Sandbrook and Halfani, (eds.), *Empowering People* (op. cit.), p. 2.

51. Ibid

52. Claude Ake "Government Instability in Nigeria," *Nigerian Forum* 8, 1-3 (January March 1988):28-29.

53. Mohammed Halfani, "Constraints on Empowerment" (op. cit.), p. 33.

SELECT
BIBLIOGRAPHY

"A Radical Programme of Action for UNIP," (The Zero Option Plan), *The National Mirror* (March 15-21, 1993).

Achebe, Chinua, *A Man of the People*. London: Heinemann, 1966.

Adedeji, Adebayo, Economic Progress: What Africa Needs," *TransAfrica Forum* Vol. 7, (2) (Summer 1990).

————, "Putting the People First." Opening Address, International Conference on Popular Participation in the Recovery Process in Africa, Arusha, Tanzania, February 12, 1990.

————, "The Case for Remaking Africa," in Douglas Rimmer, ed., *Action in Africa*. London: James Currey and Heinemann, 1993.

————, ed., *Africa Within the World: Beyond Dispossession and Dependence*. London: Zed Books, 1993.

Adedeji, Adebayo, Rasheed, Sadiq and Melody Morrison, eds., *The Human Dimensions of Africa's Persistent Economic Crisis*. London: Hans Zell, 1990.

Adedeji, Adebayo, and Timothy M. Shaw, eds., *Economic Crisis in Africa: African Perspectives on Development Problems and Potentials*. Boulder, Colorado: Lynne Rienner, 1985.

Africa Leadership Forum, Organization of African Unity, and Economic Commission for Africa, *Report on the Brain Storming Meeting for a Conference on Security. Stability*

Development and Cooperation in Africa. Addis Ababa, 17-18 November, 1990.

Africa Watch, *Zambia: Model For Democracy Declares State of Emergency*. New York: Africa Watch, Volume V, Issue 8, June 10, 1993.

Ake, Claude, "Explaining Political Instability in New States," *Journal of Modern African Studies* Vol. 11, (3) (1973).

———, "The African Context of Human Rights," *Africa Today* Vol. 34, (1987).

———, The Case for Democracy," in Carter Center at Emory University, *African Governance in the 1990s*. Atlanta: African Governance Program, 1990.

———, "As Africa Democratises," *Africa Forum* Vol. 1, (2) (1991).

———, "Rethinking African Democracy," *Journal of Democracy* Vol. 2, (1) (1991).

———, "Devaluing Democracy," *Journal of Democracy* Vol. 3, (3) (July 1992).

———, "Is Africa Democratizing?" 1993 Guardian Lecture, Nigerian Institute of International Affairs, Lagos, Nigeria, December 11, 1993.

———, "Academic Freedom and Material Base," in Mahmood Mamdani and Mamadou Diouf, eds., *Academic Freedom in Africa*. Dakar: CODESRIA, 1994.

Akwetey, E., "State, Unions and Structural Adjustment: A Comparative Study of Ghana, Tanzania, and Zambia." Project Proposal, SAREC, Department of Political Science, University of Stockholm, 1990.

Allen, C., "Restructuring an Authoritarian State: Democratic Renewal in Benin," *Review of African Political Economy* (54) (July 1992).

Amin, Samir, "Democracy and National Strategy in the Periphery," *Third World Quarterly* Vol. 9 (4) (1987).

Anglin, Douglas G., "Confrontation in South Africa: Zambia and Portugal," *International Journal* Vol. 25, (3) (Summer 1970).

Anyang'Nyongo, Peter, *Popular Struggles for Democracy in Africa*. London: Zed Press, 1987.

———, "Political Instability and the Prospects for Democracy in Africa," *Africa Development*, Vol. XIII (1) (1988).

———, "Democratization Processes in Africa," *CODESRIA Bulletin* (2) (1991).

————, "Africa: The Failure of One-Party Rule," *Journal of Democracy* Vol. 3, (1) (January 1992).

————, "Regional Integration, Security and Development in Africa," in Olusegun Obasanjo and Felix G. N. Mosha, eds., *Africa: Rise to Challenge*. New York: Africa Leadership Forum, 1993.

Armah, Aya Kwesi, *The Beautiful Ones Are Not Yet Born*. Boston: Houghton Miflin, 1968.

Assimeng, J. M., "Sectarian Allegiance and Political Authority: The Watch Tower Society in Zambia, 1907-1935," *The Journal of Modern African Studies* Vol. 8, (1) (1970).

Atwood, Brian, "The U.S. Agenda for International Development," *International Politics and Society* No. 1, (1995).

Ayisi, R. A., "Mozambique: Back to the Stone Age," *Africa Report* Vol. 36 (1) (1991).

Bakary, Tessy D., "An Ambiguous Adventure: Transition From Authoritarian Rule and Economic Reforms," in *Economic Reform in Africa's New Era of Political Liberalization: Proceedings of a Workshop for SPA Donors*. Washington, D.C.: USAID, 1993.

Bangura, Yusuf and Peter Gibbon, "Adjustment, Authoritarianism and Democracy in Sub-Saharan Africa: An Introduction to Some Conceptual and Empirical Issues," in Peter Gibbon, et. al, eds, *Authoritarianism, Democracy and Adjustment*, Uppsala: SIAS, 1992.

Bates, Robert H., "Input Structures, Output Functions and Systems Capacity: A Study of Mineworkers' Union of Zambia," *Journal of Politics* Vol. 32, (4) (November 1970).

————, *Unions. Parties and Political Development: A Study of Mineworkers in Zambia*. New Haven and London: Yale University Press, 1971.

————, *Rural Responses to Industrialization: A Study of Village Zambia*, New Have and London: Yale University Press, 1976.

————, "UNIP in Post-Independence Zambia: The Development of an Organizational Role," Ph.D Dissertation, Harvard University, 1977.

———— and Paul Collier, *The Politics and Economics of Policy Reform in Zambia*. Papers in International Political Economy, Working Paper 153, Durham: Duke University,

1992.

Bauzon, Kenneth E., ed., *Development and Democratization in the Third World: Myths, Hopes, and Realities*. Washington, D.C.: Crane Russak, 1992.

Baylies, C., "Class Formation and the Role of the State in the Zambian Economy." Lusaka: University of Zambia, Seminar Paper, 1974.

———, and M. Szeftel, "The Rise of a Zambian Capitalist Class in the 1970s," *Journal of Southern African Affairs* Vol. 8, (2) (1982).

———,"The Rise and Fall of Multi-party Politics in Zambia," *Review of African Political Economy*, (54) (July 1992).

Beckman, Bjorn, "State Capitalism and Public Enterprise in Africa," in Ghai, Y, ed., *Law in the Political Economy of Public Enterprise: African Perspectives*. Uppsala: Scandinavian Institute for African Studies, 1977.

———, "Imperialism and the National Bourgeoisie," *Review of African Political Economy* (22) (1981).

———, "When Does Democracy Make Sense? Problems of Theory and Practice in the Study of Democratization in Africa and the Third World," Paper to AKUT Conference on Democracy, Uppsala, October 1988.

———, "Whose Democracy? Bourgeois Versus Popular Democracy," *Review of African Political Economy* (45-46) (1989).

———, "Empowerment or Repression? The World Bank and the Politics of African Adjustment," in Peter Gibbon, Yusuf Bangura and Arve Osftad, eds., *Authoritarianism, Democracy and Adjustment: The Politics of Economic Reform in Africa*. Uppsala: The Scandinavian Institute of African Studies, 1992.

———, "Comments on Economic Reform and National Disintegration," in *Economic Reform in Africa's New Era of Political Liberalization: Proceedings of a Workshop for SPA Donors*. Washington, D.C.: USAID, 1993.

Berger, E., *Labour, Race and Colonial Rule: The Copperbelt From 1942 to Independence*. London: Oxford University press, 1974.

Berger, Peter E., "The Uncertain Triumph of Democratic Capitalism," *Journal of Democracy* Vol. 3, (3) (July 1992).

Beveridge, A.A., "Varieties of African Businessmen in Emerging

Zambian Stratification System." Paper at the 16th Annual Meeting of the African Studies Association, Syracuse, New York, 1973.

————, "Converts to Capitalism: The Emergence of African Entrepreneurs in Lusaka, Zambia," PhD Dissertation, Yale University, 1973.

————, "Economic Independence, Indigenization, and the African Businessman: Some Effects of Zambia's Economic Reforms," *African Studies Review* Vol. 17, (3) (1974).

———— and Anthony R. Oberschall, *African Businessmen and Development in Zambia*. Princeton: Princeton University Press, 1979.

Bhagwati, Jagdish, "Democracy and Development," *Journal of Democracy* Vol. 3, (3) (July 1992).

Bhatt, T. A., *A Biographical Sketch of Indians in Africa. Vol. 1. Zambia*. Nairobi: United Africa Press, 1969.

Biermann, Werner, "The Development of Underdevelopment: The Historical Perspective," in Ben Turok, ed., *Development in Zambia*. (London: Zed Press, 1979).

Billing, M.G., "Tribal Rule and Modern Politics in Northern Rhodesia," *African Affairs* Vol. 58, (231) (April 1969).

Bing, Adotey, "Salim A. Salim on the OAU and the African Agenda," *Review of African Political Economy* (50) (March 1991).

Binsbergen, Wim van, "Aspects of Democracy and Democratisation in Zambia and Botswana," *Journal of Contemporary African Studies* Vol. 13, (1) (January 1995).

Bjornlund, E., M. Bratton, and C. Gibson, "Observing Multiparty Elections in Africa: Lessons from Zambia," *African Affairs* Vol. 91, (364) (July 1992).

Bloom, L. "Some Values and Attitudes of Young Zambians: Studies of Three Spontaneous Autobiographies," *African Social Research* (14) (1972).

Boahen, Adu, "Military Rule and Multi-party Democracy: The Case of Ghana," *Africa Demos* Vol. 1, (2) (January 1991).

Bobbio, N., "Gramsci and the Concept of Civil Society," in J. Keane, ed., *Civil Society and the State*. London: Verso, 1988.

Boyle, P. "Beyond Self-Protection to Prophecy: The Catholic Church and Political Change in Zaire," *Africa Today* Vol. 39, (3) (1992).

Bratton, Michael, *Peasant and Part-State in Zambia: Political Organization and Resource Distribution in Kasama District*. PhD Dissertation, Michigan State University, 1977.

Bratton, Michael, *The Local Politics of Rural Development: Peasant and Party State in Zambia*. Hanover: University of New England Press, 1980.

———, "Beyond the State: Civil Society and Associational Life in Africa," *World Politics*, Vol. XLI (3) (1989).

———, "The Politics of government-NG0 Relations in Africa," *World Development*, (April 1989).

———, "Non-Governmental Organizations in Africa, " *Development and Change*, Vol. 21 (1) (January 1990).

———, "Zambia Starts Over," *Journal of Democracy* Vol. 3, (2) (April 1992).

———, "Political Liberalization in Africa in the 1990s: Advances and Setbacks," in *Economic Reform in Africa's New Era of Political Liberalization: Proceedings of a Workshop for SPA Donors*. Washington, D.C.: USAID, 1993.

———, "Economic Crisis and Political Realignment in Zambia," in Jennifer Widner, ed., *Economic Change and Political Liberalization in Sub-Saharan Africa*. (Baltimore: The Johns Hopkins Press, 1994).

——— and Beatrice Liatto-Katundu, "Political Culture in Zambia: A Pilot Survey." MSU Working Papers on Political Reform in Africa, Michigan State University, January 1994.

Bratton, Michael and Nicholas van de Walle, "Popular Protest and Political Reform in Africa," in Goran Hyden and Michael Bratton, eds., *Governance and Politics in Africa*. Boulder: Lynne Rienner, 1991

———, "Popular Protest and Political Reform in Africa," *Comparative Politics*, Vol. 24 (4) (July 1992).

Browne, Robert S., "Africa: Time for a New Development Strategy," in M. Martin and T. Randal, eds., *Development and Change in the Modern World*. New York: Oxford University Press, 1989.

———, "The Continuing Debate on African Development," *TransAfrica Forum* Vol. 7 (2) (Summer 1990).

Burawoy, M., "Zambianisation: A study of the Localisation of a Labour Force." Mimeo, University of Zambia, 1971.

———, "Industrial Conflict: The Relationship Between Effort, Remuneration and Output." Mimeo, University of Zambia, 1972.

———, "Another Look at the Mineworker," *African Social Research* (14) (1972).

———, *The Colour of Class on the Copper Mines*. Lusaka: UNZA, Institute for African Studies, 1972.

———, "Consciousness and Contradiction: A Study of Student Protest in Zambia," *British Journal of Sociology* Vol. 27, (1) (1976).

Burdette, M. M., "Zambia," in Timothy Shaw and Olajide Aluko, eds., *Political Economy of African Foreign Policy*. Aldershot: Gower Publishers, 1984.

Callaghy, Thomas, "Lost Between State and Market: The Politics of Economic Adjustment in Ghana, Zambia and Nigeria," in Joan M. Nelson, ed., *Economic Crisis and Policy Choice: The Politics of Economic Adjustment in the Third World*. Princeton: Princeton University Press, 1990.

———, "Political Liberalization and Economic Policy Reform in Africa," in *Economic Reform in Africa's New Era of Political Liberalization: Proceedings of a Workshop for SPA Donors*. Washington, D.C.,: USAID, 1993.

Camdessus, Michel, "The IMF: Facing New Challenges," *Finance and Development* (25) (June 1988).

———, "The IMF and the Global Economy: Three Addresses." Washington, D.C.: International Monetary Fund, 1989.

———, "Good News Out of Africa," *Finance and Development* (28) (December 1991).

Campbell, Bonnie and John Loxley, eds., *Structural Adjustment in Africa*. New York: St. Martins Press, 1989.

Campbell, Horace, "Angolan Woman and the Electoral Process in Angola, 1992," *Africa Development*, Vol. XVIII (2) (1993).

———, and Howard Stein, eds., *Tanzania and the IMF: The Dynamics of Liberalization*. Boulder, Colorado: Westview Press, 1992.

Caplan, G. L., "Barotseland: The Secessionist Challenge to Zambia," *The Journal of Modern African Studies* Vol. 6, (3) (1968).

"Capturing the Continent: U.S. Media Coverage of Africa," *Africa News Special Report*, Durham, NC: Africa News,

1990.

Carter Center of Emory University, *Beyond Autocracy in Africa* Atlanta: Africa Governance Program, 1989.

———, *Perestroika Without Glasnost in Africa*. Atlanta: Conference Report Series Vol. 2, No. 1, 1989.

———, *African Governance in the 1990*. Atlanta: African Governance Program, 1990.

Chabal, Patrick, ed., *Political Domination in Africa: Reflections on the Limits of Power*. Cambridge: Cambridge University Press, 1986.

Chalker, Lynda, "The Proper Role of Government," in Douglas Rimmer, ed., *Action in Africa*. London: James Currey and Heinemann, 1993.

Chaput, M. J., "Zambian State Enterprises: The Politics and Management of Nationalized Development." PhD Dissertation, Syracuse University, 1976.

Charlton, Leslie, *Spark in the Stubble: Colin Morris of Zambia*. London: Epworth, 1969.

Chazan, Naomi, "The New Politics of Participation in Tropical Africa," *Comparative Politics* Vol. 14 (1982).

———, "Planning Democracy in Africa: a Comparative Perspective on Nigeria and Ghana," *Policy Sciences* (22) (1989).

———, "Africa's Democratic Challenge: Strengthening Civil Society and the State," *World Policy Journal* (Spring 1992).

Chege, Michael, "Remembering Africa," *Foreign Affairs* Vol. 71, (1) (1991-92).

Cheru, Fantu, "The Politics of Desperation: Mozambique and Nkomati," *TransAfrica Forum* (Spring 1986).

———, *The Silent Revolution in Africa: Debt, Development and Democracy*. London and Harare: Zed Books and Anvil, 1989.

Chikulo, Bornwell C., "Elections in a One-Party Participatory Democracy," in Ben Turok, ed., *Development in Zambia*. London: Zed Press, 1979.

Chiluba, Frederick, Address to the Nation on the Eve of Local Government Elections. n.d. Typescript.

———, "Inauguration Speech to the Nation," Lusaka: Government Printer, November 2, 1991.

———, Speech on the Occasion of the National Release of the State of the World's Children Report, 19th December,

1991. Typescript.

———, Statement to ZUFIAW Annual General Meeting, 28th December, 1991. Typescript.

———, "Marching Towards a Common Market," Opening Statement on the Occasion of the Opening Ceremony of the 10th P.T.A. Summit, Mulungushi Conference Centre, Lusaka, Zambia, 30th January, 1992.

———, "Brief Statement on Drought," Arusha, Tanzania, 28th April, 1992. Typescript.

———, Speech on the Occasion of the Official Launching of the "Community Awareness Week" on the Problem of Vandalism in Institutions of Learning on Both Radio and Television, 15th June, 1992.

———, Speech on the Occasion of the Pass Out Parade of Squads 13 to 24 at Lilayi Training School, Lilayi, Zambia, 30th July, 1992. Typescript.

———, Press Statement, 4 August, 1992. Typescript.

———, Speech at the Independence Reception Day, 24th October, 1992. Typescript.

———, Speech on the Occasion of the Installation Ceremony of Mr. John M. Mwanakatwe as Chancellor of the University of Zambia, Mulungushi Conference Centre, 27th November, 1992. Typescript.

———, "Opening Address to the ICFTU/ZCTU Conference on Social Dimension of Adjustment," 19th December, 1992.

———, Address to the Nation to Inaugurate 1993 Youth Week Celebrations, Lusaka: Typescript, 5th March, 1993.

———, Speech at the Pastors and Church Leaders Global Advance Conference at Chongwe Secondary School, 12th April, 1993.

Chitala, Derrick, "Towards Accountability in a Democracy: The Case of Zambia." Paper presented to Workshop on Civil Society and Consolidation of Democracy in Zambia, February 27, 1992.

Chivuno, L. S., "Opening Address," Delivered at the International Conference on the Auctioning of Foreign Exchange, Lusaka, Zambia, 29 June-3 July, 1987.

Chomsky, Noam, "The Struggle for Democracy in a Changed World," *Review of African Political Economy* (50) (March 1991).

Christian Michelsen Institute, *Zambia: Country Report and Norwegian Aid Review*. Bergen: CMI, 1986.

Clark, J., *Democratizing Development: The Role of Voluntary Organizations*. West Hartford: Kumarian Press, 1991.

—— and Caroline Allison, *Debt and Poverty: A Case Study of Zambia*. Oxford: Oxfam, 1987.

Clarke, D. G., "The Political Economy of Discrimination and Underdevelopment in Rhodesia, With Special Reference to African Workers, 1940-1973." PhD Dissertation, St. Andrews University, 1975.

Clausen, Lars, "On Attitudes Towards Industrial Conflict in Zambian Industry," *African Social Research* (2) (December 1966).

Cliffe, Lionel, "Labour Migration and Peasant Differentiation: Zambian Experiences," in Ben Turok, ed., *Development in Zambia*. London: Zed Press, 1979.

Cliffe, Lionel and David Seddon, "Africa in a New World Order," *Review of African Political Economy* (50) (March 1991).

Clough, Michael, "Beyond Constructive Engagement," *Foreign Policy* (61) (Winter 1985-86).

——, "Africa in the 1990s," *CSIS Africa Notes* (107) (1990).

——, "The United States and Africa: The Policy of Cynical Disengagement," *Current History* Vol. 91, (May 1992).

——, "Africa Finds Reasons to Hope for Democracy's Future," *The New York Times* (March 22, 1992).

——, *Free at Last? U.S. Policy Toward Africa and the End of the Cold War*. New York: Council on Foreign Relations, 1992.

Colclough, Christopher, "Zambian Adjustment Strategy- With and Without the IMF," *IDS Bulletin* Vol. 19, (1) (January 1988).

——, "The Labour Market and Economic Stabilization in Zambia," Washington, D.C.: World Bank PPR Working Paper No. 272, November 1989.

Collins, J. and I. Muller, "Economic Activity, the Informal Sector and Household Income: Some Findings from a Survey of Chawama, Lusaka." Mimeo, University of Zambia, 1975.

Commander, Simon, ed., *Structural Adjustment and Agriculture: Theory and Practice in Africa and Latin America*. London: Overseas Development Institute, 1989.

Copans, Jean, "No Short Cuts to Democracy: The Long March Towards Modernity," *Review of African Political Economy* (50) (March 1991).

Copeland, D. S., "Structural Adjustment in Africa," *International Perspectives* Vol. XVIII, (2) (March-April 1989).

Cornia, Giovanni Andrea, Richard Jolly, and Frances Stewart, eds., *Adjustment With a Human Face: Protecting the Vulnerable and Promoting Growth 2 Volumes*. Oxford: Clarendon Press, 1987.

Coulon, C., "Senegal: The Development and Fragility of Semidemocracy," in L. Diamond et. al., eds., *Democracy in Developing Countries: Africa*. Boulder, Colorado: Lynne Rienner, 1988.

Crook, R. E., "State, Society and Political Institutions in Cote d'Ivoire and Ghana," *IDS Bulletin* Vol. 21 (4) (1990).

Cross, S., "Politics and Criticism in Zambia," *Journal of Southern African Studies* Vol. 1, (1) (1974).

Curry, R. L. Jr., "Global Market Forces and the Nationalization of Foreign-Based Export Companies," *Journal of Modern African Studies* Vol. 14, (1) (1976).

Cowan, L. Gray, "Zambia Tests Democracy," *CSIS Africa Notes* (141) (October 1992).

Dahl, Robert A., "Why Free Markets Are Not Enough," *Journal of Democracy* Vol. 3, (3) (July 1992).

Daniel, Philip, "Zambia: Structural Adjustment or Downward Spiral?" *IDS Bulletin* Vol. 16, (3) (1985).

Decalo, Samuel, "Regionalism, Political Decay and Civil Strife in Chad," *Journal of Modern African Studies* Vol. 18 (1980).

―――, "The Process, Prospects and Constraints of Democratization in Africa," *African Affairs* Vol. 91 (362) (January 1992).

Diamond, Larry, "Nigeria's Search for a New Political Order," *Journal of Democracy* Vol. 2, (2) (Spring 1991).

―――, *An American Foreign Policy for Democracy*. Washington, D.C.: Progressive Policy Institute, Policy Report No. 11, July 1991.

―――, "Promoting Democracy," *Foreign Policy* (87) (1992).

Diamond, Larry; Juan J. Linz, and Seymour Martin Lipset, eds., *Democracy in Developing Countries: Africa*. Boulder: Lynne Rienner Publishers, 1988.

Dillion-Malone, Cleve, *Zambian Humanism, Religion, and Social Morality*. Ndola, Zambia: Mission Press, 1990.

Dodge, D.J., *Agricultural Policy and Performance in Zambia:*

301

History Prospects and Proposals for Change. Berkeley:
Institute for International Studies, Berkeley Research
Series No. 32, 1977.

Dore, M.H.I., "Planning Industrial Development in Zambia."
PhD Thesis, Oxford University, 1975.

Dotson, Floyd and Lillian Dotson, *The Indian Minority of
Zambia, Rhodesia and Malawi*. New Haven: Yale
University Press, 1968.

Draisma, Tom, *The Struggle Against Underdevelopment in
Zambia Since Independence: What Role for Education*.
Amsterdam: Free University Press, 1987.

Dresang, D.L., "The Zambian Civil Service: A Study in
Development Administration." PhD Dissertation,
University of California-Los Angeles, 1971.

———, "Entrepreneuralism and Development Administration
in Zambia," *African Review* Vol. 1, (3) (1972).

———, "Ethnic Politics, Representative Bureaucracy and
Development Administration: The Zambian Case,"
American Political Science Review Vol. 68, (4) (1974).

———, "The Political Economy of Zambia," in R. Harris, ed.,
The Political Economy of Africa. Cambridge, Mass.:
Schenkmann, 1975.

———, *The Zambian Civil Service: Entrepreneuralism and
Development Administration*. Nairobi, Kenya: East
African Publishing House, 1975.

Due, Jean M., "Female Farm Households in Zambia: Further
Evidence of Poverty." Urbana-Champaign: University of
Illinois, Department of Agricultural Economics, n.d.
Mimeo

—— and Timothy Mudenda (with Patricia Miller and Marcia
White), *Women's Contributions to Farming Systems and
Household Income in Zambia*. Ann Arbor: Michigan State
University, Women in Development Series Working Paper
No. 85, 1985.

Economic Commission for Africa, *The African Charter for
Popular Participation in Development and
Transformation*. Addis Ababa: ECA, 1990.

Economist Intelligence Unit, *Zambia: Country Profile*. London:
Business International Limited, 1987.

Elliot, C., "The Zambian Economy," *East African Journal* Vol.
5, (12) (December 1968).

———, ed., *Constraints on the Economic Development of*

Zambia. Nairobi, Kenya: Oxford University Press, 1971.

Ellis, Stephen, "Democracy in Africa: Achievements and Prospects," in Douglas Rimmer, ed., *Action in Africa*. London: James Currey and Heinemann, 1993.

Ergas, Zakis, ed., *The African State in Transition*. New York: St. Martins Press, 1987.

Etheredge, D. A., "The Role of Education in Economic Development: The Example of Zambia," *Journal of Administration Overseas* Vol. 6, (4) (October 1967).

Evans, Peter, *Dependent Development: The Alliance of Multinationals, State and Local Capital in Brazil*. Princeton: Princeton University Press, 1979.

———, "Predatory, Developmental and Other Apparatuses: A Comparative Political Economy Perspective on the Third World State," *Sociological Forum* Vol. 4 (4) (1989).

Faber, Mike, *Zambia-The Moulding of a Nation*. London: Africa Bureau, 1968.

Fatton, Robert, "Liberal Democracy in Africa," *Political Science Quarterly* Vol. 105, (3) (1990).

———, *Predatory Rule: State and Civil Society in Africa*. Boulder, Colorado: Lynne Rienner, 1992.

Fincham, R. and Grace Zulu, "Labour and Participation in Zambia," in Ben Turok, ed., *Development in Zambia*. London: Zed Books, 1979.

Fortman, Bastiaan de Gaay, ed., *After Mulungushi: The Economics of Zambian Humanism*. Nairobi: East Africa Publishing House, 1969.

Fry, J., "The Turner Report: A Zambian View." Discussion Paper, Economics Department, University of Zambia, 1970.

———, "An Analysis of Employment and Income Distribution in Zambia." PhD Thesis, Oxford University, 1974.

———, "Rural-Urban Terms of Trade, 1960-1973," *African Social Research* (19) (1975).

Fundanga, Caleb, "Impact of IMF/World Bank Policies on the Peoples of Africa: The Case of Zambia," in Bade Onimode, ed., *The IMF. The World Bank and the African Debt: The Economic Impact*. London: Institute for African Alternatives and Zed Press, 1989.

Gappert, Gary, *Capital Expenditure and Transitional Planning in Zambia*. New York: Syracuse University, Program of East African Studies, 1966.

Getzel, Cherry, "Labour and State: The Case of Zambia's
    Mineworkers Union," *Journal of Commonwealth and
    Comparative Politics* Vol. 13, (3) (1975).
————, "Industrial Relations in Zambia to 1975," in Ukandi
    Damachi, ed., *Industrial Relations in Africa*. New York:
    Macmillan, 1979.
————, "Dissent and Authority in the Zambian One-Party State,
    1973-80," in Getzel, C., C. Baylies, and M. Szeftel, eds,
    The Dynamics of the One-Party State in Zambia.
    Manchester: University of Manchester Press, 1984.
————, Carolyn Baylies and Moris Szeftel,eds. *The Dynamics of
    the One Party State in Zambia*. Manchester: University of
    Manchester Press, 1984.
Gibbon, Peter, Yusuf Bangura and Arve Ofstad,
    *Authoritarianism. Democracy and Adjustment: The
    Politics of Economic Reform in Africa*. Uppsala:
    Scandinavian Institute of African Studies, 1992.
Global Coalition for Africa(GCA), *African Social and Economic
    Tends: The 1992 Annual Report*. Washington, D.C.: The
    GCA, 1992.
Godsell, Bobby, "Six Strategies for African Development," in
    Douglas Rimmer, ed., *Action in Africa*. London: James
    Currey and Heinemann, 1993.
Good, Kenneth, "The Reproduction of Weakness in the State
    and Agriculture: The Zambian Experience," *African
    Affairs*, Vol. 85 (339) (April 1986).
————, "Systematic Agricultural Mismanagement: The 1985
    'Bumper Harvest' in Zambia," *Journal of Modern African
    Studies*, Vol. 24 (1) (June 1986).
————, "Debt and the One-Party State in Zambia," *Journal of
    Modern African Studies* Vol. 27, (2) (1989).
Government of Zambia, *Restructuring in the Midst of Crisis*.
    Background Paper for the Consultative Group for Zambia
    Meeting in Paris, May 1984.
————, *Annual Agricultural Statistical Bulletin*, Lusaka:
    Ministry of Agriculture and Water Development, Planning
    Division, 1984.
————, *An Action Programme for Economic Restructuring*.
    Consultative Group for Zambia Meeting, Lusaka, June 4-5,
    1985.
————, *Economic Report 1984*. Lusaka: National Commission
    for Development Planning, January 1985.

————, 1990 Census Population, Housing, and Agriculture: Preliminary Report. Lusaka: Central Statistical Office, December 1990.

————, Ministry of Finance and National Commission for Development Planning, *New Economic Recovery Programme: Economic and Financial Policy Framework 1991-1993*. Lusaka: Government Printers, 1991.

————, National Commission for Development Planning, *Economic Report*. Lusaka: Government Printers, 1991.

————, *Report of the Committee on Local Administration for the First Session of the Seventh National Assembly Appointed on 5th December, 1991*. Lusaka: Government Printer, September, 1992.

————, *Annual Report for the Year 1992*. Ministry of Home Affairs, Drug Enforcement Commission, Lusaka: Government Printer, 31st December 1992.

————, *Action-Taken Report on the Parliamentary Committee Financial Services Presented by the Vice-President for the First Session of the Seventh National Assembly Appointed on 5th December. 1991*. Lusaka: Government Printer, February, 1993.

Graham, Carol, "Zambia's Democratic Transition: The Beginning of the End of the One Party State in Africa?" *Brookings Review* (Spring 1992).

————, *Safety Nets, Politics and the Poor: Transitions to Market Economies*. (Washington, D.C.: The Brookings Institution, 1994.

Greenfield, C.C., "Manpower Planning in Zambia," *Journal of Administration Overseas* Vol. 7, (4) (October 1968).

Gulhati, Ravi, "Impasse in Zambia: The Economics and Politics of Reform." Washington D.C.: World Bank Economic Development Institute Analytical Case Study No. 2, July 1989.

Gupta, Anirudha, "The Zambian National Assembly: Study of an African Legislature," *Parliamentary Affairs* Vol. 19 (Winter 1965).

————, "The Lusaka Summit: An Assessment," *Africa Quarterly* Vol. 10, (3) (October–December 1970).

Hall, Richard, *Kaunda: Founder of Zambia*. London: Longmans, 1965.

————, *Zambia*. London: Pall Mall, 1965.

————, "Zambia's Search for Political Stability," *World Today*

Vol. 25, (11) (November 1969).

———, *The High Price of Principles: Kaunda and the White South*. London: Hodder and Stoughton, 1969.

Ham, Melinda, "End of Honeymoon," *Africa Report* (May-June, 1992).

———, "Zambia: Luring Investment," *Africa Report* (September-October 1992).

———, "Zambia: One Year On," *Africa Report* (January-February 1993).

———, "Zambia: History Repeats Itself," *Africa Report* Vol.38, (3) (May-June 1993).

———, "Malawi: Banda's Last Waltz," *Africa Report* Vol. 38 (3) (May-June 1993).

———, "Zambia: An Outspoken Opposition," *Africa Report* Vol. 38, (6) (November December 1993).

Hamalengwa, Munyonzwe, "The Political Economy of Human Rights in Africa," *Philosophy and Social Action* Vol. IX, (3) (July-September 1983).

———, "The Legal System of Zambia," in Peter Sack, Carl Wellman and Mitsukuni Yasaki, eds., *Monistic or Pluralistic Legal Culture? Anthropological and Ethnological Foundations of Traditional and Modern Legal Systems*. Berlin: Dunker and Humbolt, 1991.

———, "Economic Crisis, Human Rights Violations and Prospects for Democratization in Africa: The Case of Zambia." Paper presented at the Conference on Structural Adjustment, Peace and Prospects for Security in Africa, Park Plaza Hotel, Toronto, Canada, October 1990.

———, *Thoughts are Free: Prison Experience and Reflections on Law and Politics in General*. Toronto: Africa in Canada Press, 1991.

———, *Class Struggles in Zambia 1889-1989 and the Fall of Kenneth Kaunda 1990-1991*. Lanham: University Press of America, 1992.

Han, H. C., "The Structure of the Manufacturing Industry in Zambia and its Implications for the Development of the Informal Sector." SARFP Working Papers, ILO, Lusaka, Zambia, August 1982.

Hansen, A., "Refugee Dynamics: Angolans in Zambia 1966 to 1972," *International Migration Review* Vol. 15 (1981).

———, "Refugee Settlement Versus Settlement on Government Schemes: The Long-Term Consequences for Security,

Integration and Economic Development of Angolan
Refugees (1966-1989) in Zambia." UNSRID Discussion
Paper, No. 17, November 1990.

Harden, Blaine, "Zambia Puts Hammer to its Foreign Debt," *The
Washington Post* (29 June 1987).

Harries-Jones, P., "Tribe, Politics and Industry on the Zambian
Copperbelt," PhD Thesis, Oxford University, 1970.

Harvey, C., "The Control of Credit in Zambia," *Journal of
Modern African Studies* Vol. 11 , (3) (1973)

——, "The Structure of Zambian Development," in Ukandi
Damachi et. al., eds., *Development Paths in Africa and
China*. London: Macmillan, 1976.

Hatch, John, *Africa Emergent: Africa's Problems Since
Independence*. Chicago: Henry Regnery, 1974.

——, *Two African Statesmen: Kaunda of Zambia and
Nyerere of Tanzania*. London: Secker and Warburg, 1976.

Hawkins, Jeffrey, J., "Understanding the Failure of IMF Reform:
The Zambian Case," *World Development*, (19) (1991).

Hawkins, Tony, "Now Zambia Points Way to Fiscal Rectitude in
Adversity," *The Financial Times* (London) (February 10,
1993).

Heisler, Helmuth, "Continuity and Change in Zambian
Administration," *Journal of Local Administration
Overseas* Vol. 4, (3) (July 1965).

——, "The Creation of a Stabilized Urban Society in Northern
Rhodesia/Zambia," *African Affairs* Vol. 70, (279) (April
1971).

——, *Urbanization and the Government of Migration: The
Inter-Relation of Urban and Rural Life in Zambia*.
London: C. Hurst, 1974.

Hellen, J. A., *Rural Economic Development in Zambia, 1890-
1964*. Munchen: Weltforum Verlag, 1968.

Henderson, I., "The Origins of Nationalism in East and Central
Africa: The Zambian Case," *Journal of African History*
Vol. 11, (4) (1970).

——, "Labour and Politics in Northern Rhodesia, 1900-1953:
A study in the Limits of Colonial Power." PhD
Dissertation, University of Edinburgh, 1972.

——, "Wage Earners and Political Protest in Colonial Africa,"
African Affairs (72) (1973).

——, "The Limits of Colonial Power: Race and Labour
Problems in Colonial Zambia, 1900-1953," *Journal of*

Imperial Commonwealth History Vol. 2, (3) (1974).

———, "Early African Leadership: The Copperbelt Disturbances of 1935 and 1940," *Journal of Southern African Affairs* Vol. 2, (1) (1975).

Heron, Alastair, "Zambia: Key Point in Africa," *World Today* Vol. 21, (2) (February 1965).

Hodges, Tony, "Zambia's Autonomous Adjustment," *Africa Recovery* Vol. 2, (4) (December 1988).

Holman, Michael, "Fresh Start for Africa's Newest Democracy," *Financial Times* (17 December, 1992).

Huntington, Samuel P., "Democracy's Third Wave," *Journal of Democracy* Vol. 2, (2) (Spring 1991).

———, *The Third Wave: Democratization in the Late Twentieth Century*. Norman, Oklahoma: Oklahoma University Press, 1992.

———, "Clash of Civilizations?" *Foreign Affairs* Vol. 72, (3) (Summer 1993).

Ihonvbere, Julius, O., "Contradictions of Multi-Party Democracy in Peripheral Formations: The Rise and Demise of Nigeria's Second Republic, 1979-83," in Peter Meyens and Dani Wadada Nabudere eds., *Democracy and the One-Party State in Africa*. Hamburg: Institute for African Studies, 1988.

———, "The African Crisis in Historical and Contemporary Perspective," in Julius O. Ihonvbere, ed., *The Political Economy of Crisis and Underdevelopment in Africa: Selected Works of Claude Ake*. Lagos: JAD Publishers, 1989.

———, "Structural Adjustment in Nigeria," in Ben Turok, ed., *Alternative Development Strategies for Africa Vol. III-Debt and Democracy*. London: Institute for African Alternatives, 1991.

———, "The Economic Crisis in Sub-Saharan Africa: Depth, Dimensions and Prospects for Recovery," *Journal of International Studies* (27) (July 1991).

———, "Economic Crisis in Sub-Saharan Africa: Constraints and Prospects for Recovery," *Pakistan Horizon* Vol. 44, (4) (October 1991).

———, "The African Crisis, The Popular Charter and Prospects for Recovery in the 1990s," *Zeitschtift fur Afrikastudien (ZAST)* (11-12) (1991).

———, "Surviving at the Margins: Africa and the New Global

Order," *Current World Leaders* Vol. 35, (6) (December 1992).

———, "Africa and the New World Order: Prospects for the 1990s," *Iranian Journal of International Affairs* Vol. IV, (3-4) (Fall-Winter 1992).

———, "Is Democracy Possible in Africa?: The Elites, The People and Civil Society" *QUEST: Philosophical Discussions* Vol. VI, (2) (December 1992).

———, "The Persian Gulf Crisis and Africa: Implications for the 1990s," *International Studies* Vol. 29, (3) (1992).

———, The Third World and the New World Order," Futures Vol. 24, (10) (December 1992).

———, "Changes in Eastern Europe and Africa's Role in the World Political Economy," in Chronis Polychroniou ed., *Perspectives and Issues in International Political Economy*. Westport, CT: Praeger, 1992.

———, "The 'Irrelevant' State, Ethnicity and the Quest for Nationhood in Africa," *Ethnic and Racial Studies* Vol. 17, (1) (January 1994).

———, "Why African Economies Will Not Recover," *Iranian Journal of International Studies* (Spring-Summer 1994).

———, "Between Debt and Disaster: The Politics of Africa's Debt Crisis," *In Depth: A Journal of Values and Public Policy* Vol. 4, (1) (Winter 1994).

———, *Nigeria: The Politics of Adjustment and Democracy* New Brunswick, NJ: Transaction Publishers, 1994.

———, "From Movement to Government: The Movement for Multiparty Democracy and the Crisis of Democratic Consolidation in Zambia," *Canadian Journal of African Studies*. (1) (1995).

———, "Government and Opposition Politics in Africa: A Study of the 'Zero Option' Controversy in Zambia," *Afrika Spectrum* (1) (1995).

———, "Threats to Democratization in Sub-Saharan Africa: The Case of Zambia," *Asian and African Studies: Journal of the Israeli Oriental Society* Vol. 28, (1) (1995).

International Forum for Democratic Studies, *Nigeria's Political Crisis: Which Way Forward ?* (Conference Report) Washington, D.C.: IFDS, 1995.

International Labour Office, *Zambia: Basic Needs in an Economy Under Pressure*. Addis Ababa: Jobs and Skills Programme for Africa, 1981.

International Monetary Fund, *Surveys of African Economies: Zambia Volume 4*. Washington, D.C.: IMF, 1971.

Javaheri, F., *Soyabean: Combatting Malnutrition in Zambia*. Lusaka: Government of the Republic of Zambia, 1990.

Jere, Susan, "Resolving Conflicts and Building Linkages Among NGOs in Zambia," in Richard Sandbrook and Mohamed Halfani, eds., *Empowering People-Building Community, Civil Associations, and Legality in Africa*. Toronto: Center for Urban and Community Studies, University of Toronto, 1993.

Jolly, Richard, "Skilled Manpower as a Constraint to the Development of Zambia." Sussex: University of Sussex, Institute of Development Studies Communications Series No 48, January 1970.

———, "How Successful was the First National Development Plan ?" *African Development* Special Issue on "Zambia: Six Years After," (October 1970).

———, "The Seers Report in Retrospect," *African Social Research* (11) (1971).

Joseph, Richard, "Africa: The Rebirth of Political Freedom," *Journal of Democracy* Vol. 2, (4) (1991).

———, "Zambia: A Model for Democratic Change," *Current History* (May 1992).

Kalula, E., ed., *Some Aspects of Zambian Labour Relations*. Lusaka: National Archives of Zambia, 1975.

Kandeke, T., *A Systematic Introduction to Zambian Humanism*. Lusaka: NecZam, 1977.

Kansteiner, Walter, H., "U.S. Interests in Africa Revisited," *CSIS Africa Notes* (157) (February 1994).

Kapferer, B., *Strategy and Transaction in an African Factory: African Workers and Indian Management in a Zambian Town- Kabwe*. Manchester: Manchester University Press, 1972.

———, "Conflict and Process in a Zambian Mine Community: An Appreciation of Some of Max Gluckman's Theories of Conflict," *Political Anthropology* Vol. 1, (3-4) (1976).

Kaplan, Robert D., "The Coming Anarchy," *Atlantic Monthly* (February 1994).

Kashoki, Mubanga E. ed., *Language in Zambia*. Manchester: Manchester University Press, 1978.

———, "Indigenous Scholarship in African Universities: The Human Factor," in Ben Turok, ed., *Development in*

Zambia. London: Zed Press, 1979.

Kasoma, Francis, *The Press in Zambia*. Lusaka: Multimedia, 1986.

————, *Communication Policies in Zambia*. Tempere, Finland: University of Tempere, 1990.

Katona, Emic, *National Development Plans and the Standard of Living in Black Africa: The Zambian Case*. Budapest: Institute for World Economics of the Hungarian Academy of Sciences, 1982.

Kaunda, Kenneth D., *Zambia Shall be Free: An Autobiography*, London: Heinemann Educational Books, 1962.

————, *Humanism in Zambia and a Guide to its Implementation Part 1*. Lusaka: Zambia Information Service, 1967.

———— and C.M. Morris, *A Humanist in Africa*. London: Longmans, 1967.

————, "Ideology and Humanism," *Pan African Journal* Vol. 1, (1) (Winter, 1968).

————, "Zambia's Economic Reforms," *African Affairs* Vol. 67, (269) (October 1968).

————, "Zambia's Economic Revolution." Address to the National Council of UNIP at Mulungushi, April 19, 1968. Lusaka: Zambia Information Service.

————, "Zambia's Guideline for the Next Decade." Address to the National Council of UNIP at Mulungushi, November 9, 1969. Lusaka: Zambia Information Service.

————, "Towards Complete Independence." Address to the National Council of UNIP, Matero Hall, Lusaka, August 11, 1969. Lusaka: Zambia Information Service.

————, *Africa in the Sixties: The Decade of Decision and Definition*. Lusaka: Zambia News Agency, 1969.

————, "A Path For the Future." Address to the National Council of UNIP, Mulungushi Hall, 7-10 November, 1970. Lusaka: Zambia Information Service.

————, *Ten Thoughts on Humanism. Humanism in the Party: Humanism in the Trade Unions*. Mimeo, 1970.

————, *No Cause for Concern. Address on the Occasion of the Opening of the National Council at Mulungushi Hall- 1st October. 1971*. Lusaka: Government Printer, 1971.

————, *Humanism in Zambia and a Guide to its Implementation Part II*. Lusaka: Government Printer, 1974.

————, "The Watershed Speech." Address to the National Council of the United National Independence Party, Lusaka, June 30, 1975.

————, "Opening Address" to the Leaders' Seminar of the United National Independence Party, Mulungushi Rock, 14th September, 1976.

————, Address at the Occasion of the Opening of the Ninth National Council of the United National Independence Party, Mulungushi Rock, 20th September, 1976.

————, Address at the Closing of the Ninth Session of the National Council of the United National Independence Party, Mulungushi Rock, 24th September, 1976.

————, *Communocracy: A Strategy for Constructing a People's Economy Under Humanism*. Lusaka: Zambia Information Services, 1976.

————, Guidelines Issued to ZIMCO Director-General, Executive Directors, Managing Directors, Deputy Managing Directors and General Managers of all ZIMCO Subsidiaries and other Parastatal Organizations," Lusaka: Zambia Information Services, 1st February, 1983.

————, Address to the Inaugural Meeting of the ZIMCO Council of Members of the Board of Directors of ZIMCO and the Chief Executives of ZIMCO Member of Companies, Lusaka: Zambia Information Services, 9th May, 1983.

————, Speech to the 9th General Conference of the United National Independence Party, Mulungushi Rock of Authority, 22nd August, 1983.

————, *Politics in Zambia. Volume I*. Lusaka: Kenneth Kaunda Foundation, 1988.

————, Address at the Opening of the 25th National Council of the United National Independence Party, Mulungushi International Conference Centre, September 24-29, 1990.

————, Address to Parliament on the Opening of the Third Session of the Sixth National Assembly, 26th October, 1990. Lusaka: Government Printer.

————, Brief Introductory Remarks to the Special Meeting of Church Leaders, State House, Lusaka, 26th November, 1990.

————, "Observations on MMD Position Statement on Constitution Proposals," n.d. Typescript.

————, Address to a Businessmen's Dinner Held at State House, 3rd April, 1991. Typescript.

————, Speech on the Occasion of the Official Opening of the Kabwe and Kafue Roundabout Fountains, Cairo Road, Lusaka, 1st July, 1991.

Kay, George,"Agricultural Progress in Zambia's Eastern Province," *Journal of Administration Overseas* Vol. 5, (2) (April, 1966).

————, *A Social Biography of Zambia*. London: University of London Press, 1967.

————, "A Regional Framework for Rural Development in Zambia," *African Affairs* Vol. 67, (266) (January 1968).

Kayizzi-Mugerwa, Steve, "External Shocks and Adjustment in a Mineral Dependent Economy: A Short-run Model for Zambia," *World Development* (19), (July 1991).

Keane, J., *Democracy and Civil Society*. London: Verso, 1988.

"Kenneth Kaunda of Zambia Governs in Classic 'Big Man' Style," *Washington Post*, (11 September 1988).

Kelly, Michael, A., "Democracy and Economic Liberalism: The Foundations of Hope for Africa," *The Midsouth Political Science Journal* Vol. 13 (Spring 1992).

Kessel, N., "The Mineral Industry and its Contribution to Development of Zambian Economy." PhD Dissertation, University of Leeds, 1971.

————, "Mining and Factors Constraining Economic Development," in C. Elliot, ed., *Constraints on the Economic Development of Zambia*. Nairobi: Oxford University Press, 1971.

Klein, Martin, A., "Back To Democracy," Presidential Address to the 1991 Annual Meeting of the African Studies Association, St, Louis, Missouri, November 1991.

Klepper, Robert, "Zambian Agricultural Structure and Performance," in Ben Turok, ed., *Development in Zambia*. London: Zed Press, 1979.

Kolakowski, Leszek, "Uncertainties of a Democratic Age," *Journal of Democracy* Vol. 1, (1) (Winter 1990).

Koleso, B. J., "Zambia: Hunting for Conservation," *Africa Report* (July-August 1993).

Koloko, J., "Rural to Urban Migration in Zambia." M.A. Thesis, University of Pittsburgh, 1974.

————, "The Manpower Approach to Educational Planning: Theoretical Issues and Evidence from Zambia." PhD Thesis, University of Pittsburgh, 1976.

Krishnamurthy, B.S., *ChaChjaCha: Zambia's Struggle for*

Independence. Lusaka: Oxford University Press, 1972.

Kydd, J., "Changes in Zambian Agricultural Policy Since 1983: Problems of Liberalisation and Agrarianisation," *Development Policy Review* Vol. 4, (3) (September 1986).

———, "Coffee After Copper" Structural Adjustment, Liberalisation and Agriculture in Zambia," *The Journal of Modern African Studies* Vol. 26, (2) (June 1988).

———, "Zambia," in Charles Harvey, ed., *Agricultural Pricing and Marketing in Africa*. London: Macmillan, 1988.

———, "Zambia in the 1980s: The Political Economy of Adjustment," in Commander, S., ed., *Structural Adjustment and Agriculture: Theory and Practice in Africa and Latin America*. London: ODI and James Currey, 1989.

Lancaster, Carol, "Economic Reform in Africa: Is it Working?" *The Washington Quarterly* (13) (Winter 1990).

———, "Governance in Africa: Should Foreign Aid Be Linked to Political Reform," in The Carter Center, *African Governance in the 1990s*. Atlanta: Emory University, 1990.

———, "The New Politics of U.S. Aid to Africa," *CSIS Africa Notes* (120) (1991).

———, *African Economic Reform: The External Dimension*. Washington, D.C. Institute for International Economics, 1991.

———, *United States and Africa: Into the Twenty-First Century*. Washington, D.C.: Overseas Development Council, Policy Essay No. 7, 1993.

———, and John Williamson, eds, *African Debt and Financing*. Washington, D.C.: Institute for International Economics, 1986.

Legum, Colin, ed., *Zambia: Independence and Beyond- The Speeches of Kenneth Kaunda*. London: Thomas Nelson, 1966.

Lemarchand, Rene, "African Transitions to Democracy: An Interim (and Mostly Pessimistic) Assessment," *Africa Insight* Vol. 22, (3) (1992).

Liatto-Katundu, Beatrice, "Social Consequences of Structural Adjustment: Effects on Zambian Workers and Workers' Coping Strategies." Lusaka: Department of African Development Studies, University of Zambia, November 1991.

————, "The Women's Lobby and Gender Relations in
Zambia," *Review of African Political Economy* (56)
(1993).

Linz, Juan, "Transitions to Democracy," *The Washington
Quarterly* (Summer 1990).

————, "The Perils of Presidentialism," *Journal of Democracy*
Vol. 1, (1) (Winter 1990).

Lipset, Seymour Martin, "Some Social Requisites for
Democracy: Economic Development and Political
Legitimacy," *American Political Science Review* Vol. 53,
(1) (1959).

Lombe, Chris, "Thousands of Striking Zambian Miners Sacked,"
Africa Now (August 1985).

Loxley, J., "Structural Adjustment Programmes in Africa:
Ghana and Zambia," *Review of African Political Economy*
(47) (1991).

Maketla, Neva Seidman, "Theoretical and Practical Implications
of IMF Conditionality in Zambia," *Journal of Modern
African Studies*, Vol. 24 (September 1986).

Makoba, J. W., "The Impact of Government Policy on the
Performance of Industrial Public Enterprises in Two
Selected Sub-Saharan African Countries: A Comparative
Study of Public Policy and Public Enterprise Behavior in
Tanzania and Zambia, 1964-1984." PhD Dissertation,
University of California at Berkeley, May 1991.

Malila, Mumba, "The State of Emergency, Multi-Party
Democracy and Constitutional Change." Mimeo,
University of Zambia, 1990.

Mandazza, Ibbo, "The State and Democracy in Southern Africa:
Towards a Conceptual Framework," in Eghosa Osaghae,
ed., *Between State and Civil Society in Africa*. Dakar:
CODESRIA, 1994.

Markakis, John and Robert L. Curry, "The Global Economy's
Impact on Recent Budgetary Politics in Zambia," *Journal
of African Studies* Vol. 3, (4) (Winter 1976-77).

Martin, A., *Minding Their own Business: Zambia's Struggle
Against Western Control*. London: Penguin Books, 1975.

Martin, Guy, "Preface: Democratic Transitions in Africa," Issue
Vol. XXI, (1-2) (1993).

Martin, M., *The Crumbling Facade of Africa's Debt
Negotiations: No Winners*. London: Macmillan, 1991.

————, "Neither Phoenix not Icarus: Negotiating Economic

Reform in Ghana and Zambia, 1983-8," in Callaghy, T and J. Ravenhill, eds., *Hemmed In: Responses to Africa's Economic Dilemma*. New York: Columbia University Press, 1994.

Mbikusita-Lewanika, Akashambatwa, "Role of the Press in the Third Republic." Address to the University of Zambia Press Club, Lusaka, January 23, 1991.

———— and Derrick Chitala, eds., *The Hour Has Come: Proceedings of the National Conference on the Multi-Party Option Held at Garden House Hotel, Lusaka, Zambia, 20-21 July, 1990*. Lusaka: Zambia Research Foundation, 1990.

Mbozi, Parkie, "The Zambian Media Has Betrayed the People," *The Watchdog*, University of Zambia, Vol. 1, (4) (September 1990).

McKay, Vernon, "The Propaganda Battle for Zambia," *Africa Today* Vol. 18, (2) (April 1971).

Meebelo, H. S., *Reaction to Colonialism: A Prelude to the Politics of Independence in Northern Zambia. 1893-1939*. Manchester: University of Manchester Press, 1971.

Mehta, M.M., "Economic Development of Zambia: Selected Economic and Statistical Indicators." Mulungushi: President Citizenship College, Monograph No. 1, 1971.

Meyns, Peter, "The Political Economy of Zambia," in Klaas Woldring et. al, eds, *Beyond Political Independence: Zambia's Development Predicament in the 1980s*. Berlin and New York: Mouton Publishers, 1984.

Meyns, Peter and Dani Wadada Nabudere, eds., *Democracy and the One-Party State in Africa*. Hamburg: Institute for African Studies, 1989.

Michaels, Marguerite, "Retreat From Africa," *Foreign Affairs* Vol. 72, (1) (1993).

Mijere, Nsolo, *The Mineworkers' Resistance to Governmental Decentralization in Zambia*. Ph.D Thesis, Brandeis University, 1985.

Minter, William, ed., *U.S. Foreign Policy: An Africa Agenda*. Washington, D.C.: Africa Policy Information Center, 1994.

Mlenga, Kenin L., *Who is Who in Zambia*. Lusaka: Zambia Information Service, 1968.

Mohane, Guy, "Employment and Incomes in Zambia in the Context of Structural Adjustment." Lusaka: ILO/SATEP, 1987.

Molteno, Robert V., "Zambia and the One-Party State," *East African Journal* Vol. 9, (2) (1972).

———, "Zambian Humanism: The Way Ahead," *African Review* Vol. 3, (4) (1973).

———, *The Zambian Community and its Government*. Lusaka: NecZam, 1974.

———, "Cleavage and Conflict in Zambian Politics: A Study in Sectionalism," in W. Tordoff, ed., *Politics in Zambia*. Los Angeles and Berkeley, CA.: University of California Press, 1974.

Moore Jr., Barrington, *Social Origins of Dictatorship and Democracy: Lord and Peasant in the Making of the Modern World*. Boston: Beacon Press, 1966.

Movement for Multi-Party Democracy, *Manifesto*. Lusaka: MMD Secretariat, Campaign Committee, n.d.

———, "Programme of National Reconstruction and Development Through Democracy." Draft Discussion Paper, MMD Secretariat, Lusaka, February 1991.

Mtshali, B. Vulindlela, "Zambia's Foreign Policy," *Current History* Vol. 58, (343) (March 1970).

———, "Zambia's Foreign Policy: The Dilemma of a New State." PhD Dissertation, New York University, 1972.

Mudenda, G., "Class Formation and Class Struggle in Contemporary Zambia," in B. Magubane and G. Nzongola-Ntalaja, eds., *Proletarianization and Class Struggle in Africa*. San Francisco: Synthesis Publications, 1983.

———, "The Process of Class Formation in Contemporary Zambia," in Klaas Woldring, ed., *Beyond Political Independence: Zambia's Development Predicament in the 1980s*. London: Mouton, 1984.

———, "MMD Two Years Later," *Southern Africa Political and Economic Monthly* (1992).

Muigai, Githu, "Kenya's Opposition and the Crisis of Governance," *Issue* Vol. XXI, (1-2) (1993).

Mulford, D., *Zambia: The Politics of Independence*. Oxford: Oxford University Press, 1967.

Mulwila, J. M., "Economic Independence in Zambia and the Role of Law in Economic Development." LLM Thesis, University of Zambia, 1976.

Muntemba, Dorothy C., "The Impact of the World Bank/IMF on the Peoples of Africa with Special Reference to Zambia and Especially on Women and Children," in Bade

Onimode, ed., *The IMF, The World Bank and the African Debt-The Social and Political Impact.* London: Institute for African Alternatives and Zed Press, 1989.

Muntemba, M.S., "The Evolution of Political Systems in South Central Zambia, 1894-1953." M.A. Thesis, University of Zambia, 1973.

———, "Rural Underdevelopment in Zambia: Kabwe Rural District, 1850-1970." PhD Dissertation, University of California, Los Angeles, 1977.

Musiker, Naomi, *Kaunda's Zambia, 1964-1991. A Select and Annotated Bibliography.* Johannesburg: South Africa Institute of International Affairs, Bibliographical Series No. 26, 1993.

Mutua, Makau wa, "U.S. Foreign Policy Towards Africa: Building Democracy Through Popular Participation," in William Minter, ed., *U.S. Foreign Policy: An Africa Agenda.* Washington, D.C.: Africa Policy Information Center, 1994.

Mwanakatwe, J. M., *The Growth of Education in Zambia Since Independence.* London: Cambridge University Press, 1968.

Mwanawina, I., *An Input-Output and Econometric Approach to Analyzing Structural Change and Growth Strategies in the Zambian Economy.* Konstanz: Hartung-Gorre-Verlag, 1990.

———, "Zambia," in Aderanti Adepoju, ed., *The Impact of Structural Adjustment on the Population of Africa.* Portsmouth, NH and London: Heinemann and James Currey, 1993.

Mwalimu, Charles, "Police, State Security Forces and Constitutionalism of Human Rights in Zambia," *Georgia Journal of International and Corporate Law* Vol. 21, (Summer 1991).

Mwangilwa, Goodwin, "The Future of Journalism in Zambia." Address at the Law and Media Seminar, African Literature Center, Kitwe, Zambia, April 13-14, 1990.

Mwanza, Jacob M. "Rural-Urban Migration and Urban Employment in Zambia," in Ben Turok, ed., *Development in Zambia.* London: Zed Press, 1979.

National Democratic Institute for International Affairs and Carter Center of Emory University, *The October 31. 1991. National Elections in Zambia.* Washington, D.C.: National Democratic Institute, 1992.

Ncube, P., M. Sakala and M. Ndulo, "The IMF and the Zambian Economy: A Case Study," in Havnevik, K., ed., *The IMF and the World Bank in Africa*. Uppsala: The Scandinavian Institute of African Studies, 1987.

Ndulo, Manenga and Martin Sakala, "Stabilization Policies in Zambia, 1976-85," Geneva: International Labour Office, World Employment Programme, Working Paper No. 13, May 1987.

Ndulo, Muna, "Domestic Participation in Mining in Zambia," in Ben Turok, ed., *Development in Zambia*. London: Zed Press, 1979.

Ndulo, Muna and Kaye Turner, *Civil Liberties Cases in Zambia*. London: The African Law Reports, 1984.

Nelson-Richards, M., *Beyond the Sociology of Agrarian Transformation: Economy and Society in Zambia, Nepal and Zanzibar*. Leiden: Brill 1988.

Ng'ethe, Njuguna, "Strongmen, State Formation, Collapse, and Reconstruction in Africa," in I. William Zartman, ed., *Collapsed States*. Boulder: Lynne Rienner, 1995.

Novicki, Margaret A., "Zambia: Lesson in Democracy," *Africa Report* (January-February, 1992).

———, "Frederick Chiluba: Champion of Zambia's Democracy," (Interview), *Africa Report* (January-February 1993).

Nyirenda, V. G., "Social Change and Social Policy in a Developing Country: The Zambian Case." PhD Dissertation, University of California, Los Angeles, 1977.

Nzomo, Maria, "Women, Democracy and Development in Africa," in Walter O. Oyugi, et., al, eds., *Democratic Theory and Practice in Africa*. London: Heinemann and James Currey, 1988.

Ohadike, Patrick O., "The Nature and Extent of Urbanization in Zambia," *Journal of Asian and African Studies* Vol. 4, (2) (April 1969)

———, "Counting Heads in Africa: The Experience of Zambia, 1963 and 1969," *Journal of Administration Overseas* Vol. 9, (4) (October 1970).

Ollawa, P., "Rural Development Policies and Performance in Zambia: A Critical Study," The Hague: Institute of Social Studies, Occasional Paper, No. 4, 1977.

———, "Politics, Institutions and Participatory Development in Rural Zambia," *Labour and Society* Vol. 2, (3) (1977).

————, *Participatory Democracy in Zambia*. Devon: Ilfracombe, 1979.

Organization of African Unity(OAU), *The Lagos Plan of Action for the Economic Development of Africa 1980-2000*. Geneva: International Institute for Labour Studies, 1982.

————, *Africa's Priority Programme for Economic Recovery, 1986-1990*. Addis Ababa: OAU Secretariat, 1986.

————, "Africa's Submission to the Special Session of the United Nations General Assembly on Africa's Economic and Social Crisis." Addis Ababa: OAU Secretariat, 13 May 1986.

————, "External Debt Crisis of Africa: Summary of Information, Statistical Data, and Proposed Actions." Addis Ababa: OAU Secretariat, 20-21 November 1987.

Osaghae, Eghosa, ed., *Between State and Civil Society in Africa*. Dakar: CODESRIA, 1994.

Oyugi, Walter, E.S. Atieno Odhiambo, Michael Chege and Afrifa K. Gitonga, eds., *Democratic Theory and Practice in Africa*. London: James Currey, 1988.

Parfitt, Trevor W., "Lies, Damned Lies and Statistics: The World Bank/ECA Structural Adjustment Controversy," *Review of African Political Economy* (47) (Spring 1990).

————, and Stephen P. Riley, *The African Debt Crisis*. London: Routeledge, 1989.

Parpart, Jane., *Labour and Capital on the African Copperbelt*. Philadelphia: Temple University Press, 1983.

————, and Timothy Shaw, "Contradictions and Coalitions: Class Fractions in Zambia, 1964-1984," *Africa Today* Vol. 30, (3) (1983).

Pearce, Richard, "Food Consumption and Adjustment in Zambia." Food Studies Group, Queen Elizabeth House, Oxford University, Working Paper No. 2, December 1990.

Pettman, Jan, "Zambia: The Search for Security, 1964-1970." PhD Dissertation, University of London, 1971.

————, *Zambia: Security and Conflict*. London: Davison Publishing Limited, 1974.

————, "Zambia's Second Republic: The Establishment of a One-Party State," *Journal of Modern African Studies* Vol. 12, (2) (1974).

Pletcher, J. R., "The Political Uses of Agricultural Markets in Zambia," *The Journal of Modern African Studies* Vol. 24, (4) (1986).

Prithvish, Nag, *Population, Settlement, and Development in Zambia*. New Delhi: Concept Publishing Company, 1990.

Pullan, R. A., "The Utilization of Wildlife for Food in Africa: The Zambian Experience," *Singapore Journal of Tropical Geography* (26) (1981).

Ranger, Terrence and Olufemi Vaughn, eds., *Legitimacy and the State in Twentieth Century Africa: Essays in Honour of A. H. M. Kirk-Greene*. London: Macmillan, 1993.

Rasmussen, Thomas, "Political Competition and One-Party Dominance in Zambia," *The Journal of Modern African Studies* Vol. 7, (3) (October 1969).

Ravenhill John, ed., *Africa in Economic Crisis*. London: Macmillan, 1986.

Reinikka-Soininen, R., *Theory and Practice in Structural Adjustment: The Case of Zambia*. Helsinki: Helsingin Kauppakorkeakoulin Julkaisuja D-126, 1990.

Roberts, Andrew Dunlop, "Zambia: White Judges Under Attack," *The Round Table* (236) (October 1969).

———, *A History of Zambia*. London: Heinemann, 1976.

Rostow, Dankwart, "Transitions to Democracy: Toward a Dynamic Model," *Comparative Politics* Vol. 2, (3) (1970.)

——— and Kenneth P. Erickson, eds., *Comparative Political Dynamics: Global Research Perspectives*. New York: Harper Collins, 1991.

Rotberg, Robert I., "The Leshina Movement in Northern Rhodesia," in *Human Problems in British Central Africa* No. 29, 1961.

———, "Race Relations and Politics in Colonial Zambia: The Elwell Incident," *Race* Vol. 7, (1) (July 1965).

———, "Tribalism and Politics in Zambia," *Africa Report* (December 1967).

———, *Black Heart: Gore-Browne and the Politics of Multi-Racial Zambia*. Berkeley: University of California Press, 1977.

Rothchild, Donald, "Rawlings and the Engineering of Legitimacy in Ghana," in I. William Zartman, ed., *Collapsed States*. Boulder: Lynne Rienner, 1995.

Rothchild, Donald and Michael W. Foley, "African States and the Politics of Inclusive Coalitions," in D. Rothchild and N. Chazan eds., *The Precarious Balance: State and Society in Africa*. Boulder, Colorado: Westview Press, 1988.

Sakala, M. et. al., *Stabilization Policies in Zambia*. Mimeo.
    Lusaka: University of Zambia/ Bank of Zambia, 1987.
Sakala, Martin and Manenga Ndulo, "The International
    Monetary Fund and the Zambian Economy," in K. J.
    Havnevik, ed., *The IMF and the World Bank in Africa*.
    Uppsala: Scandinavian Institute of African Studies, 1987.
————, *The Zambian Foreign Exchange Auction*. Mimeo
    University of Zambia/ Bank of Zambia, 1987.
Salim, Salim A., "Africa in Transition," in William Minter, ed.,
    U.S. Foreign Policy: An Africa Agenda. Washington, D.C.:
    Africa Policy Information Center, 1994.
Sandbrook, Richard, "Liberal Democracy in Africa: A Socialist-
    Revisionist Perspective," *Canadian Journal of African
    Studies* Vol. 22, (1988).
————, *The Politics of Africa's Economic Recovery*. London:
    Cambridge University Press, 1993.
———— and Mohamed Halfani, eds., *Empowering People-
    Building Community, Civil Associations and Legality in
    Africa*. Toronto: Center for Urban and Community
    Studies, University of Toronto, 1993.
Sanderson, M., "Why Zambia's Auction Failed." Paper to the
    Economic Association of Zambia Conference, Lusaka,
    June 1987.
Sano, H. O., "The IMF and Zambia: The Contradictions of
    Exchange Rate Auctioning and De-Subsidisation of
    Agriculture," *African Affairs* Vol. 87, (349) (October
    1988).
————, *Big State, Small Farmers: The Search for an
    Agricultural Strategy for Crisis-Ridden Zambia*.
    Copenhagen: Centre for Development Research, 1990.
Sayagues, Mercedes, "Zambian Villagers Struggle with
    Drought," *Africa Recovery* (November 1992).
Sayila, Alfred, "Zambia Opens South Africa Trade Links,"
    Africa Recovery Vol. 6, (1) (April 1992)
Scarritt, J., "The Analysis of Social Class, Political Participation
    and Public Policy in Zambia," *Africa Today* Vol. 30, (3)
    (1983).
Scott, Earl P., "Lusaka's Informal Sector in National Economic
    Development," *Journal of Developing Areas* Vol. 20,
    (October 1985).
Scott, Ian, "Party Politics in Zambia." PhD Thesis, University of
    Toronto, 1976.

———, "Ideology, Party and the Cooperative Movement in Zambia," *Journal of Administration Overseas* Vol. 19, (October 1980).

Scott, Ian and Robert Molteno, "The Zambian General Elections," *Africa Report* (January 1969).

Seers, Dudley, "The Use of a Modified Input-Output System for an Economic Program in Zambia." Sussex: Institute for Development Studies Communications No. 50, University of Sussex, 1970.

Sehamani, Venkatash, "Structural Adjustment in Zambia: Industrial Policy Issue." Paper presented at the Annual Meeting of the Economic Association of Zambia, 12-14 December 1986.

———, "The Human Crisis in Africa: The Experience of Zambia." Paper prepared for the International Conference on the Human Dimension of Africa's Economic Recovery and Development, Khartoum, 5-8 March, 1988. UN Document ECA/ICHD/88/5.

Seidman, Ann, "The Distorted Growth of Import-Substitution Industry: The Zambian Case," *The Journal of Modern African Studies* Vol. 12, (4) (1974). Also in Ben Turok, ed., *Development in Zambia*. London: Zed Press, 1979.

———, "The Economics of Eliminating Rural Poverty," in Ben Turok, ed., *Development in Zambia*. London: Zed Press, 1979.

Seshamani, Venkatesh, "Towards Structural Transformation with a Human Focus: The Economic Programs and Policies of Zambia in the 1980s," *Innocenti Occasional Papers No.* 7 Florence: Spedale degli Innocenti, 1980.

Seymour, T, "Squatter Settlements and Class Relations in Zambia," *Review of African Political Economy* (3) (1975).

———, "Squatters, Migrants and the Urban Poor: A Study of Attitudes Towards Inequality, with Special Reference to a Squatter Settlement in Lusaka, Zambia." PhD Dissertation, University of Sussex, 1976.

Shaw, Timothy. M., "The Foreign Policy of Zambian Interests and Ideology," *Journal of Modern African Studies* Vol. 13, (1) (1976).

———, "The Political Economy of Energy in Southern Africa: Oil, the OAU and the Multinationals," *Africa Today* Vol. 23, (1) (1976).

———, "The Foreign Policy System of Zambia," *African*

Studies Review Vol. 19, (1) (1976).

———, "Zambia and Southern Africa: From Confrontation to Co-existence," in Olajide Aluko, ed., *The Foreign Policies of African States*. London: Hodder and Stoughton, 1976.

———, "The Political Economy of Zambia," *Current History* (March 1982).

———, "Zambia After Twenty Years: Recession and Repression Without Revolution," *Issue-A Journal of Opinion* Vol. XII, (1-2) (1982).

———, "Africa in the 1990s: From Economic Crisis to Structural Adjustment," *Dalhousie Review*, Vol. 68 (1-2) (1988).

———, "Structural Readjustment: New Framework," *Africa Recovery* Vol. 2, (4) (December 1988).

———, "Africa's Conjuncture: From Structural Adjustment to Self-Reliance," in *Third World Affairs 1988*. London: Third World Foundation, 1988.

———, "Africa in the 1990s: Beyond Continental Crisis to Sustainable Development?" World University Service of Canada (WUSC), Background Series in International Development, Annual Assembly 1990 Edition.

———, "Reformism, Revisionism, and Radicalism in African Political Economy During the 1990s," *Journal of Modern African Studies* Vol. 27 (1) (March 1991).

——— and A. Mugombe, "The Political Economy of Regional Detente: Zambia and Southern Africa," *Journal of African Studies* Vol. 4, (4) (1977-78).

Shivji, Issa, *Fight My Beloved Continent: New Democracy in Africa*. Harare: SAPES Trust, 1988.

———, "The Pitfalls of the Debate on Democracy," *IFDA Dossier* (79) (October-December 1990).

Sibanda, Arnold, "Case Studies of IMF and World Bank Impact on Africa: Zambia and Zimbabwe." Paper presented at the IFAA Conference, London 7-10 September 1987.

Sichalwe, Mann V., "Democratizing Media Structures in Southern Africa: The Case of Zambia." Address to the Seminar on the Democratization of the Media, Livingstone, Zambia, November 13, 1990.

Sichone, Owen B., "One-Party Participatory Democracy and Socialist Orientation: The De-Politicization of the Masses in Post-Colonial Zambia," in Peter Meyns and Dani Wadada Nabudere, eds., *Democracy and the One-Party*

State in Africa. Hamburg: Institute for African Studies, 1989.

Siddle, D. J., "Rural Development in Zambia: A Spatial Analysis," *The Journal of Modern African Studies* Vol. 8, (2) (July 1970).

Simmons, H. J., "Zambia's Urban Situation," in Ben Turok, ed., *Development in Zambia*. London: Zed Press, 1979.

Simwinga, G. K., "Corporate Autonomy and Government Control: A Study of Three State Enterprises Under a National Planned Developing Economy: INDECO, KDC and NCCM of Zambia." PhD Thesis, University of Pittsburgh, 1977.

Sirleaf, Ellen Johnson, "Some Reflections on Africa and the Global Economy," in William Minter, ed., *U.S. Foreign Policy: An Africa Agenda*. Washington, D.C.: Africa Policy Information Center, 1994.

Sithole, Masipula, "Is Zimbabwe Poised on a Liberal Path? The State and Prospects of the Parties," *Issue* Vol. XXI, (1-2) (1993).

Small, N. J., "Citizenship and Education for a National Ideology, With Reference to Zambia." MSc Dissertation, University of Edinburgh, 1975.

Soremekun, Fola, "The Challenge of Nation-Building: Neo-Humanism and Politics in Zambia, 1967-1969," *Geneve-Afrique* Vol. 9, (1) (1970).

Southall, Roger, "Zambia: Class Formation and Government Policies in the 1970s," *Journal of Southern African Studies* Vol. 7, (1) (1989).

Spring, Anita, "The Underside of Development: Agricultural Development and Women in Zambia," *Agriculture and Human Values* Vol. 2, (1) (1985).

Stadler, Alf, "Strong States Make for a Strong Civil Society," *Theoria* (79) (May 1992).

Steel, William F., "Recent Policy Reform and Industrial Adjustment in Zambia and Ghana," *Journal of Modern African Studies*, Vol. 26 (1) (March 1988).

Stokes, Eric and Richard Brown eds., *The Zambian Past: Studies in Central African History*. Manchester: The University of Manchester Press, 1966.

Strickland, R. S., "Stabilisation Strategies of the International Monetary Fund and the Effects on Income and Welfare: The Case of Zambia." PhD Thesis, University of Sussex,

1991.

Sutcliffe, R. B., "Zambia and the Strains of UDI," *World Today* Vol. 23, (12) (December 1967).

Szeftel, M., "Elite Conflict and Socio-Political Change in Zambia." PhD Dissertation, University of Manchester, 1978.

———, "Conflict, Spoils and Class Formation in Zambia" Ph.D. Dissertation, University of Manchester, 1978.

———, "The Political Process in Post-Colonial Zambia: The Factional Bases of Factional Conflict," in *The Evolving Structure of Zambian Society*. Edinburgh: Centre for African Studies, 1980.

———, "Political Graft and the Spoils System in Zambia-the State as a Resource in Itself," *Review of African Political Economy* (24) (May-August 1982).

Tordoff, William, "Democracy and the One-Party State," *Government and Opposition* Vol. 2, (4) (July-October, 1967).

———, "Provincial and District Government in Zambia, Parts I and II," *Journal of Administration Overseas* Vol. 7, (3-4) (July and October 1968).

———, "Provincial and Local Government in Zambia," *Journal of Administration Overseas* Vol. 9, (1) (January 1970).

——— ed., *Politics in Zambia*. Berkeley: University of California Press, 1974.

———, "Residual Legislature: The Case of Tanzania and Zambia," *The Journal of Commonwealth and Comparative Politics* Vol. XV, (3) (November 1977).

———, "Zambia: The Politics of Disengagement," *African Affairs* Vol. 76, (302) (1977).

———, *Administration in Zambia*. Manchester: University of Manchester Press, 1980.

Taylor, P. L., "Local Government Training in Zambia," *Journal of Local Administration Overseas* Vol. 5, (1) (January 1966).

Tomkys, Roger, "Implementing Africa's Second Revolution," in Douglas Rimmer, ed., *Action in Africa*. London: James Currey and Heinemann, 1993.

Turok, Ben, ed., *Development in Zambia: A Reader*. London: Zed Press, 1979.

———, "The Penalties of Zambia's Mixed Economy," in B. Turok, ed., *Development in Zambia*. London: Zed Press, 1979.

United Nations Economic Commission for Africa (UNECA), *Report of the UN/ECA/FAO Economic Survey Mission on the Economic Development of Zambia*. (The Seers Report) Ndola, Zambia: Falcon Press, 1963.

Van Binsbergen, Wim, *Religious Change in Zambia*. London: Keagan Paul International, 1981.

———, "The Post-Colonial State, 'State Penetration' and the Nkoja Experience in Central Western Zambia," in Van Binsbergen, W., Hasseliong, G. and Reijntjens, F. eds., *State and Local Community in Africa*. Brussels: Cahiers du CEDAF, 1986.

———, *Tears of Rain: Ethnicity and History in Central Westeren Zambia*. London: Keagan Paul International, 1992.

———, "Aspects of Democracy and Democratisation in Zambia and Botswana," *Journal of Contemporary African Studies* Vol. 13, (1) (January 1995).

Van Donge, J, "Religion and Nationalism in Zambia." Paper presented at the conference on "Culture and Consciousness in Southern Africa," Manchester 23-26 September 1986.

Vaughn, Olufemi, "The Politics of Global Marginalization," *Journal of African and Asian Studies* Vol. XXIX, (3-4) (1994).

Vickery, K. P., "Saving Settlers: Maize Control in Northern Rhodesia," *Journal of Southern Africa Studies* Vol. 11, (2) (1985).

Volman, Daniel, "Africa and the New World Order," *The Journal of Modern African Studies* Vol. 31, (1993).

Wanjohi, N. Gatheru, "The Relationship Between Economic Progress and Democracy in Kenya and Tanzania," in Walter O. Oyugi, et. al., eds., *Democratic Theory and Practice in Africa*. London: Heinemann and James Currey, 1988.

West, Tina, "The Politics of the Implementation of Structural Adjustment in Zambia, 1985-1987," in *The Politics of Economic Reform in Sub-Saharan Africa*. Final Report Prepared by the Center for Strategic and International Studies, Washington, D.C., March 1992.

Wina, Arthur, "The Mass Media." Draft Working Paper of the Movement for Multi-Party Democracy, MMD Secretariat, Lusaka, Zambia, February, 1991.

Wincott, N. E.,"Education and the Development of Urban Society in Zambia," in B. Pachai et. al., *Malawi: Past and Present*. Manchester: University of Manchester Press, 1967.

Wiseman, John, A., *Democracy in Black Africa: Survival and Revival*. New York: Paragon House, 1990.

Woldring, Klaas, "Corruption and Inefficiency in Zambia: Recent Inquiries and their Results," *Africa Today* Vol. 30, (3) (1983).

—— ed., *Beyond Political Independence: Zambia's Development Predicaments in the 1990s*. London: Mouton Press, 1984.

"World Bank Hits Nigeria on Oil Earnings Report," *Platt's Oilgram News* Vol. 70, (55) (March 19, 1992).

World Bank, *Accelerated Development in Sub-Saharan Africa: An Agenda for Action*. Washington, D.C.: The World Bank, 1981.

——, *Industrial Strategy for Late Starters: The Experience of Kenya Tanzania and Zambia*. Washington, D.C.: World Bank Staff Working Papers No. 457, 1981.

——, *Zambia: Policy Options and Strategies for Agricultural Growth: Supplementary Volume on Methodology and Commodity Analysis*. Washington, D.C.: Eastern Africa Projects Department, 1984.

——, *Zambia: Country Economic Memorandum-Issues and Options for Economic Diversification*. Washington, D.C.: Eastern Africa Country Programmes Department 1, 1984.

——, *Report of the Consultative Group on Zambia on Progress Towards Economic Restructuring*. Eastern and Southern Africa Regional Office, April 1985.

——, *Zambia: Agricultural Pricing and Parastatal Performance*. Eastern and Southern Africa Projects Department, July 1985.

——, *Improving Parastatal Performance in Zambia*. Washington, D.C.: Public Sector Management Unit, 1986.

——, *Sub-Saharan Africa: From Crisis to Sustainable Growth*. Washington, D.C.: The World Bank, 1989.

——, *A Framework for Capacity Building in Policy Analysis and Economic Management in Sub-Saharan Africa*. Washington, D.C.: World Bank, 1990.

Wright, Rob, "Chiluba Sets Zambia on a New Course," *Africa Recovery* Vol. 6, (1) (April 1992).

Wulf, Jurgen, "Zambia Under the IMF Regime," *African Affairs* Vol. 87, (349) (October 1988).

Yaker, Laiyashi, Keynote Address at the International Conference on "Africa in Transition: Challenges and Opportunities," AGSIM, Glendale, Arizona, 18-20 February, 1993.

Young, A., "Patterns of Development in Zambian Manufacturing Industry Since Independence," *Eastern African Economic Review* Vol. 1, (2) (December 1969).

Young, Crawford, *Ideology and Development in Africa*. New Haven: Yale University Press, 1982.

———, "Patterns of Social Conflict: State, Class and Ethnicity," *Daedalus* Vol.III, (2) (1982).

———, "Beyond Patrimonial Autocracy: The African Challenge," in The Carter Center, *Beyond Autocracy in Africa*. Atlanta: Emory University, 1989.

Young, Roger, *Zambia: Adjusting to Poverty*. Ottawa: North-South Institute, 1988.

Young, R. and John Loxley, *Zambia: An Assessment of Zambia's Structural Adjustment Experience*. Ottawa: North-South Institute, 1990.

"Zambia Debt Rescheduled by Paris Club," *The Herald* (7 March 1986).

"Zambia Relieved of Debt Worry," *The Herald* (29 May 1986).

"Zambia Moves to Stem the Tide of Imported Goods," *The Financial GAZETTE* (20 June 1986).

"Zambia Sacks 5,000 Workers," *The Herald* (13 May 1986).

"Zambia Shuts Two Embassies," *The Herald* (January 1986).

"Zambian Celebrations Could Cost Millions," *The Herald* (1 November 1984).

"Zambian Loan Deal With West Germany," *The Herald* (30 May 1986).

Zartman, I. William, "Africa in the Year 2000: Some Key Variables," *CSIS Africa Notes* (161) (June 1994).

———, ed., *Collapsed States: The Disintegration and Restoration of Legitimate Authority*. Boulder: Lynne Rienner, 1995.

Newspapers and Periodicals

Financial Mail
Malawi Democrat
National Mirror
Search
Sunday Times of Zambia
The Times of Zambia
The Weekly Post
Weekly Standard
Zambia Daily Mail

INDEX